SECONDARY SCHOOLS
in a
CHANGING SOCIETY

SECONDARY SCHOOLS
in a
CHANGING SOCIETY

Frederick R. Smith

Indiana University

C. Benjamin Cox

University of Illinois

Holt, Rinehart and Winston

New York   Chicago   San Francisco   Atlanta
Dallas   Montreal   Toronto   London   Sydney

373.73
Sm 55
98870
oct 1976

Library of Congress Cataloging in Publication Data

Smith, Frederick Robert, 1929–
  Secondary schools in a changing society.

  Includes index.
  1. Education, Secondary—United States.   I. Cox,
Charles Benjamin, joint author.   II. Title.
LA222.S56   373.73   75-43578
ISBN 0-03-089179-5

for our Patricias
and our children

Preface

This book was written for persons who have to know about secondary schools in the United States. Although we fashioned it as a textbook for college students in education, we predict the book will be of value to many others. School board members, school administrators, teachers, students, and concerned citizens in general will find many chapters helpful in gaining a better understanding of current educational concepts, problems, issues, and innovations.

We believe this text focuses on matters affecting the quality of public secondary education; and a basic assumption upon which our work rests is that the teachers' ability to cope with these matters will be a prime factor in determining the future success of our schools. We have attempted to offer a broad and thoughtful consideration of emerging social and professional issues while avoiding the pretense of proposing simple solutions to hard problems.

The material in the book is drawn from contemporary professional literature, research, theory; writings in sociology, history, psychology, philosophy, and their educational counterparts; and the authors' combined experiences gained over forty years of involvement in public education. We have tried throughout to expose our data and analyses to enable readers to see how we came to judge the desirability of alternatives as we did. We invite our readers to consider the reading of this book only one of many experiences necessary for becoming active participants in the process of improving schools.

The book views schools in a societal panorama. This perspective is basic to the development of rational responses to the educational problems attending changes in the purposes or structure of institutions, technological developments, the persuasions of individuals or groups, and the many other pressures that may emerge in a dynamic pluralistic society.

In such a complex society—constantly shaken by social, political, economic, and technological eruptions—old solutions may not fit new problems. The choice to ignore social changes in the hope that conventional institutions and standard practices will outlast the new disruptions is dysfunctional. A willingness to change, a desire to modify old responses, and a determination to invent new responses that match new circumstances are imposing normative challenges. But beyond the challenge to respond, there remains the imperative that man, because he is man, will shape circumstances to increase the likelihood that some things will happen and others will not.

A teacher, we believe, qualifies to assume educational leadership when he can make rational judgments on matters of educational importance. Being rational, we should emphasize, does not preclude being creative, inventive, and even artistic in one's work and life. There are many ways to conceptualize, many models to apply, and many points of view to take.

Thus a major goal of this text is to assist teachers and others sharing their concerns to think rationally about hard questions facing public education. We propose to accomplish this goal by viewing secondary schools in the perspective of a rural society which rapidly became urban in character; by providing contemporary analyses of students, teachers, and curriculum; and by describing processes that we believe are fundamental to the development of appropriate educational experiences for students in our society.

We have attempted to provide credible analyses of existing conditions in education. In carrying out this task, we have identified basic topics and developments to which we believe teachers ought to be sensitive. We present these as problem-generating areas that must be penetrated by the rational decisions of educators. In discussing these areas, we deliberately attempted to avoid imposing our own prescriptions. Instead we endeavored to challenge our readers to form their own conclusions and answers.

A teacher, rationally pursuing the study of schooling, is prepared to reject, accept, or modify the conclusions of others only when he probes their analyses and weighs the evidence on his own.

Our justification for the topics included in the book is neither profound nor unnatural. We simply try to say what we think we see. We think we see the school as a highly adaptable institution, and we try to say so. We see the school as a social being plying its trade according to its clients' whims, though we pray for some theoretical basis upon which substantive decisions may be made. We believe it is incontrovertible that whatever schools do will be done mainly in town, because that is where most people live; so we say that. We see teachers suddenly realizing that they spend half their lives in school and that they ought to have more to say about what happens there.

Finally, we notice that everyone around seems to have an axe that needs grinding, and an ox that is either in a ditch or has been gored. Somehow, which are to be accommodated must be sorted out; once sorted out, they must be negotiated into some kind of sensible social machine. We think we say these things.

In the final chapter we have departed from the main format of the text by presenting some of our own thinking about the topics, problems, and alternatives present in earlier chapters. In doing this, we are not abandoning our position that there are few definitive responses to the complex problems facing educators. Rather, we anticipate that the perspectives this chapter presents will serve to stimulate further reader reactions and encourage our readers to mount their own alternative proposals for improving public secondary education. Following each chapter is a section entitled "Questions and Activities" that can assist readers in reflecting on some of the major points and issues raised.

Unavoidably, the book remains ambitious. We would not wish it otherwise. It will certainly disappoint those who seek simple remedies for the many issues confronting public education. Nevertheless, we believe that the answers will be forthcoming through diligent study and imaginative response. But first we must attempt to understand the problems.

Bloomington, Indiana   F. R. S.
Urbana, Illinois   C. B. C.
December 1975

Acknowledgments

Many persons helped us write this book—most of them unknowingly. Foremost among these, perhaps, are the scores of researchers and authors who, before us, wrote on the several topics and problems which we have discussed in the book. Brief citations and footnotes seem minimal recognition of their contributions in shaping many of our ideas and analyses.

In addition we note our debt to the hundreds of teachers with whom we have worked over the past quarter of a century or so. Insights coming out of our interactions with them surfaced in this manuscript. Indirectly our public school colleagues conceptualized this book by increasing our sensitivity to some matters and desensitizing us to others.

Moreover, we acknowledge the salutary effect that our several thousand students in a half dozen public junior and senior high schools, colleges, and universities have had on us and, hence, on this text. They have been at the center of our professional interests for nearly three decades. Whether we shaped them as much as they shaped us is no less mooted by the fact that we were their teachers.

During the course of the writing of this manuscript, numerous individuals added materially to it either by what they did or by what they said and, in some cases, by what they left unsaid. We are most appreciative for the counsel, reactions, and suggestions given along the way by many of our colleagues at Indiana University and the University of Illinois, our editors at Holt, Rinehart and Winston, and several anonymous reviewers.

Specific individuals who helped in preparing the manuscript include Dr. Floyd Coppedge of Indiana University; Thayer Warshaw, Newton, Massachusetts, Public Schools; Dr. Jerry Walker of the University of Illinois, and Don Cassady, graduate assistant, Indiana University. We applaud their editorial comments and suggestions for improving the manuscript. Notwithstanding, we absolve them from accountability.

Patti Jennings of Bloomington, Indiana, patiently typed several versions of sections of the text and deserves special thanks for a job well done.

More important than any of the above in teaching us about the anxieties and aspirations of young persons in our society are our children.

They have affected and have been affected by teachers and schools in a half dozen midwestern cities. Nursery school through university, they have kept us enrolled as school patrons for twenty years. We could not have written so honestly without them, though without them we would have written faster.

But for our wives we reserve that very special measure of gratitude for tolerating our hiatuses of husbandhood when lesser tasks seemed momentarily more important; for typing and retyping to the point of memorization the phrases and paragraphs that kept surviving the several "cut-and-paste" versions of the manuscript; and for proofing and critiquing, while always encouraging. If patience and forbearance, like all virtues, were not self-rewarding, our indebtedness to Patricia Smith and Patricia Cox would go largely unpaid.

Contents

Preface *vii*

1. Society and School   1

The Latin Grammar School   2
The Academy   3
The High School   4
Public Secondary Education   5
New Goals for the New School   6
The Seven Cardinal Principles   7
The Progressive Education Movement   7
Social Norms, Institutions, and Schools   9
Questions and Activities   10

2. Purposes for Schools in a Transitional Era   13

American Value Core   14
Social Change   17
A Transitional Era   17
Teacher Responses to Traditional/Emergent Value Conflicts   20
A Framework for a Rationale for Secondary Education   21
A Framework for Developing a Rationale for
     Secondary Education   22
Summary   27
Questions and Activities   28

3. The Metropolitan Context of Public Schools   31

The Urban Process   32
The Institutional Crisis in the Metropolis   35
The Central Problems of Authenticity and Identity   36
Race and Class in the Metropolitan Area   38
Segregation in Metropolitan Schools   40
Legitimacy   42
Explanations for Class and Racial Differences
     in Achievement   44

The Denial of Mobility   47
Questions and Activities   48

4. Alternatives for Metropolitan Schools   51
Desegregation   51
Alternatives for Metropolitan Schools   55
Some Tentative Judgments   60
Questions and Activities   62

5. The Developing Adolescent in School   64
Adolescent Variability and Similarity   65
Adolescent Subcultures   66
The Factor of Intelligence   67
Social Class and Intelligence   69
Race as a Factor in Understanding Adolescents   73
Reading and Language Variance in Adolescence   75
The Factor of Sex   77
The Factor of Development   78
The School and Student's Development   80
Questions and Activities   81

6. The Rights of Students   85
Dimensions of Student Dissent   86
In Loco Parentis   88
Freedom of Speech, Press, and Assembly   89
Personal Rights of Students   92
Problems in Adjusting to the Change   98
Some Conclusions   103
Questions and Activities   103

7. Teachers and Their Emergent Professional Power   106
The Gargantuan Enterprise   106
Is Education a Profession?   107
Factors Related to the Image of Teachers   108
Societal Attitudes toward Teaching   111
Extending the Scope of Professional Power   112
Questions and Activities   123

8. Developing the School Curriculum   126
Major Categories of the Curriculum   126
Making Decisions about Curriculum   128
Broad Goals and Instructional Objectives   132
Classifying Instructional Objectives   132

Summary   *135*
Questions and Activities   *135*

9. Forces Affecting the Curriculum   137
Higher Education   *137*
Instructional Materials   *138*
Legislated Curriculum   *140*
Leadership at the State Level   *141*
Accrediting Associations   *141*
Local Influences on the Curriculum   *142*
National Commissions and Reports   *144*
Summary   *147*
Questions and Activities   *147*

10. Innovative Organizational Patterns   149
Stress on Change and Innovation   *149*
Criteria for the Evaluation of Innovative Organizational
    Patterns   *151*
Organizational Patterns   *152*
Flexible Scheduling   *153*
Alternative Schools   *156*
Summary   *159*
Questions and Activities   *160*

11. Implementing Change   162
Dimensions of Change   *162*
The Process of Change   *165*
Factors Related to Change   *167*
A Generalized Model for Change   *170*
The Teacher as Change Agent   *171*
Summary   *172*
Questions and Activities   *174*

12. An Essay on Schools   176
Society and School   *176*
Purposes for Schools   *177*
Metropolis Schools   *179*
The Adolescent Student   *181*
Professional Power   *187*
Changing Schools   *188*
Preparation of Teachers   *189*
Questions and Activities   *192*

Index   195

SECONDARY SCHOOLS
in a
CHANGING SOCIETY

CHAPTER 1

Society and School

Since World War II, American education has been buffeted by critics, internal disagreements, and social disruptions. It has been an era of crises. The crises, as we all know, have not abraded the schools alone; they have been pervasive. None of our institutions has escaped the critics' rhetoric; all have suffered the aches of change and adjustment.

Unfortunately for those who prefer tranquillity, most views of the future evoke no less dismay than a review of the past. The institutional aches of the last quarter of a century are not over. It has not yet been decided which of our institutions, if any, will survive the twentieth century nor which, if any, are doomed.

Although the hazards are many, we are not persuaded that American public education is doomed. We doubt that critics, Sputnik, Vietnam, busing, the drug culture, black power, failing referendums, the tax revolt, the free school movement, urban decay, the armaments race, or the population explosion will destroy public education. The glint of optimism is fitful, however, for the future of the society is also endangered by many of these same problems. Because of the dependence of the society on rational citizens, we are convinced that if the educational choices of this generation are flawed, the future of this society is imperiled.

We are not prepared to present a definitive solution toward the relief of our institutional aches and social ailments. Although we have preferred resolutions, their predictable success in curing the complaints of

1

the schools is certainly no greater than that of the surgeon who radically treats melanosis or the psychiatrist who sets out to reintegrate his psychotic patient. On occasion our educational preferences will be exposed, but we intend mainly to present ways of structuring the problems of secondary education. We intend to conceptualize, probe, and examine the problems in an effort to isolate the issues and lay the groundwork for eventual resolution.

We suggested earlier that most of the crises in education are shared by other institutions in the society. An awareness of these problems actually argues for the continued or eventual health of the institutions. When a society or its institutions are no longer aware of their aches and ails, death is very near.[1] Further encouragement extends from the fact that today's crises are only the most recent in a history of crises. In part, this chapter traces the history of the responses to crises in the development of secondary education in America.

American secondary education has had repeated threats to its survival in its history of three and a half centuries. It has always known financial deprivation. It has been at the center of philosophical debates that have required the painful examination of the goals of the society, the place of the individual, the nature of knowledge, and the very meaning of life itself. It has been the child of conflict in colonial assemblies, state legislatures, and community councils. Its basic propositions, modes of operation, and institutional forms have been contested in colonial, county, state, and federal courts. Our argument is not that secondary education has been uncommonly disfavored; its various institutional forms have waxed and waned in popularity for a number of reasons. But, rather, we suggest that secondary education has had a history of adversities and that its present plight as an institution beleaguered by critics must be viewed in that perspective. In this chapter we attempt to build that perspective.

The Latin Grammar School

The initial form of secondary education in America appeared in 1635 in the Massachusetts Bay Colony where the Boston Latin Grammar School was organized for the aspiring young men of the colony. The Latin schools, typified by their rigorous and tedious treatment of classical Latin and Greek and catechistical religion, were modeled after the elitist English Latin grammar schools previously known by the Bay colonists and other New England settlers. The American version, like its English progenitor, aimed to perpetuate an elitist society. Organized primarily to prepare subteen boys for matriculation at Harvard, which began accepting students in 1636, the Latin grammar school was a means of preparing young men for church and state leadership. Although they persisted through most of the colonial period, the Latin schools were of little concern to many and of no use to most colonial settlers. Their tuition was beyond the means and their subject matter was beyond the ability and interest of all but a few favored colonists. The farmers, tradesmen, mechanics, and merchants of New England had neither an overpowering interest nor much use for facility in classical Latin and Greek; and they learned their religion in church from a classical scholar in the Anglican pulpit.[2]

By 1750 life in the colonies had changed. In the last half century alone, the population along the coast and up the river valleys that fingered their way into the wilderness had increased by more than five times. New population centers had developed apart from the original colonial sites, and along the coast America boasted of five "major" cities.[3] An energetic merchant class had evolved, tainting and threatening the old theocracy of New England and laying a financial base for the impending claims of American independence. Furthermore, the frontier had become a powerful political, social, economic, and military force in American life. The cumulative effect of these factors was a different kind of society composed of a far more heterogeneous population than had been the case in the seventeenth century.

As the society changed, so did its needs in education. In New England disaffection for the old Latin grammar school grew. It came to be seen as unsuited for the developing American society. As a result a new kind of secondary school, the academy, was invented. It would become the dominant institutional form of secondary education in America for a century. Vestiges of the academy remain in secondary schools today. Some would suggest that the ghosts of the Latin school are there also.

The Academy

The first academy was established in Philadelphia in 1750 at the suggestion of Benjamin Franklin. Franklin's Academy was a result of an effort to liberalize American secondary education. Franklin had argued that it was time to provide a school in which both boys and girls might "learn those things that are likely to be most useful and most ornamental." By the end of the Revolutionary War, the academy had replaced the Latin grammar school as the major institutionalized form of secondary education.

Purportedly sensitive to the needs of the society and largely unfettered by legislative prescriptions, academies developed considerable diversity in subject matter and clientele. Most offered instruction in English grammar and literature, mathematics, and history and made some accommodation to the new sciences. Some offered training leading to a vocation such as surveying or accounting. Some offered military training as a basic ingredient in their curriculum. Today's secondary military academies display remnants of these curriculums. Still others offered courses in pedagogy which were sometimes available to both boys and girls who aspired to teach in the elementary schools. For the most part, however, girls attended female seminaries or finishing schools where they learned to be cultured ladies. A few female seminaries were as intellectually engaging as the best of the academies.

Taken as a whole, the academy system appeared to offer a diverse and liberal curriculum for American youth in the century preceding the Civil War (1750–1850). Taken individually, however, academies had quite narrow offerings. One academy's curriculum might resemble closely that of a Latin grammar school; another's might feature mathematics, science, and "modern" literature.[4]

Furthermore, though often supported by churches, philanthropies, or corporations, academies were exclusively for the few who were lucky enough to win scholarships or wealthy enough to pay the usually high tuitions. Following the Revolution, Americans became less willing to support such an elitist philosophy. Their newly won equality among the nations of the world was reflected in a fierce egalitarianism and individualism which were applied as the new social norms. Just as an elitist Latin school had been found unsuited for the developing colonies, the academy was to be judged not to fit the needs of the expanding nation.

The High School

While the academy was the dominant form of secondary education in antebellum America, it had a more egalitarian competitor in the decades prior to the Civil War. The prototype of the new institutional invention was Boston's English Classical School, established in 1821. This Boston English High School, as it was renamed in 1824, was the firmly established model for secondary education in America by the end of the nineteenth century.

The advantages of the new school to the growing nation were impressive. It recognized both girls and boys as potential social contributors who merited the benefits of further education beyond the elementary school. It marked the first serious application of the principle of public support for secondary education. That principle, which had been applied to elementary schools since 1647, had been frequently legislated, but randomly applied to secondary education from the time of the Latin grammar school. It represented the first distinct attempt to loosen the chain that bound secondary education to the university.

In effect, the English high school was secondary education's first halting step toward joining the elementary school in the broad task of general education. It offered to a wider population an access to postelementary schooling, previously available only to the wealthy or the lucky. At the same time, the new high school was an alternate route to the university.

The early high schools, like the academies, varied greatly. Some closely resembled the older academies despite the expectation that the high schools would offer more popular and practical courses of study, while the academies would continue to serve as the main college preparation schools. Most of the early high schools offered a practical education leading to many vocations and professions; however, some reverted to curriculums that mimicked those of the academies in order to capture a prestige associated with the older institution.[5]

Public Secondary Education

Differing interpretations notwithstanding, by the mid-nineteenth century a design for public education had appeared that included a *public* secondary school. Heretofore, as we have documented, public elementary schools were widely available and *non-public* Latin schools and academies were in existence for an elite minority. By 1860 half of the nation's children were in school, and the majority of the states had public school systems. Some states had free public secondary schools and a few had state universities which were identified as part of the public education system. In the Midwest, where no tradition of private schools had developed, most of the school children were in public schools. In New England, however, private schools continued to flourish, and in the South few public schools were developed until after the Civil War.[6]

One interpretation has it that the new high school was an institution devoted to the preparation of youth for life. Since its curriculum was both general and common, it philosophically joined the elementary school system in offering educational experiences of a more general nature for all youth. Thus the high school was designed to attract young persons from all classes and walks of life because "only with a heterogeneous group of students could the unifying goals of the common school be achieved."[7]

In another interpretation, however, the truly broader aims for secondary education emerged only when larger portions of middle-class students actually began to attend public high schools, say, in the last quarter of the nineteenth century. It was only after 1875 that the so-called practical and useful studies, for example, citizenship training, home-living, and the use of leisure time, became important goals for secondary schools.[8]

Supporting this latter interpretation is the fact that public high schools were not regularly tax supported until after Michigan's supreme court ruling in the *Kalamazoo* case in 1872. While the old English high school model entailed public support, and while several state legislatures provided public support for secondary education, the precedent had been to provide public funds from sources other than taxes, often through the sale of public lands as prescribed in the Northwest Ordinance of 1787. The *Kalamazoo* case confirmed that a state legislature could pass legislation enabling communities to tax directly for the support of *both* elementary and secondary schools. As a result most states had such laws by the end of the nineteenth century. In addition many had state educational funds derived from land sales and state taxes to be distributed to local school authorities, a move that allowed state surveillance of public education and the eventual establishment of state systems of education.

It was the direct tax support for high schools that made secondary education available to the masses. And it was the subsequent invasion of the public high school by large numbers of middle-class children that precipitated the liberalization of the curriculum. The Boston English High School had been the philosophical conception of the modern high school; the *Kalamazoo* case was its final birth pang.[9]

New Goals for the New School

The era of the modern high school began sometime in the last quarter of the nineteenth century. With its development came a proliferation of colleges and universities eager to accept the new high school graduates, an increased interest in the preparation of teachers, and the organized involvement of teachers and administrators in public education. The National Education Association (NEA), formed in 1870 from a coalition of public school teachers' and administrators' organizations, became the most powerful voice of the organized profession.[10]

One of the early and notable pronouncements of the National Education Association is referred to as the Report of the Committee of Ten. That report, appearing in 1892, and a subsequent report in 1895 by the NEA's Committee on College Entrance Requirements were powerfully influential in establishing college preparation as a primary goal of the high school. Although the reports recognized that high school students have many goals besides college attendance and that many courses are important besides those required for admission to college, the effect of the reports was to align the high school with its antecedent institutions, the academy and Latin school.

The reports represented a retrenchment with respect to goals; they were narrower than those that were emerging for the new high school. They were set well in the center of the academic tradition, now expressed for the masses. Everyone needed the hard subjects, for example, Latin and Greek classics, mathematics, and science, for mental discipline and training in memory, expression, and reasoning. The decision would remain as the official position of the NEA for twenty-five years; its effect on the high school curriculum would last much longer.[11]

The Seven Cardinal Principles

At least one other major pronouncement on secondary education is historically noteworthy. The commission that issued the statement, in contrast with the two college-dominated committees just discussed, was laced heavily with teachers and administrators from the public schools. As a result this commission's report reflected the broader goals that had continued to gain importance in the high schools themselves. Thus in 1918, a quarter of a century after the affirmation of the high school as a college preparation institution, the NEA-sponsored Commission on the Reorganization of Secondary Education issued a report asserting that the functions of secondary education are contained in "Seven Cardinal Principles of Education" relating to health, fundamental processes ("the three R's," etc.), home membership, vocational preparation, civic education, leisure use, and ethical character. The new dogma was to be preparation for life.[12]

Strongly utilitarian, the seven cardinal principles, in effect, mandated the schools to influence the entire gamut of a child's personal development and social relationships. As a departure from the Report of the Committee of Ten, the commission's report served as a license for high schools to expand their curriculums into many new realms. The release of the Seven Cardinal Principles report was the harbinger of a movement that intended to transform American schools.

The Progressive Education Movement

In the twenty-five years between World War I and World War II, the progressive education movement attempted to liberalize, humanize, and reorganize the American high school. Although its intentions were not wholly realized, the influence of progressivism on secondary education was impressive.

The attraction and holding power of the secondary school were greatly increased by the development of the junior high school, which aimed to attend more directly to the needs of pubescent children, and by greatly expanded curriculum offerings in the trades, agriculture, home economics, physical education, and the arts.

The attractiveness of secondary education was also enhanced by extracurricular activities, such as clubs, sports, and music organizations. Guidance programs were improved in an effort to serve the needs of individual students. Learning itself became more palatable as new teaching methods, such as the project method, became more widely utilized. Teacher training attended more to teaching skills and the problems of motivation in classrooms. School buildings became more attractive places to be in as school architecture began to reflect curricular needs and student needs.

Finally, the administration and control of schools became professionalized and somewhat more democratic. Although parents, teachers, and local communities were able to exercise more power in the formulation of educational policy, administration of schools became the specialized function of trained administrators. Many of the effects of progressivism on education remain. Due to its influence, schools are more liberal, humane, and democratic today than they would have been otherwise. An unintended consequence partly due to the effects of progressivism is that schools today are also bureaucratic organizations.[13]

The Progressive Education Association, the fountainhead of progressive education, was disbanded in the mid-1950s as the progressive movement collapsed. When it mounted its final reformist attack after World War II as "life adjustment education," the progressives appeared to embrace conformity at a time when conformity was being rejected in American life and thought. The error was significant. It precipitated a barrage of criticism of the entire progressive educational movement.[14]

The world had become a different place after the war. The mind molding of the prewar years and the intensive efforts of the war years to build an America unified in spirit and strength had turned into rampant individualism and nonconformity. The atom and hydrogen bombs at once obliterated all concepts of security and depreciated all previous notions of power. Automation was changing the nature of work and making an anachronism of vocational education. Computers were generating new knowledge and information at rates and in amounts that only computers themselves could accommodate. The mass media were inundating the society with a limitless flood of perceptual data.

The schools, said the critics, were not helping students to make sense of the social maelstrom in which they were entangled. Instead, they seemed to be advising students to adjust to the devious currents in nearly every aspect of their lives. Two influential critics of the period, Arthur Bestor and Hyman Rickover, felt the schools had attempted too much, had gone too far, and should now return to their primary task, "the deliberate cultivation of the ability to think."[15] Thinking is certainly not the only function and may not be the most important function in life, these and other critics were saying, but it is the most important concern of the schools. Furthermore, "intellectual training, particularly through the academic disciplines, may not be the only function of the schools," but in the final analysis it is their *raison d'être*.[16]

The mood of the society had changed. The vocal critics of the period had come full circle from the progressives who had argued that the schools needed to extend their functions in order to serve the national interest. Now it was being argued that the national interest would be better served by a contraction of those functions.[17]

One voice of the education professions followed suit. In 1960 the NEA's Educational Policy Commission expressed that secondary education should aim toward the transfer of learning and the development of the ability to think.[18] Fifteen years earlier the Educational Policy Commission had endorsed the programs of the progressives. To the extent that the commission reflected the thinking of professional educators in both instances, they too had come full circle. A contraction of the function of schools in American society appeared imminent.[19]

Social Norms, Institutions, and Schools

In the end it is the social norms that provide the standards by which the purposes and programs of schools are judged. Although social norms, at least in a pluralistic society such as ours, are not static, neither do they ordinarily shift rapidly. As a result, old norms seem not to die at all. They, like old soldiers, simply fade away to be replaced almost surreptitiously by some new norm which seems more fitting and whose strength and popularity have waxed seemingly overnight.

The period between the dominance of one norm and the dominance of the norm that eventually replaces it is frequently referred to as a period of transition. When the waxing and waning norms are of nearly equal strength, often called a crisis period, the society is thoroughly ambivalent in its choice of competing standards. We apply this crisis hypothesis often throughout this book.

When, for one reason or another, the society experiences a change in values, there are many consequences. In the midst of the transition, many consequences seem dire and threatening; but once the new standard has been accommodated, a new perspective emerges. The change from the Ptolemaic system to the Copernican system in astronomy must have been a devastating experience for many. Today we are not much shaken by the loss of Ptolemy's theory.

One important consequence of a value shift relates to institutions. An institution, in effect, is the social structure of a value or set of values. It organizes the rules, roles, and activities by which the value is implemented in the society. Further, it provides for the application of criteria to its interacting parts as a self-monitor. The institution is thus self-perpetuating. It maintains its own rules, trains persons to play its roles, and monitors the role players' activities. A well-constituted institution can maintain itself in a society long after its value foundation has crumbled. Without the moral authority that proceeds from an accepted social value, however, the structure also crumbles or becomes a meaningless ritual. The British throne is an example.

But institutions are also amazingly adaptive. When their value bases erode and new sets of values emerge, institutions are often capable of assuming new social postures reflecting the new standards. In time, the rules governing the intricate mechanisms of the structure are amended to fit the new standards, new institutional roles are invented and old roles are canceled or redefined, training and retraining procedures are developed, and activities appropriate to the new standards are described. Thus the old institution is refurbished. The American family would appear to be a case in point. Observers predict that the nuclear family as an institution will survive the presently occurring shift from an authoritarian–patriarchal to a companionship–equalitarian value base, but not without significant alterations in its rules, roles, and activities.[20]

We believe the American secondary school is also a case in point. From the historical sketch presented in this chapter, there seems no contesting that the public secondary school in America has been sensitive to the tenor of the society. It has been, and we believe it remains, an adaptive institution. In at least two instances in the past, the concept of adaptation may not seem applicable. The academy did replace the Latin school and the high school superseded the academy. The question is mooted, however, by the remarkable likenesses among these institutions, for example, by the continuity of some common elements like teachers, students, administrators, courses, classrooms, and textbooks. Other incidents point more clearly to adaptiveness, for example, the shifts from an academic to a utilitarian posture and back again.

Whether the school's adaptiveness extends back to colonial America, we will leave for others to resolve; but through the remainder of this book we assume that an adaptive capability obtains today. Alternatives notwithstanding, American public secondary schools are in an adaptive mood. They will survive.

QUESTIONS AND ACTIVITIES

1. Identify some of the significant historical developments in early American education which provide a backdrop for the study of the contemporary

high school. This should include the period from 1635 up to, but not including, the events of 1892.

2. In what ways do the historical events identified above provide insights into the nature of the problems facing contemporary American educators?

3. What, if any, influence did each of the following developments have on the growth of the modern high school?
   a. The Report of the Committee of Ten (1892).
   b. NEA's Committee on College Entrance Requirements (1895).
   c. The Seven Cardinal Principles (1918).
   d. The Progressive Education Movement (World War I to World War II period).

4. In what ways was your understanding of the modern high school broadened after a consideration of the events identified in Question 3?

5. What difference does it make whether one believes that the early high school was designed to attract young persons from all classes and walks of life or that the broader aims of the new high school actually emerged only after these persons began to attend the new school? What implications might either of these conclusions have for the design of school programs today?

6. What were some of the causal factors leading to the decline of the Progressive movement in the 1950s? Are any of these phenomena still of importance today?

7. What is meant by the assertion that an unintended consequence of progressivism is that schools became more bureaucratic?

8. To what issues did critics Bestor and Rickover address themselves in the late fifties? To what extent were their criticisms valid then and do they still have merit relative to the current educational scene?

9. Briefly describe the crisis hypothesis being used in this text. To what extent do you find it useful in analyzing various present day problems?

10. Describe various ways in which institutions adapt to change. How have the schools adapted to change?

11. What appear to be some of the more important societal functions of institutions? What specifically are the important functions of the institution called schooling?

12. The authors state that the administration and control of the schools became professionalized during the progressive period. List the criteria which you think are important in determining whether or not a specific area of work warrants being called professional.

13. Interview one or two teachers who taught through the fifties and sixties. Question them about their views and/or reactions to the nautre of change, if any, that occurred in those decades.

14. Talk to a school administrator concerning his understanding of school bureaucracy. Does he think of himself as a bureaucrat? Does he see others as bureaucrats? Are "trusted" teachers and "successful" students bureaucrats?

NOTES

[1] Harry S. Broudy, *Enlightened Cherishing* (Urbana: University of Illinois Press, 1972), p. 3.

[2] Wayne Dumas and Weldon Beckner, *Introduction to Secondary Education: A Foundations Approach* (Scranton, Pa.: International Textbook Company, 1968), p. 22.

[3] Carl Bridenbaugh, *Cities in the Wilderness; The First Century of Urban Life in America, 1625–1742* (New York: Capricorn Books, 1938, 1955, 1964), pp. 6, 143, 303.

[4] Dumas and Beckner, pp. 23–24.

[5] Dumas and Beckner, p. 25.

[6] Lawrence A. Cremin, *The Transformation of the School* (New York: Knopf, 1961), p. 13.

[7] Cremin, p. 11.

[8] Dumas and Beckner, p. 155.

[9] Dumas and Beckner, p. 27.

[10] Myron Lieberman, *Education as a Profession* (Englewood Cliffs, N.J.: Prentice-Hall, 1956), p. 260.

[11] Dumas and Beckner, p. 155.

[12] Dumas and Beckner, pp. 156–157.

[13] Cremin, pp. 306–308.

[14] Cremin, p. 336.

[15] Cremin, p. 344.

[16] Cremin, p. 244.

[17] Cremin, p. 347.

[18] Dumas and Beckner, pp. 158–159.

[19] Cremin, pp. 328–330.

[20] Charles Llewellan, *Marriage Role Expectations of High School Seniors,* unpublished doctoral dissertation, University of Illinois, Urbana, Illinois, 1974.

CHAPTER 2

Purposes for Schools in a Traditional Era

Schools exist to transmit culture traits of continuing value to the young. While all institutions share this transmission task, the schools bear a major burden. Moreover, schools are expected to perform their part of the task in a systematic way.

In a society with many cultural universals, few specialties, and no radical alternatives, this task would be fairly simple. But such does not appear to be the case in our society. Rather, our society is pluralistic in a thoroughgoing way. Unnumbered groups have different and conflicting political, economic, religious, racial, age, philosophical, sectional, ethnic, sexual, and occupational loyalties. We seem to have many alternatives and specialties and few, if any, universals. In a pluralistic society, the choice of which values, mores, traits, and skills to transmit systematically in schools may arbitrarily favor one group over others.

Furthermore, we have a conflagrant society fed by rampant industrialization, racial conflict, and urbanization. Our most cherished institutions and values appear suddenly to be transforming. The traditional traits believed once to have continuing value begin to lose popularity to emergent traits once believed to have only expedient value.

We make the assumption in this text that schools are always socially contextual: that is, the purposes schools are to serve must be extracted from the society in which they exist. However, when a society is pluralistic and transitional—claims we are making here about American society

—the problem of identifying purposes for schools becomes very complex indeed.

American Value Core

There are some values that most Americans accept. As such they seem likely candidates for influencing school purposes. These values, commonly conceded to be the central beliefs in the American value core, affirm the fundamental dignity and worth of the individual. However, the worth of the individual is not affirmed free of obligation. The value core entails an interconnected chain of personal and social responsibilities and benefits. Because the quality of the society is dependent upon the quality of individuals within the society, the individual is expected to achieve the optimum development of his own personality. Functionally, the individual's personality develops only as he extends and applies his knowledge and understanding, expands his ability to assess and evaluate, and increases his capacity to interact with others. Although the personality of the individual is dependent upon his interactions with others, personality development is best provided for under political arrangements where all individuals are protected from excessive demands from each other and from the government.[1]

Many observers of American society have noted that a creed referring to the dignity of the individual, the equality of all men, and the rights to freedom, justice, and fair opportunity is the foundation of the American society.[2] Such expressions are commonplace today; but the observation has been made about American society since before the creed was officially enshrined in the Declaration of Independence and the Constitution. It has been asserted also that the value core has been able to maintain itself for so many years in the society partly because it has great tolerance for social change and social differences as long as they do not violate the essential worth of the individual.

PLURALISM AND THE VALUE CORE

Despite the core's tolerance for differences and change, there is no actual consensus in America on the value core. For one thing, any system that values individualism, on the one hand, and cherishes a creed that every one is supposed to believe, on the other, is bound to have consensus problems. Moreover a pluralistic society reaches consensus on anything only with the greatest of difficulty. Evidence of our lack of consensus is found in the authoritarian alternatives to the creed that sporadically gain popularity in this country. More specific to this discussion is the existence of various interpretations of the core values themselves. They suggest that the American creed reinforces our diversity rather than providing us with a unifying belief. The presence of these several variations is one thing we mean when we say we have a pluralistic society.

In one variation, the value core is assumed to have face validity for most Americans; but beneath the surface, the society is fundamentally split in its interpretation of the values. This split is characterized by two contrasts. In the first of these, the belief that human nature and human institutions are governed by natural law that is independent of the society is contrasted with the belief that these are governed by the structure of the society and the character of the culture. In the second, the belief that respect for the worth of the individual demands that he should be free to function in a competitive society without interference or assistance from the government is contrasted with the belief that the society should guarantee that every individual will have ample opportunity to develop the capacities necessary to achieve the "good life."[3]

To put it more directly, the conflict is between two ideals of individual freedom. Under one ideal, the individual should be free to seek the good life with as little interference as possible from anybody or anything, including the government. Under the other, the society and all its institutions, including the government, should assist the individual as much as necessary in the quest for "the good life."

Thus, if a set of purposes for schools includes statements on individual freedom and development, it is reasonable to ask which variety of individualism has been selected and, consequently, which variety has been rejected. If the two varieties are true contrasts, which they appear to be, it would be impossible to build an integrated school program that would promote them both. An alternative would be to deny schools any purpose related to the worth of the individual; but that seems both unlikely and unreasonable.

Another variation of the value core rather cynically differentiates our verbal core from our action values:

> America has worked out a unique and creative solution to the problem of maintaining a large degree of individual freedom of choice while still providing a cohesive, integrative force within society. The solution is simple and ingenious. We act according to private beliefs, many of which are highly individualistic and rigid. Yet we think and speak publicly as if we were all bound by a highly libertarian, equalitarian creed which we seriously and conscientiously pretend controls our actions. (In time of national crisis, we may even act according to this public creed.) The most distinctive feature of the public creed is its vagueness, its lack of precise definition. We must preserve the myth that American ideals are

translatable into a single set of concrete actions, but we must be certain that no *single* translation of our ideals does in fact crystallize.[4]

While a value core may exist in verbal form and may perform an important ceremonial function in the life of the society, it does not, according to this analysis, represent a set of specific substantive values to which we require commitment in normal times. Although the core is more explicitly expressed than in most systems, it is sufficiently vague to permit many varied translations. Furthermore, none of the translations must ever become crystallized in the society, except possibly in times of national crisis.

This position comes close to allowing schools to ignore any specific commitment to the individual's development; but it also denies the schools any purpose related to the welfare of the society. If such were the case, schools might find their purposes to be, like the value core in this interpretation, largely ceremonial. More likely, given this value variation, schools would be idiosyncratic. That suggests that local community standards would prevail. That would solve some of the purpose problem, at least in homogeneous communities.

Another view has it that it is possible for our pluralistic society to function only because strategic institutions negotiate most of the profound value disagreements among conflicting groups. An elaborate system of allowable compromises, negotiations, and payoffs ordinarily prevents the occurrence of explosive public confrontations between persons with conflicting interpretations of the value core. City bosses and political machines are pertinent examples of these negotiating institutions. They trade off goods and symbols and use payoffs to keep a tolerable peace. The "gravy" they soak up in the process is simply one of the justifiable costs we pay to protect our pluralism.[5]

A purpose for schools related to the value core is suggested in this interpretation. Schools would have a specific political socialization purpose. Students would be taught the realities of the political system, the functions of bosses and machines, and the benefits and abuses of compromises and payoffs. That, at least, represents a feasible alternative, though not without denying other alternatives. But in a pluralistic society, that is the case whatever option is chosen.

There are many dimensions and probably several levels of pluralism in the United States. We have not tried to be definitive in our treatment of the condition, even relative to the limited range of values in the American value core. We have tried mainly to illustrate the fact that we are a pluralistic society. Furthermore, we have intended to show that our pluralism makes the development of purposes for schools a complex matter. Even to say out of desperation that schools should serve the purpose of helping students appreciate our social diversity offers no easy way out because there is no possible way for schools to display, let alone treat, the many social variations.

Social Change

We avoided in the discussion above on social pluralism the related phenomenon of change in American society. Although the two concepts of pluralism and change refer to different conditions in the society, they interact when they occur together. Change could occur in a uniform society and, presumably, a pluralistic society could continue without any fundamental change. When they occur together, however, for example, when a pluralistic society begins to change, the two conditions feed on each other. The social varieties are intensified and sometimes increased in number and the change is hurried along. We will not, however, attempt to explain this interaction here.

The upshot is that the American society has more trouble than what our discussion of pluralism implies. One view suggests that the conditions in the modern world have caused such a proliferation of value dilemmas that the traditional means of solution and negotiation are simply inadequate to handle the growing case load. Conflicts grow out of such conditions as increasing population pressure, unequal affluence, increasingly strained intergroup and social relations, inflated concern for personal adjustment and self-realization, and liberated sex behavior. Such disagreements relentlessly assault the stability of the individual and overwhelm the capabilities of institutions to maintain social equilibrium and justice.[6]

In the future these social conditions are likely to worsen. As a phase of a larger "Project on the Predicament of Mankind," computer experts at the Massachusetts Institute of Technology have designed a world economic growth model that algebraically treats more than 100 relationships among the elements of population, goods supply, natural resources, pollution, and industrial production. On the basis of early computer runs of the model, initial predictions suggest that human society will collapse before the year 2100 unless the geometric growth of population and industrial output can be halted.[7]

A Transitional Era

Not only is the increase of conflicts taxing the capabilities of the society to settle disputes, but also the means traditionally used to maintain social stability are being altered. These alterations appear to be an aspect of a fundamental change in the United States from a communal society to a mass society.

In a communal society, tradition is the main source of stabilizing values and beliefs. The young are sheltered from damaging outside influences and their almost perfect socialization is accomplished by frequent and rewarding contacts with adults in close-knit families and neighborhoods. While change is not impossible in a communal setting, it is well regulated by the managers of the society, with tradition as the control mechanism.

In a mass society, on the other hand, most aspects of the culture—for example, education, health, religion, recreation, and production—are managed through vast, highly centralized institutions. These huge bureaucracies, with their highly specialized tasks and occupations, function as channels through which scientific and technological developments are fed rapidly into the society. Thus the mass society is wide open to change; but it appears to have fewer accessible mechanisms for the public control of change. Although control mechanisms are available, persons caught in the transition from communal to mass operations do not know what they are, how to get to them, or how to operate them.[8]

Associated with the transition from communal to mass society is the shift from traditional to emergent values. By World War II our traditional value system, along with our communal society, was beginning to erode. The traditional values continued to function as stabilizers and behavioral standards, but with increasing discomfort and dissatisfaction. At the same time the new, mass values, vividly publicized by our efficient media systems and dramatically reflected in the many new groups and organizations that promoted new ideals and programs, were becoming competitive and often the preferred ways of looking at things.

The effects of the value competition between the old and the new continue to be evident in our confused beliefs where the emergent and traditional are in constant conflict.

> The American culture . . . is now, and for some time has been, a culture notable for the conflicts woven into the very fabric of its value system. We place a traditional value upon thrift, but we appear to believe even more strongly in the value of keeping up good appearances that depend upon mortgages and installment payments, which make thrift impossible as we play the game according to the rules of the American Dream. We believe in deferring satisfactions to the future but want the benefits of deferment now. We believe that success is to be won by hard work, but emphasize "personality" and social contacts as means to getting ahead. We laud honesty as a virtue but acknowledge the primacy of

pragmatic expediency in real life. We are egalitarian in ideal and in much of our practice, but indulge in wide-ranging and destructive expressions of invidious prejudice. We deny sexuality but titillate ourselves with sex in our mass media, dress, and imagery. Our culture is patterned in conflicts that in part mirror the struggle between the puritan ethic and the demands and opportunities of an industrializing society of abundance.[9]

The traditional, communal norm strongly reflects what we have come to call the puritan ethic which "includes emphasis on thrift, self-denial, faith in the future, a strong emphasis on success and a belief that hard work [is] the means to it, absolute moral norms, and a strong value placed on the individual." In contrast to this traditional norm, the emergent, mass norm "includes value placed upon sociability, sensitivity to the feelings of others, a relativistic attitude, a present time orientation, and high value placed upon the group."[10]

Thus the social change that we are discussing is a very complex phenomenon. It is not simply that we have different conditions, more "up-to-date" conveniences, more options and opportunities to choose among, and certainly more problems; but at another level, we are changing, or have changed, the structure of the society from a communal way of doing things to a mass way of doing things. Along with these changes, we are changing, or have changed, our way of judging and evaluating things. Since the changes are not yet complete and, in fact, may never be total, we refer to the present time as a transitional era.

Social transition has important effects on the development of purposes for the school. At the level of social conditions, where we have our day-to-day experiences, a set of purposes for the school is directly inferrable: the school should prepare youth to be intelligent and active consumers of modern conveniences and products; the school should help its students to make wise choices among the many new options available to them; the school should train students for employment in the modern world; and finally, the school should teach youth how to solve the increasing number of problems that attend rapid social change.

Those are not easy purposes to fulfill, but they are challenging and understandable. However, in a truly transitional era, the situation we are asserting for the United States, the direct treatment of conditions would be insufficient and eventually self-defeating. A purpose related to public control of social change would be more basic, but that purpose implies a certain political orientation requiring the school to opt for either traditional or emergent values. A transitional society is not disposed to accept or reject wholly either of these value options. Rather, persons in the society have varied patterns of acceptance and rejection.

VALUE RESOLUTION IN A TRANSITIONAL ERA

In a transitional era such as ours, traditional/emergent value conflicts are "resolved" in different ways by different persons. In one way of looking at these possible "resolutions," individuals and groups can be located along a scale that reflects in a general way the ratio of traditional to emergent values displayed in their own beliefs and activities. Those persons who maintain a firm hold on the values of the old communal way of life would be located near the traditional end of the continuum; others who have fully adopted the norms of the mass society would be located at the emergent end.

In a large organization, such as a school, where the participants differ by age, socioeconomic class, education, influence, responsibility, and interests, a wide spectrum of ratios may be present. The "conservative" school board members who are determined to protect the old ethic are near the traditional end of the scale along with the "concerned" parents and adult clientele of the school, the "old-fashioned" teachers, and the "model" students. Near the center of the scale are the school administrators who ply their trade in balancing and negotiating the demands that converge upon them from both ends of the scale, the arbitration-minded school board members, and the "middle-of-the-road" parents, teachers, and students. Distributed along the emergent half of the scale are the "radical" board members, the "liberal" parents and patrons, the "avant garde" teachers, and the rest of the students.

In our illustration above, we used some vague labels for the different points along the scale. "Conservative," "concerned," "old-fashioned," "middle-of-the-road," "liberal," and "avant garde" are useful terms; but they do not refer to distinct characteristics. We have adopted below a more carefully defined set of categories that can be used to classify persons according to the way they respond to tradition-emergent value conflicts. Although members of any of the groups associated with the schools—for example, parents, administrators, board members, or students—could be expected to fall into these response patterns, teachers are used in the following example. The variations in response are typified as the "reaffirmative traditionalist," the "compensatory emergentist," the "vacillator," and the "adjusted" teacher.

Teacher Responses to Traditional/Emergent Value Conflicts

The *reaffirmative traditionalist* teacher takes a rigid stance in his uncompromising projection of the traditional values. The nature and content of his assignments, his standards of success and failure, his management of classroom activities, and his most heartfelt statements faithfully represent the values of the old order in which he firmly believes.

The *compensatory emergentist* teacher uncritically appropriates all the values of the new system. He is an ardent proponent and proselytizer of the new system. Without concern for their effects on his students, he requires conformity to his newly acquired ideals.

The *vacillator* teacher superficially adopts and promotes incoherent parts of the old and the new with no sensitivity to the conflicts that his changing attitudes, directions, and standards aggravate among his students. His classroom is characterized as vacillating between different kinds of leadership and different interaction modes. Both he and his students are confused and unhappy.

The *adjusted* teacher creatively mixes the new and the old patterns into a new synthesis of his very own. The adjusted teacher rationally combines useful features from the traditional and emergent systems. He plays the role of the transitional philosopher who synthesizes the best from both worlds into a system that fits the occasion.[11]

The conceptual scheme classifies adaptive response patterns of persons confronted with changing value contexts. Since responses are contextual, a person's response may vary according to the situation in which he is functioning. An individual who is both a teacher and a parent may respond differently depending upon the role he is assuming at the moment. Obviously the response of youths in a given context may be different from that of adults.

We have suggested that purposes for public education are determined in a societal context. The conditions of the society at a given time are relevant factors in deciding on this rationale. Unfortunately the context characteristics of pluralism and transition which we have represented as important conditions in our society make the task of determining a rationale for the school extremely difficult. Further, if one assumes that the purposes of schooling should be determined cooperatively by adult clients, educators, parents, and students, the potential mix of values, experience, maturity, perspectives, and interests is mind boggling.

A Framework for a Rationale for Secondary Education

As individuals and as members of groups we represent various points on the traditional-emergent continuum, we display different adaptive patterns, and we vary in our ability to accommodate the ideas, values, and priorities of others. In a social context of pluralism and change, the effect that an individual or a group has on determining purposes for schools may depend on the ability to influence the opinions of others or to compromise during periods of impasse. But for educators, the purpose

problem has further complications. Besides having to live in and needing to understand his society, an educator has academic commitments
that transcend the immediate conditions of the society. He must see that
these commitments are also taken into account as a rationale for public
education is built. The assumption is that a rationale for secondary education must be based on judgments about the nature of knowledge,
rationality, and learners, the domains of the educator's professional
commitment, as well as on normative and empirical judgments about the
social world. We offer below a framework for such a rationale as a sum-
mation of these several concerns.

Our way of expressing this rationale framework reveals a bias we
have for putting man and his mind at the center of things. In every cell
of the frame we refer to "conception," "judgments," or "decisions" to be
made by persons in the society. So, rather than saying that a rationale
should reflect *the nature* of society, *the nature* of knowledge, *the nature*
of rationality, *and so forth*, we prefer to say that a rationale should
reflect *a judgment about* the nature of society, *a conception of* the nature
of knowledge, *a conception of* rationality, *and so forth*.

Our position does not deny that there are things "out there" in reality;
but it supposes that persons can look at that reality only through invented
concepts that predetermine what in the reality will be attended to and
what relationships will be emphasized. This position also supposes that
concepts, when held rationally, are infinitely corrigible. That means that
they are always subject to amendment when it is obvious that they are
not working well, that is, when they prevent us from seeing important
data or cause us to emphasize the wrong relationships. Moreover this
position helps to explain why the problem of developing purposes for
the school is so difficult. To say, "Different persons see the world differently" is to say, "They look at the world through different concepts."

A FRAMEWORK FOR DEVELOPING A RATIONALE FOR SECONDARY EDUCATION

I. *Judgments about the Basic Values of Society*

A rationale for secondary education must start with what are judged
to be the basic values of the society. Our discussion of the American
value core dealt with a part of this issue. We tried to make it obvious
that quite different preferences and judgments are in competition at this
basic level. Nevertheless, differences notwithstanding, whatever judgments and decisions are made in the other cells of the framework must
be validated finally with reference to the principles, assumptions, and
beliefs determined in this basic cell.

II. Normative and Analytic Conceptions and Empirical Descriptions of the Social World

Much of what was discussed previously about the conditions in the society is related to empirical conceptions and descriptions of the social world. In our discussion we examined the concepts of pluralism, transition, mass society, and communal society as they apply to what appear to be the conditions in our own society. Our definitions and descriptions, of course, must be thought of as being in competition with other conceptions and accounts of the real world.

Quite apart from the judgments of "what is" are the judgments of "what ought to be." The "ought to be" judgments are located in normative conceptions. Normative conceptions of the social world relate to ideals and visions of the good life, the good man, and the good social order. If schools are to make some contribution toward the achievement of societal goals, then such normative conceptions would constitute primary touchstones for testing the schools' objectives and activities.

III. Conceptions of the Nature of Knowledge

Although often ignored, judgments about the nature of knowledge are the cornerstones of an educational program. Judgments related to the methods of producing knowledge, the grounds for knowledge claims, and the assessment of the validity of knowledge statements are basic to the definition of the nature of knowledge. Without a commitment to knowledge, schools would have no rational justification as educational institutions and educators would become nothing more than purveyors of emotional doctrines. Unfortunately schools and teachers who claim a commitment to something they call knowledge with little or no understanding of what that commitment means have slight professional advantage over schools and teachers who wholly ignore the issues in this cell. Both groups, in effect, are functionally irrational.

IV. Conceptions of the Nature of Rationality

Also basic in the rationale for secondary education are judgments about the nature of rationality. Most expressions of purposes for schools include references to the ability to think; most school curriculums and programs imply that students must learn to think. An appropriate rationale must entail a set of concepts, judgment, and assumptions about the nature of thinking.[12] More broadly, schools and educators must stand for rationality in all human endeavors. To stand for rationality means to require good reasons for believing and doing. If anything, schools should help learners to be rational human beings.

V. Conceptions of the Nature of Learners

Further, a rationale for secondary education must accommodate judgments about the nature of learners. To be realistic and useful, such judgments must consider psychological, sociological, physical, affective, and moral characteristics of adolescents. Obviously schools without learners would not be schools; but schools where learners are treated as if they exist for the benefit of the schools may not be schools with legitimate purposes. A rationale for schools must recognize that schools exist for learners who are human beings.

VI. *Judgments on the Commonality and Generality of Secondary Education*

Another set of judgments that must be taken into account in the development of a rationale for secondary education concerns the commonality and the generality of the curriculum. The judgment on commonality involves the question of whether all students should receive the same instructional program or whether different programs should be provided as alternatives for students with different abilities, needs, and desires. Decisions would also have to be made on the matter of *requiring* secondary education for all youth. Some critics claim that inasmuch as there is little correlation between school performance and life achievement the belief that proper education for the young in an industrial society requires 12 to 20 years of schooling is a hoax.[13]

A judgment on generality relates to the question of whether secondary education should be a specialized experience, in the sense of training students for a specific employment or some other speciality, or a general experience. Also, the judgment would depend on whether general is taken to refer to central skills, ideas, and evaluations useful to deal with life in our times as opposed to a survey of generally everything.[14] For example, one position has it that

> It is not a sign that a man lacks general education if he does not know the date of the The Treaty of Utrecht, the latitude of Singapore, the formula for nitroglycerine or the author of the Four Quarters. It does denote a lack of general education if he cares nothing for any of the arts, confuses a moral judgment with an aesthetic judgment, interprets the actions of Asian political leaders in terms of nineteenth century English parliamentarianism or believes that the existence of God has been scientifically disproved.[15]

While a judgment for or against making secondary education general depends in part on the meaning applied to the term "general education," it might also depend on what alternative is being proposed. A school curriculum that specifically trains persons solely for industrial employment would not seem justifiable. On the other hand, schools that do little more than train pupils specifically for further schooling are held in high regard by some persons in our society.

It would be a contradiction in terms within this judgment area to say that the secondary school's curriculum should be common and specialized in the sense that many options are available. It could, of course, be common, that is, basically the same for all, and specialized when the one specialty, whatever it is, is all that is available.

Thus a rationale for secondary education articulates a justification for schools by means of (1) statements of the society's basic values; (2) statements about what the society is and (3) what it ought to be; (4) statements about the nature of knowledge; (5) statements that define rationality; and (6) statements that describe learners. Proceeding from these statements of justification are judgments on whether secondary education is to be (7) common or varied and (8) general or specialized. These latter judgments also serve as statements of justification for decisions about (9) school curriculums and (10) programs of instruction. We attempt to depict the relationships among these ten elements in a rationale for secondary schools in Figure 1.

EMPLOYING THE RATIONALE FRAMEWORK

Before presenting our framework for a rationale for secondary schools in the United States, we expressed the proposition that schools exist to transmit culture traits of continuing value to the young. Transmission

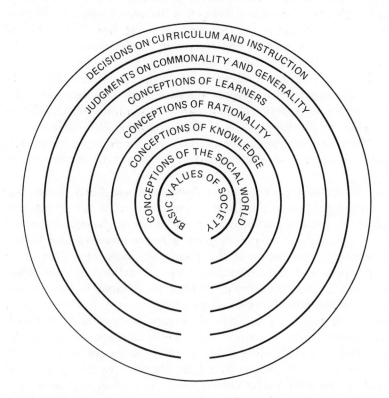

Figure 1 A Framework for Developing a Rationale for Secondary Education

difficulties arise, however, in two ways. First, schools cannot transmit *all* the desirable traits of a culture. There are too many of these and they are too varied to be transmitted by one institution. As a result the transmission task is divided up among several institutions. Problems emerge in this division of labor when the lines of responsibility begin to shift or fade. The socialization of sex was once clearly a family task in our society. Then, for a number of reasons, the school began to assume (or was given) this responsibility. Presently, neither of these institutions appears to be controlling or managing sexual norms.

Our statement of a framework for a rationale for secondary education was an effort to draw some lines of responsibility for the school. In Figure 1, the three rings referring to "Knowledge," "Rationality," and "Learners" specify the school's unique realm. The figure attempts to display, however, that judgments about these matters are made in a social context and are given meaning in school programs.

The second difficulty we have tried to show in this chapter emerges when the social context of the school is pluralistic and changing. Since most of the chapter is used to develop this theme, we will not elaborate on it here. It is sufficient to say that disagreements over the society and its values increase the number and complexity of decisions that must be made about the school's purposes.

This discussion of our framework may help in conceptualizing the different resolutions of the purpose question that have been and still are being proposed. Historically these various resolutions reflect different emphases among the conceptions in the framework. With reference to Figure 1, the conceptual content of a given ring—for example, knowledge, rationality, or learners—is put forward as the dominant concern of the school.

Some illustrations of conceptual dominance are fairly clear. Our earlier characterization of the Latin grammar school of the seventeenth and eighteenth centuries as focusing on the study of classical Latin and Greek and catechistical religion suggests a heavy dominance of knowledge concepts. In the shadow of that dominance, concern for the needs of young people and the development of rationality was minimized. Decisions and assumptions were made for each of these, to be sure; but the purpose of the school was dominated by a concept of knowledge. It does not matter that those seventeenth-century judgments about knowledge are different from our own. The framework does not specify the judgment; it specifies only the realm in which the judgment is made.

Moreover, the Latin school paid little attention to the society and its central values. It is almost inconceivable, of course, that some conception of the society had not figured in the development of the Latin school. Both the society and the school displayed overtones of theocratic elitism. Nevertheless, by mid-eighteenth century, the Latin school was so out of touch with what was occurring in the American society that a readjustment of the social concepts was inevitable.

The life adjustment advocates of the late 1940s, some progressivists in education prior to World War II, and even proponents of the Seven Cardinal Principles back in 1918 seem obviously to have been insisting that concepts of learners should have more effect in determining school purposes than had previously been the case. The social reconstructionists in education following World War II, trading on the theme of the school's role in saving, healing, and remaking the society, seem unmistakable in their emphasis in the social ring and the value center of Figure 1. The enlarged efforts to develop curriculum materials in the 1960s in the sciences, mathematics, English, and the social sciences appear, in large measure, as a resurgence of interest in knowledge as the dominant concept in establishing a purpose for schools. Advocates of critical thinking, reflective thinking, and inquiry in education make their strongest appeals in the name of rationality. Much of the literature on alternative education smacks of a learner orientation.

Our listing is very limited; it is only meant to be illustrative of the fact that powerful proposals for purposes seldom reflect an evenhanded treatment of the areas of judgment specified in our framework. Rather, the rationales that are put forward often favor one area over the others as the locus of the most important reasons for schools to exist.

Furthermore, favored school rationales tend to cycle in and out of a dominating judgment area. While we are unaware of all the social mechanisms that bring about this phenomenon, cycling appears to respond to (1) the overindulgence of one conceptual area for a period of time to the neglect of the others, (2) the advocacy of a different conceptual emphasis by powerful groups in the society, and (3) some obvious change in the social context that renders the old rationale obsolete.

If emphasis there must be in a rationale, two important questions remain to be answered. What emphasis dominates the favored rationale for secondary education today? What conceptual emphasis should we, as members of a powerful educational group, advocate for this transitional era?

SUMMARY

The schools are expected to prepare youth to assume their place in the society by teaching them useful skills, requisite knowledge, appropriate ways of thinking, and accepted ways of making judgments. The discussion of the societal context for public secondary education has focused on how a variety of factors—for example, social movements, important social events, and social pluralism—may affect decisions concerning the purposes that schools are to serve. The problem of determining purpose becomes even more complex in a society passing from a traditional communal posture to an emergent mass posture. Transitional problems tend to divide the population into segments based largely on the degree of attachment to traditional or emergent values.

Persons concerned with developing a systematic approach to the process of decision making about purposes for the secondary school must organize their thinking around the following major questions: What are the basic values of the society? What are the normative and analytic conceptions of the social world? What is the nature of knowledge? What is the nature of rationality? What is the nature of the learner? Furthermore, once a statement of purpose is formulated, its implications for the following questions must be considered: Should secondary education be a common experience for all? To what extent should secondary education be general or specific?

It may be impossible to treat the various conceptual areas equally in developing a rationale for secondary education. At least, historically, school purposes appear to cycle through periods when the issues in a single conceptual area dominate the concern of the school. If an emphasis is inevitable, what area should dominate the purposes of secondary schools in a transitional era?

QUESTIONS AND ACTIVITIES

1. In what ways do the schools in a pluralistic society differ from those in a society characterized by many cultural universals?
2. Give illustrations of how the "value core" has accommodated highly divergent points of view. How can a value be shared by two divergent points of view? Explain your answer.
3. A fundamental split in American society over the interpretation of the values of individual freedom and respect for the worth of the individual is hypothesized in this chapter. Suppose you are on the School Philosophy Committee of a newly formed high school. It is decided that the statement of philosophy which you will submit to the faculty will contain references to the individual freedom and worth values. In an effort to be persuasive, you prepare for the committee a statement that reflects your interpretation of the values. What wording do you suggest? What sort of opposition to your statement would you anticipate? In the long run, what difference does it make which interpretation is embraced by the committee or the school faculty?
4. Describe and give an example of the relationship between the *verbal* value core and the *action* value core. What problems can and do arise

out of this type of situation? What are some possible strategies for closing the gap between professed and practiced values?

5. The authors refer at one point in this chapter to a purpose for schools "related to public control of social change." How would such a purpose be expressed for a school? How would it be implemented in a school program?

6. The authors and others declare that the huge bureaucracies function as channels to bring rapid change to society. Explain the resulting predicament when the society in general does not have the control mechanisms for the public monitoring of change. What are some possible control mechanisms?

7. During a transitional era, what are some ways in which traditional/emergent value conflicts are resolved?

8. Identify the four response variations to traditional/emergent value conflicts adopted by the authors. Apply these concepts in a brief analysis of a problem situation in which you have a good understanding.

9. Prepare a two- or three-sentence summary for each segment of "A Framework for Developing a Rationale for Secondary Education." Once this is done, identify for class consideration one major educational issue which can be analyzed through the use of the "framework."

10. Identify the three rings which specify the school's "unique realm" in the aforementioned "framework." Give illustrations of how each of these areas has been singled out for emphasis by various groups in both the past and present.

11. Select one educational issue of interest to you and apply the "framework" as an analytical tool in clarifying the nature of the issue and possibly identifying strategies for reducing the magnitude of the conflict.

12. You have been asked by a local business group to present a luncheon speech on the topic "Why School?" during National Education Week. You take the request seriously and, as a part of your speech, outline a rationale for schooling. Present your rationale statement to your class for criticism.

13. Collect and analyze the statements of philosophy from several high schools. Evaluate the statements by means of the standard criteria applied by your regional accrediting agency, for example, The North Central Association of Colleges and Secondary Schools. What difference does it make what these statements say? How would you go about determining whether the statements have any meaning?

NOTES

[1] Gail M. Inlow, *The Emergent in Curriculum* (New York: Wiley, 1966), pp. 4–5.

[2] Gunnar Myrdal, *An American Dilemma* (New York: Harper & Row, 1944), pp. 3–6.

[3] William O. Stanley, *Education and Social Integration* (New York: Bureau of Publications, Teachers College, Columbia University, 1953), p. 163.

[4] Donald W. Oliver, "Educating Citizens for Responsible Individualism, 1960–1980," in Franklin Patterson, ed., *Citizenship and a Free Society: Education for The Future*, 30th Yearbook of The National Council for the Social Studies (Washington, D.C., The Council, 1960), p. 204.

[5] David Riesman, *Individualism Reconsidered* (New York: Free Press, 1954), p. 18.

[6] Frederick R. Smith and C. Benjamin Cox, *New Strategies and Curriculum in the Social Studies* (Skokie, Ill.: Rand McNally, 1969), pp. 65–69.

[7] John B. Wood, "Are We Doomed? Ask Computer," *Chicago Daily News*, April 8–9, 1972, pp. 5, 8.

[8] Harry S. Broudy, B. Othanel Smith, and Joe R. Burnett. *Democracy and Excellence in American Secondary Education* (Skokie, Ill.: Rand McNally, 1964), pp. 24–25, 27.

[9] George D. Spindler, "The Transmission of American Culture," in George D. Spindler, ed., *Education and Culture* (New York: Holt, Rinehart and Winston, 1963), p. 149.

[10] Spindler, p. 156.

[11] Spindler, pp. 158–159.

[12] James P. Shaver and Harold Berlack, eds., *Democracy, Pluralism, and the Social Studies* (Boston: Houghton Mifflin, 1968), pp. 2–3.

[13] Paul Goodman, "Freedom and Learning: The Need for Choice," *Saturday Review* 51, no. 20: 73, May 18, 1968. See also Christopher Jencks et al., *Inequality: A Reassessment of the Effect of Family and Schooling in America* (New York: Basic Books, 1972), pp. 221–225.

[14] Broudy, Smith, and Burnett, p. 10.

[15] Oxford University Department of Education, *Arts and Sciences Sides in the Sixth Form* (Abingdon-Berkshire, England: The Abbey Press, 1960), p. 13.

CHAPTER **3**

The Metropolitan Context
of Public Schools

The context of public education in the United States is metropolitan. Most of the schools in this country are metropolitan institutions serving a metropolitan clientele. By 1980, 75–80 percent of our elementary and secondary students will be in metropolitan schools. Secondary education in the last quarter of the twentieth century is overwhelmingly metropolitan education.

A study of a population density map of the United States will show that ours is an urban society. A projection of our urban character in the United States can be seen in the Ekistical maps of Doxiadas (see Figure 2) in which he charts the development of Ecumenopolis in the United States. He depicts the United States as becoming a massive and interconnected urban system.[1]

It takes very little insight on the part of persons living in the United States to recognize that both the primary vitality and the major problems of this nation have their source in our great metropolitan centers. The heartwarming stories of life on the farm told by grandparents who have long since moved to town represent experiences without analogy in the lives of most present and future residents of the United States. The popularity of television's "The Waltons," "The Little House on the Prairie" and "Apple's Way,"and, to some extent, that of "Bonanza" and "Gunsmoke" demonstrates our capacity for nostalgia rather than our concern for what the real world has become.

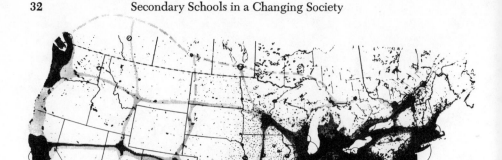

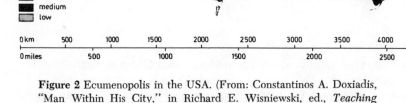

Figure 2 Ecumenopolis in the USA. (From: Constantinos A. Doxiadis, "Man Within His City," in Richard E. Wisniewski, ed., *Teaching About Life in the City*, 42nd Yearbook of The National Council for the Social Studies. Washington, D.C.: The Council, 1972, p. 237.)

In an earlier chapter we looked at the historical development of the school as an institution. We will attempt in this chapter to look at that institution in its present primary context, the metropolis. While neither the school nor any of our social institutions were born of the city, all of them must now function mainly in that setting. It is the function of an institution to order our lives into meaningful patterns and to help us apply the best knowledge and technology to our life problems. In a sense, it is the function of the city in our time to test the viability of these institutions. All, some, or none of them may survive the trial.

The Urban Process

By 1980 it is estimated that between 75 and 80 percent of all Americans will live in urban territory. Considering the population growth of a decade, there will be as many persons living in an urban environment in 1980 as there were in the entire population in the United States in

1970.[2] While the prediction may be in error by a few million, there would appear to be no way to arrest the continued urbanization of our country unless we close the universities, stop all research, and quit producing automobiles.[3] Neither these events nor even more catastrophic occurrences short of an all-out nuclear holocaust, such as economic depression, famine, and pathogenic epidemic, would likely keep persons from coming to the cities. Persons in deep trouble go to the cities where they believe more help and more hope is available.

In the United States we have undergone and are continuing to undergo a process of *systematic* urbanization. In a country that is systematically urbanized, the towns and small- and medium-size cities are regularly distributed and are functionally related to the large cities. The rural producers ship their surpluses to the population centers for sale and, in exchange, seek goods and services that are available in the city. A systematically urbanized country sustains very little subsistence farming. In effect, interdependent satellite systems are developed with large metropolitan centers as nuclei.

Havighurst identifies five stages in the development of a metropolitan nucleus. In the beginning (*stage one*) is a small, trading-center town which in time grows to a medium-size city of 25,000 to 50,000. A socioeconomic structure begins to appear, featuring high-status residential areas, an area on the "wrong side of the tracks" where mainly the working-class people live, and a slum area. If the city has a strategic commercial location, it begins to develop industry and attract more people.

By the time its population has reached 100,000 or more, the city will have emerged into *stage two* as a structured city. Industrial centers with slum areas surrounding them will develop where the well-to-do have evacuated their houses for the choice residential areas on the outskirts of the city. Schools will begin taking on the socioeconomic characteristics of their surrounding areas. Additional high schools are built to assume special functions, such as vocational training or college preparation.

In *stage three*, suburban communities begin to appear beyond the reaches of the central city but along the major railway or highway accesses to the city. The first suburbs tend to be exclusively residential, housing middle- and upper-class persons who have evacuated the city. Some later suburbs will develop industries of their own and become, in effect, small cities, though still retaining their attachment to the main urban center.

The *fourth stage* in the development of a metropolitan area is characterized by a plethora of suburbs, each with its own character and each with its own special attachment to the city. In this period, industry in the central city begins to decentralize and some of the suburbs become its new homes. As the city ages, persons who are financially able, largely middle class, increasingly leave the central city to take up residence in the burgeoning suburbs. As the middle class moves out, the poor move in. During stage four, also, the earliest formed suburbs, now aging, begin to experience an exchange of population. The older, well-to-do, middle-class residents move out farther away from the city into new suburbs, while the poor move into the older suburbs.

In the *fifth stage*, which historically began in the United States with the Housing Act of 1949, some of the depreciated areas of the central city are reclaimed in an effort to reverse the out-migration of middle-class whites. This stage of urban renewal aims both to make the living conditions of the poor in the central city more tolerable and to make the central city a more attractive place for all kinds of people to work and reside. At a minimum, urban renewal intends to replace slum areas with attractive housing and other structures. Beyond that it intends to plan for the growth of the metropolitan area from the central city to its farthest suburb.[4]

During the process of metropolitan growth the metropolitan area becomes stratified both socially and economically. The inner shells of the city come to contain largely persons with low income, for example, blacks, Puerto Ricans, Chicanos, and Latinos. The middle-income people live in the outer shells of the city, while at the outer edges and in the suburbs are the people who have high incomes.[5] There is a general sorting out of areas into wealthy estates, industrial enclaves, middle-class bedroom communities, and the central city. The central city is at one extreme with an increasing percentage of poor families. At the other extreme are the wealthy suburbs.[6]

The suburbs themselves become stratified also, with high-status residential areas developing in certain favored directions, heavy industry in another direction, and middle-class suburbs in still another. The suburbs become differentiated into three basic types: dormitory, employing, and manufacturing.

In a dormitory suburb, at least half of the mainly middle-class residents commute to work in the city or in another suburb. There are only small, local businesses in the dormitory suburb. The dormitory suburb may also contain a high-status residential area. More than half the persons who live in an employing suburb work in that suburb. However, relatively few nonresidents come into the suburb to work. Economically the employing suburb tends to be self-sufficient with local business, light industry, an airport, and sometimes a college existing there. The manufacturing suburb imports workers for its industry. The local residents, who also work in the large manufacturing plants, are usually below average in socioeconomic rank with a high percentage of manual laborers.[7]

As they age, suburbs tend to decrease in their average socioeconomic status. In part, this decrease occurs because the suburban housing and business become obsolescent and the higher-status families move out to newer suburbs or back into the city. Status depreciation also occurs as working employees seek to live near their employing business, industry, or shopping center that has moved into the suburb.[8]

The gradual decrease in socioeconomic status of the aging suburbs nearest the city can also be viewed as a phenomenon related to the process of integrating new people into the life of the city. The new-comers to the city, often members of ethnic minorities, settle in the deteriorating slums of the inner city forcing, in effect, the older and more financially able residents, themselves earlier ethnic immigrants to the city, to move out into the outlying areas. As the displaced persons continue to succeed financially, they move successively through outlying zones and finally into the suburbs, where they often lose their original ethnic identity and become a part of the mainstream of the society. Other newcomers arrive, settle in the inner city, and the process continues.[9]

The question now is whether this integration pattern of spinning off into the suburbs will continue with no new inputs into the central city to push the old residents out. In the past the newcomer was of a different ethnic origin or race than the old resident. At present, the blacks are the major residents of the central city, and there is no new incoming group of sufficient size to expel them in this same way. There is some evidence, however, that the spinning-off process is continuing anyway. Middle-class blacks are beginning to seek refuge in the suburbs from the problems of the central city.

The Institutional Crisis in the Metropolis

The black, Latino, and other ethnic urban migration of the last quarter of a century is the central human event that is forcing a reevaluation of our social institutions. As a result of this minority migration, our urban centers and suburbs have been polarized between nonwhite and white, and the inner cities have become surfeited with social and welfare problems. New York City is a recent and classic case in point. Partly because of its liberal welfare policies and other efforts to provide institutional services for its people, this richest of all cities sought financial help desperately in 1975 from the state, the Federal government, banks, and labor unions to save it from virtual bankruptcy. The incapacitation of our institutions is pervasive. With the possible exception of a few medium-size cities in Northern Europe, no major city in the world has been able to provide housing, health services, and welfare for its poor which meet modern and humane standards.[10] The indictment extends to education.

Technically our incapacity to deal with many of these disturbing human problems is nonsensical. Technically we know how to solve the urban problems of noise, dirt, congestions, housing, parking, traffic flow, transportation, recreation, pollution, health, welfare, and possibly even education. In the face of these technical capabilities, the hypothesis is strongly suggested that our failure to do the technically possible has its source in the life outlooks and beliefs of people and in the institutional arrangements that are the traditional keeps of these paralyzing beliefs and outlooks. Although many of the outlooks and attitudes are patently unjustifiable and many of these beliefs are known to be false— for example, that a man's home is his castle and his neighborhood is his fief, that only the lazy accept welfare, and that those who pay more into the public till deserve more of the public largess—we hold to them tenaciously and neglect to tell our youth that they are false and unjustifiable.[11] As a result the problems persist, and the anachronistic institutions are perpetuated.

The primary indictment of institutions in the city, then, is that they are illegitimate. The assumption supporting this indictment is that in the humanized city the people have a right to be served by institutions legitimated in their own lives, by institutions that help them apply to their real problems the full power of the best technology in the full light of our best knowledge. Anything less than that smacks of custodial welfare and dehumanization. We hypothesize in these chapters that many metropolitan schools, especially in the inner city, display these characteristics of illegitimacy.

The Central Problems of Authenticity and Identity

The city presents us with myriad problems that warrant our concern. Most of them can be shown to have some relationship to education. We will, however, focus on only a few that have immediate repercussions in the conduct of schools in the city, including a look at two of these that have immediate psychological effects on students throughout the metropolitan area. The two concepts that help to define these two interrelated problems are authenticity and identity.

AUTHENTICITY

Advances in science and technology have created so complex a culture in the modern metropolis that it seems to metropolitan man that what he knows and understands is either no longer the case or is a minuscule part of his buzzing new world. Change is so rapid that the culture in which the young are socialized portrays the world that may have been, but certainly no longer is.

Science and technology are not the only dramatic change mechanisms in our society. Some changes occur by the confluence of masses of people who share an engaging idea. In a country of over 200 million persons almost any movement can assemble and unite a half million followers. Woodstock, Bull Island, Guru Maharaj Ji, and the Jesus Freaks are prime examples. It is the nature of the urban system that large numbers of persons are exposed to new ideas.[12]

One of the consequences of living in an environment in which new alternatives are constantly emerging is that the individual who is unused to accommodating himself to change and choice will find it difficult to feel psychologically at ease. He may come to see his own restricted way of life as inauthentic with respect to the larger world which he becomes aware of by accident or design.[13] Thus, a person previously shielded from the diversity of the city may not perceive his limited environment, say, the suburb or the inner city, as an authentic part of the larger metropolitan reality. It is the same for the suburbanite who has retreated from the city as for the inner-city resident who feels compelled to protect himself from the city. Both suburbanization and the closure of the inner city are partially a result of fear. A part of that fear is "a fear of the richness of urban life."[14]

The nearly frantic search for relevance by many middle-class metropolitan youth is in part a result of their having grown up in protected suburbs. Their parents' escape from the city's problems has resulted in these youths growing up in a setting that seems not a part of the vital metropolis.[15] Minority youths in the inner city also suffer similar consequences, though for quite different reasons. They too perceive themselves as separated from the vital reality of the metropolis, even though they are imprisoned in its very center. In a sense their dilemma is more poignant. On the one hand, they are shielded from the larger reality by their own self-isolation. On the other hand, they are prevented from any meaningful participation in the society by racial and socioeconomic barriers.

In the face of wild discrepancies between his present concepts and the alien data that besiege him, the individual must negotiate his alternatives. He can attempt to isolate himself from the new, disturbing data and continue to try to organize his life within the confines of his old, inadequate concepts. He can attempt to accommodate himself to the new whole by continuously amending his existing concepts to incorporate that which is relevant in the new and that which is useful in the old. He can reject his old beliefs and and concepts as unworthy of the new world and seek some new ideal that offers him more satisfaction. He may choose one alternative for some aspects of his life, another for other aspects, and still another for others. Nonetheless, each of the alternatives presents its own set of consequences.

IDENTITY

The immediate personal and psychological consequence of the perception of inauthenticity of one's limited environment and life-style is centered around the concept of identity. When the individual begins to perceive of his life experiences and the environment in which he lives as being inauthentic, he also begins to think of himself as inauthentic and to doubt or deny his own identity which has grown out of his past experiences. To ease his discomfort, he may rationally reevaluate his condition and seek a new accommodation with the world as he now views it. At the other extreme, he may give up entirely and sink into a condition of utter hopelessness, a state of permanent anomie. In trying to reestablish a nonbanal identity, he may join thousands of his compatriots in what are actually mass voyages of identiy, for example, in drugs, crusades, hero worship, rituals and cults, style rebellions, and endless fads.[16]

The two concepts of environmental authenticity and personal identity are interactive. Unless a person's surroundings are perceived as real and authentic, he will experience difficulty with his own personal identity perceptions. Conversely, unless he achieves an identity that expresses his selfness, his surroundings are likely to seem ethereal and unsubstantial. The two conditions have implications for the conduct of schools throughout the metropolitan area. Too often schools ignore the problems of environmental authenticity and personal identity. By providing no assistance to the individual, they actually may aggravate his problems.

Race and Class in the Metropolitan Area

Two other conditions that have great effect on metropolitan education are neither new in origin nor uniquely urban; however, their conquences are magnified in the urban context. The two conditions, racial and class segregation, are pervasive characteristics of metropolitan life. In a later chapter we will treat their specific ramifications in the schools.

Outside the considerations of health, safety, and public welfare, it is difficult in a democracy to find a justification for legislating where a person may or may not live. Nevertheless, we have done so from time to time in the United States with respect to blacks, Indians, Jews, Orientals, several other minorities, and the poor. The systems that have been utilized for this purpose include slavery, indentures, reservations, segregation, covenants, and codes. Each in its own way had its realm and era of effectiveness; together, they have left us with a legacy of racist and elitist outlooks and attitudes.

SOCIAL CLASS SEGREGATION

Most of the metropolitan area is characterized by homogeneous communities segregated on the bases of race, ethnic origins, and social class. Communities segregated by race or ethnic origin are highly visible and easily labeled. They are identified usually by the single factor of race or ethnic origin and take on the name of the majority residents, for example, the black, Spanish-American, or Polish community. Communities segregated by social class are subject to a more complex system of categorization. Sociologists attempting to determine the social class of the residents of a community will look at such variables as the type of housing, the geographic location of the area, and the occupation, amount of income, amount of education, cultural interests, and child-rearing practices of the residents. On the basis of these variables, persons can be classified as being members of the lower, middle, or upper class. Sometimes additional strata, such as lower-middle and upper-middle, are added to the hierarchy. Similarly whole communities can be characterized with respect to their social class according to the classification of the majority of their residents. The most reliable single indicator of social class membership is the occupation of the household head.

Persons in our society are quite sensitive to the social class status of other persons and very sensitive to the socioeconomic level of their communities. They are especially aware of a deterioration in the socioeconomic ratio of their communities when persons of lower occupational status begin moving in. When this sort of class invasion occurs, the higher-class residents who are financially able move out of the community. Moving to a better neighborhood from a socioeconomically deteriorating neighborhood is one of the means used in our society to maintain social class segregation. Restricted building codes are another mechanism used to protect the socioeconomic level of communities and maintain class segregation. Home building in middle-class and upper-middle-class subdivisions in the metropolitan area typically is regulated by fixing minimum limits on the size and cost of houses, standards of lot usage and development, and rules of occupancy.

RACIAL SEGREGATION

Historically relationships between blacks and whites in the United States have been characteristic of a caste system. Extensive and rigid lines were drawn between the two races, with the blacks always in a subordinate position. That earlier cast relationship is reflected in the present socioeconomic distribution of whites and blacks across socioeconomic status levels. Although both whites and blacks are now represented in all the socioeconomic status levels, they are not equitably represented. There is a smaller proportion of blacks in the upper half of the distribution than of whites. The trend, however, is toward an equalization of these distributions. In the future the distribution of blacks may approximate that of the whites.[17]

Racial segregation in the cities was simultaneous with the heavy in-migration of southern blacks to northern cities in the post–World War I era. From World War I to the close of World War II, segregation was enforced in the cities by "restrictive covenants." The covenant was a device written into real estate deeds to prevent blacks, Orientals, and non-Christians from moving into certain areas of the city. A covenant required the owner to pledge not to sell his home to the types of persons identified in the covenant. An owner who violated a restrictive covenant could be brought into court. This device effectively confined blacks moving into the cities to areas unprotected by restrictive covenants or to areas where covenants were not being enforced by agreement of the owners and real estate companies. Such areas were the least desirable in the city because of age or location.[18]

When covenants were declared illegal, owners and real estate dealers successfully maintained racial segregation in many desirable areas by the use of "gentlemen's agreements." White owners in an area would promise not to sell their houses to in-migrating blacks, and real estate agents would cooperate by not showing these houses when offered for sale to prospective black buyers. Such agreements were not enforceable in the courts and, in fact, were patently illegal.

Even the efforts after World War II to refurbish the inner cities have served inadvertently to perpetuate the conditions of segregation. The Housing Act of 1949 provided federal aid for slum clearance, housing projects, and what has come to be called urban renewal. While many of the most bitter poverty pockets in major metropolitan areas have been reconstructed by this process, a result has been the intensification of segregation by the grouping of the poor and racial minorities in huge housing complexes in certain areas. The creation of such housing complexes can change almost overnight the racial distribution in the schools serving the area. Few schools are able to adjust quickly to such dramatic changes.

Segregation in Metropolitan Schools

We have indicated that a basic condition of metropolitan education is racial and class segregation in the schools. That condition is a result of population distribution patterns in the metropolitan area and of traditional social policies relative to the separation of races. Although the condition has been determined illegal, the residential patterns unworthy, and the social policies unjustifiable, all three are retained with some vigor in the attitudes and actions of the majority of metropolitan dwellers.

The existential cause of racial isolation in the urban public schools is residential segregation. For example, 80 percent of the blacks* who live in the metropolitan area reside in the inner city. At the same time, 50 percent of the whites in the metropolitan area live in the suburbs. The resultant, residential-based segregation in the schools is often referred to as *de facto* segregation. De facto segregation is reinforced in the metropolitan area by "the antimetropolitan nature of school district organization." The division of the educational system into a large number of independent districts throughout the metropolitan area precludes the intermixing of inner-city and suburban students.[19] While the racial mixing of students within the central city is possible by the pairing and mixing of black and white schools or the cross busing of black and white students, it is extremely difficult to pair, mix, or bus between city and suburbs. In medium-size cities where outlying residential areas are included within the school district or in suburbs that have significant black populations, racial mixing has occurred in several ways. But in the great metropolitan areas where the suburban school districts are sacrosanct and never include central city areas, the massive mixing of students is largely prevented.

Sacrosanctity notwithstanding, in some locations, Federal district judges have ordered busing programs involving more than one school district that take city blacks to suburban schools and suburban whites to city schools in an effort to even out racial ratios. In Louisville, the court-ordered desegregation plan reformed the separate districts of Louisville and Jefferson County into a single district.

The situation is no better within the central city itself, even with the legal district barriers removed. In fact the larger the city, the smaller the percentage of mixed classes and the larger the percentage of homogeneous middle-class or lower-class schools.[20] In 1967, thirteen years after the Supreme Court's landmark decision in *Brown* v. *Topeka* outlawing segregation in the public schools, in the twenty largest cities in the United States, 70 percent of the black pupils attended schools that were 90 to 100 percent black.[21] By 1980, white pupils will be in the minority in most northern city schools.[22] Experiences in Washington, D.C., dramatically illustrate the trend. Before the 1954 Supreme Court decision, the District's schools were 55 percent white. By 1968 they were only 10 percent white. Furthermore, half of the students in the District's schools were from families beneath the poverty line of $3,000 income per year and the dropout rate was 50 percent. An irony of the

---

* The authors recognize that there are many minorities in the city. It is not accurate to call all of them black nor fair to call any of them nonwhite. On occasion we generalize across these racial and ethnic groups. But most often, we refer to the vast majority, which is black.

situation, though not a sociological contradiction, is that middle-class blacks were deserting the school system or demanding class segregated schools.[23]

The point to be made is that school segregation is a direct result of the segregated residential patterns in the metropolitan area and that this condition proceeds from the outlooks and attitudes of the majority of the metropolitan dwellers. When they are financially able, the middle-class whites seek refuge from the problems of the central city and from the in-migrating blacks in the relatively protected suburbs of the metropolitan area. The blacks are rapidly becoming or have become the majority residents of the central city and, along with Latinos, Chicanos, and other ethnic groups, nearly the exclusive residents of the inner city. As a result the schools of the central city are becoming or have become predominantly black while most schools in the suburban areas remain predominantly or exclusively white. Some of the older suburbs, generally those closer to the central city, are also exhibiting the same racial exchange residential pattern. The residential preferences of the majority of the metropolitan dwellers, together with the anti-metropolitan nature of independent school districts, work to thwart efforts to integrate the races in public school classrooms.

Legitimacy

The exchange of clientele in the urban schools produces many anomalies in the schools. For one thing, the faculties ordinarily do not change as the clients change. The result is often a mismatching of community and school values. From one view, this community-school mismatch calls into question the legitimacy of the school. We stated earlier that to be legitimate, a school must help the persons whom it serves to apply knowledge to their own real problems. When schools do not have legitimacy with respect to the lives of their clientele, they become nothing more than custodial for these persons. Custodial programs do not encourage creativity or participation. Worse, they may be dysfunctional in the lives of these educationally denied persons. The indictment has been focused primarily on the inner city. As a result of their alleged custodial programs, the inner-city schools have been characterized as shambles without order or learning.[24]

Rhody McCoy so characterized the schools in the Ocean Hill-Brownsville area of New York prior to his assuming the position of administrative head of the district.

> Mrs. Smith—that's a fictitious lady—used to go into the school and she'd say to the principal, "Will you tell me about my little boy?" And

the principal would pass you on to the teacher and the teacher would say, "Mrs. Smith, Johnny is the nicest boy in the world, comes to school neat and clean, it's a pleasure to have him in my class, he's so well behaved," and poor Mrs. Smith! At the end of the year, Johnny can't read his name.[25]

One explanation for the alleged illegitimacy of these inner-city schools centers on the educational ideals of professional autonomy and political sterility. Educators have opposed political decisions on educational programs; administrators are presumably appointed without regard for political affiliation; school boards are supposedly appointed or elected without political identification. The assumption is that education should be shielded from political influence.

But as a result of the political isolation of educators, schools are often unresponsive to groups in the city whose only influence is political. Presumably the politicization of the schools would assure a sensitivity to any group capable of wielding political power within the city.[26] Political power, of course, cannot be equated with representativeness. A power group does not necessarily represent the real needs of the community.

As another result of being nonpoliticized, schools find themselves shielded from effective political support. In part, political support is denied the school because of the traditional isolation of the schools from party politics. But in a broader sense, political support separate from party concerns is denied the urban school by the body politic because of the ingrained racism of the American people. White suburbanites reject out of hand any proposals for sharing the social burdens and economic costs of neighboring, black, central city schools.

The legitimacy of the inner-city school especially has been questioned by many concerned persons who believe that students in these schools are being failed for life rather than educated for life. Despite the conclusions of Jencks that "differences between schools have rather trivial long-term effects," these persons see the inner-city student destined for a life of economic insecurity because of the irreversible effects of a custodial school program.[27]

Specifically, in this view the well-known economic and social inequities suffered by persons from inner-city schools in their adult life are causally linked with their obviously depressed achievement in school. If the schools were better, that is, legitimated for inner-city students, the argument is made, the achievement of these students would be improved and hence their life chances would be increased. The argument is only partly valid. Although the quality of schooling has an effect on school achievement, other factors may be more influential both on achievement in school and in life after school.

The fact that certain groups of persons consistently achieve below average in school and in life after school has stimulated researchers to seek explanations. In particular, they are trying to account for the lower achievement of lower-class and black students in school. What factors, they are asking, consistently function in a negative way to depress the achievement of these students?

Explanations for Class and Racial Differences in Achievement

Scholars who have studied the data on the differential achievement of students across socioeconomic levels and races have arrived at disagreeing explanations for the slower development of minority and lower-class children. Their varying explanations emphasize social-environmental, school-situational, physiological, and genetic-racial factors. Most of the expert opinions can be classified under these broad categories.[28]

A popular explanation of the 1960s, which we referred to earlier, indicts the school itself as defeating the urban ghetto child. The compassionate critics of the school—for example, Holt, Herndon, Kohl, Kozol, Hentoff, Silberman, and others—dramatized the educational genocide perpetrated on blacks and other minorities by the white middle class through the instrument of the middle-class school.

Inner-city teachers have been especially severely criticized for their failure to improve the instructional programs in inner-city schools. There are obvious reasons for any such failure. The staffs of inner-city schools often are economically and culturally alien to the school neighborhoods and students. When students are predominantly lower-class black and teachers are typically middle-class white, the disparity between teacher and student reflects class-related belief systems, views of self and others, and other values.[29] The inner-city staff is likely to consist of uncertain, young recruits still in culture shock along with veteran teachers who have been stigmatized for their long identification with the slum school.[30]

This school quality factor also includes the general and special purposes of the school and the matching of these purposes with the concerns of the students; the nature of the rules governing the conduct of students and faculty within the school; the attitude of the administration toward the staff and toward the students; the authority structure of the school; the content and the flexibility or rigidity of the curriculum; the standard classroom procedure; the richness of the extracurriculum; the relationship of the school to the community; the condition of the building; the crowdedness of the school; the kind and amount of materials available for instruction; and the general amount of financial and moral support afforded the school by the community.

The more recent research of Jencks has questioned the validity of this indictment as a serious explanation of differential achievement of students from different socioeconomic levels and races. He concludes that equalizing the quality of both elementary and high schools would reduce the inequality in achievement by 4 percent or less.[31]

Robert Coles, in his *Children of Crisis*, makes a strong case that the social-environmental conditions under which the inner-city child must live and develop is so severe as to be pathological. The morbidity of the inner city and its slums is so pervasive as to irrevocably mar the potential mental development of inner-city children. He would see radical social change as the only possible way to ameliorate the crippling conditions of the inner city. Other observers, while agreeing that the conditions are intolerable and that they are the primary cause of arrested development and depressed school achievement, believe these social-environmental conditions to be more easily remediable. The divisions among these opinions are not on the effect of the environment on the child, but on the remedies required to counter this effect.[32]

Another set of environmentalist opinions centers on the effects of the home on the development of the child. The shared assumption of these opinions is that the school is largely unable to contribute to any development beyond the contribution of the home. If the home and the school are in agreement on important experiences, beliefs, and values, the school can amplify the prior contributions of the home. If the school and the home are in basic disagreement, the child comes to discover that what the school teaches does not relate to his life and experiences in his real world. The school reinforces the teachings of middle-class homes, but fails to relate to the behaviors of students from other socioeconomic backgrounds.[33] Important in this respect would appear to be the interests and preoccupations of family members, the variety of activities of the family, the types and amount of social contacts maintained by the family, the family's "cultural" interests, the kind and amount of reading material available in the home, and the kind and level of conversation carried on by family members. Other important contributions of the family that affect success in school are related to attitudes toward work, responsibility, authority, and other people, as well as training in promptness, neatness, diligence, and thoroughness.

Contemporary studies on the effects of malnutrition, ill health, and drug addiction during pregnancy has precipitated a renewed interest in a physiological explanation for the slow development of inner-city children. Although the power of this physiological hypothesis to explain the entire effect of poor achievement in school is in question, the specific debilitating effects of malnutrition, ill health, and drug addiction are well documented. Furthermore, the incidence of these crippling pre- and postnatal conditions is known to be higher among the poor than in affluent groups.

Another explanation relates to the inborn ability of the individual. Ability by definition is a personal factor and by observation is infinitely variable. Variability in individual ability has intrigued observers for centuries and has been a major preoccupation of psychologists in the last century. Some aspects of inborn ability have been elaborately defined and are purportedly measurable. Due to their relatively stable, genetic origins, their occurrence is even predictable. For example, intelligence has been voluminously defined, is measurable by the intelligence quotient, or IQ, and furthermore, can be predicted with reasonable probability from parental intelligence.

In this regard, a view that had been largely abandoned by most authorities was revived in the late 1960s by Arthur Jensen. This position has it that the simplest explanation for the differential functioning of inner-city and middle-class children is also the oldest. The differences in intellectual capacity and academic potential are related to race.[34] While views hypothesizing the genetic inequality of the black and white races are at least as old as Negro slavery in this country, their acceptability has been regional and expedient. This most recent expression of the racial hypothesis, while enjoying the support of some, is hotly contested by others in the scientific community.[35]

Another hypothesis is that the motivation level, aspirations, and self-concepts of majority and minority students are critical factors in their different levels of achievement. This position emphasizes the contrast between the educational expectations of middle-class students, largely white, and inner-city students, largely black. Most middle-class, white students attend school with the high expectation of learning subject matter that will contribute directly to their further educational and occupational aspirations. Their apparent healthy and positive self-concepts allow them to approach this task with a high degree of tolerance and a presumption of success. In the inner city, however, the climate is presumed to be one of negative expectations.[36] The students ordinarily display lower aspirations toward further education or occupations for which the school curriculum is largely preparatory. Furthermore, their approach to the task of school is not buoyed by a healthy self-concept which anticipates success. The "Black is beautiful" movement notwithstanding, the argument continues, "Most black children live within a world where black connotes evil and shame." They "are trapped in the delusion of worthlessness so carefully engineered by an exploitative larger society." Thus their approach to schooling is that of a worthless person doing a worthless task for a worthless purpose.[37]

Some of the experiences in the Ocean Hill-Brownsville area of New York suggested that elements of this negative climate as well as the defeatist attitude of students can be alleviated by increased community participation and control in the schools. Given more relevant purposes and experiences, both teachers and students exhibited new expectations for learning.[38]

We will not attempt to judge among these explanations. We express them here as tentative hypotheses that warrant the further examination of the profession and the society. An aspect of this examination involves the tracing of their implications in the formation of urban school policy, an exercise we intend to perform in the next chapter.

The Denial of Mobility

The tone of this chapter suggests a normative frame for our discussion of race and class segregation in the metropolitan area. Segregation is detrimental in a democracy because it denies the opportunity to the segregated minority for important growth-producing experiences with the social mainstream majority. Both racial and socioeconomic segregation affect the entire society by restricting opportunities for growth and development. Growth naturally occurs when persons from mixed backgrounds are allowed to learn and socialize together.[39]

The persons for whom socioeconomic and racial segregation produce the most disastrous consequences are the poor and the racial and cultural minorities. It is these adults and children who are specifically denied the opportunity to learn what is needed to succeed in the larger society. In many instances the learnings refer to behaviors associated with the middle class.

The position presented in this line of argument is both defensible and popular. It parallels the position taken by the Supreme Court in support of its 1954 decision which outlawed segregation in the public schools and is posited in many statements supporting increased educational opportunities, better schools, and equalized employment. Persons favoring this view, however, should examine its assumptions before wholly ascribing to it. One of these assumptions is that the middle-class way of life is appropriate, if not preferable, for living in our society. This assumption was affirmed by Coleman in his report on educational opportunity[40] and tends to be supported in most school programs. This assumption implies another: that persons in the lower-socioeconomic level are desirous of moving from lower-working-class status into occupations normally associated with middle-class status. Still another prejudicial assumption suggests that the blacks, the poor, and other denigrated minorities are the sole beneficiaries in interactions with middle-class whites.

Jencks, in his study of inequality, avoids such jaundiced assumptions by viewing the desegregation of schools as "part of a political process in which diverse people (adults as well as children) are forced to accept the fact that they have to live with one another." He assumes simply that in the long run "this will be a good thing for society."[41]

It is our view that it is essential for educators in the public schools to examine with care these and other assumptions and the positions they support. The discussions in the following chapter will assist in this examination.

QUESTIONS AND ACTIVITIES

1. The authors discussed the process of systematic urbanization. What are some educational implications of the process for decisions on school districts, programs of study, teacher salaries, and desegregation?
2. Identify the five stages in the development of a metropolitan nucleus and then indicate what types of educational problems might be associated with the various stages.
3. How are the suburbs stratified and what implications does this have for those responsible for the management of suburban school environments?
4. Briefly describe the nature of the metropolitan institutional crisis. What are some beliefs that contribute to the malaise of the cities?
5. What are some of the contributing factors to that cluster of problems conceptualized as inauthenticity?
6. How do the problems associated with identity manifest themselves among persons inhabiting metropolitan areas?
7. What could be done in schools to deal with the problems of environmental authenticity and personal identity?
8. Explain the ways and means by which metropolitan areas become racially and socially segregated.
9. What are some of the significant characteristics of segregation in metropolitan schools and how do these contribute to the problems facing urban educators?
10. Identify the important aspects of the "legitimacy" problem faced by many metropolitan schools and then apply the concept to a problem with which you are familiar.
11. Identify both the explicit and implicit values which are involved in the various issues which arise out of the subject of school achievement.
12. Several explanations were hypothesized in this chapter for differences in achievement across races and classes in the United States. How would you set about to test the plausibility of any of these explanations?
13. Suppose you are at a party where the subject of "Jensenism" comes up. You are asked your opinion as an educator. What do you say?

14. How does immobility violate some of the most cherished values of our society?
15. Do you think Jencks' view of desegregation as a political process which forces persons "to accept the fact that they have to live with one another" offers an adequate justification for the policy? How do you justify your opinion?
16. Prepare as a group project a summary of Jensen's "How Much Can We Boost I.Q. and Scholastic Achievement." Prepare as a follow-up activity a summary of Hirsch's "Jensenism: The Bankruptcy of 'Science' without Scholarship."

NOTES

[1] Constantinos A. Doxiadis, "Man Within His City," in Richard Wisniewski, ed., *Teaching About Life in the City*, 42nd Yearbook of The National Council for the Social Studies (Washington, D.C.: The Council, 1972), p. 237.

[2] William Van Til, *The Year 2000: Teacher Education* (Terre Haute: Indiana State University, 1968), pp. 9–35.

[3] Doxiadis, p. 227.

[4] Robert J. Havighurst, *Education in Metropolitan Areas*, (Boston: Allyn and Bacon, 1966), pp. 33–44.

[5] Havighurst, *Education in Metropolitan Areas*, p. 52.

[6] Havighurst, *Education in Metropolitan Areas*, p. 67. See also John Shannon, "Tax Policy and Educational Expenditure," *The Encyclopedia of Education*, vol. 8 (New York: Macmillan and Free Press, 1971), pp. 590–595.

[7] Havighurst, *Education in Metropolitan Areas*, pp. 68–69.

[8] Havighurst, *Education in Metropolitan Areas*, p. 70.

[9] Louis Wirth, *The Ghetto* (Chicago: University of Chicago Press, 1928).

[10] Dan W. Dodson, "The Metropolitan Racial Shift and Three Questions for Inquiry," in Richard Wisniewski, ed., *Teaching About Life in the City*, 42nd Yearbook of The National Council for the Social Studies (Washington, D.C.: The Council, 1972), p. 79.

[11] Lawrence E. Metcalf, "Urban Studies, Reflectively Speaking," *Social Education* 33: 657, October 1969.

[12] Doxiadis, p. 229. See also Richard J. Woods, "Jesus Freaks, Gurus, and Dissent," *The Progressive* 38, no. 6: 27–30, June 1974.

[13] David U. Levine, "The Unfinished Identity of Metropolitan Man," in Richard Wisniewski, ed., *Teaching About Life in the City*, 42nd Yearbook of The National Council for the Social Studies (Washington, D.C.: The Council, 1972), pp. 26–27.

[14] Richard Sennet, *The Uses of Disorder: Personal Identity and City Life* (New York: Knopf, 1970), p. 72.

[15] Levine, p. 37.

[16] Orrin E. Klapp, *Collective Search for Identity* (New York: Holt, Rinehart and Winston, 1969), p. 331.

[17] Havighurst, *Education in Metropolitan Areas*, p. 16.

[18] Havighurst, *Education in Metropolitan Areas*, p. 56.

[19] Thomas F. Pettigrew, "The Negro and Education: Problems and Proposals," in Irwin Katz and Patricia Gurin, eds., *Race and Social Sciences* (New York: Basic Books, 1969).

[20] Robert J. Havighurst, "Urban Development and the Educational System," in A. Harry Passow, ed., *Education in Depressed Areas* (New York: Teachers College Press, 1963), pp. 24–25.

[21] Robert A. Dentler and J. Elsberg, "Big City School Desegregation: Trends and Methods," *Papers Prepared for National Conference on Equal Educational Opportunity in American Cities* (Washington, D.C.: Government Printing Office, 1967), p. 307.

[22] Charles A. Glatt, "Selected Demographic Factors That Affect School Planning: A Look at Four Northern Cities," *Urban Education* 2, no. 1: 35–49, 1965.

[23] George R. LaNoue, "Political Questions in the Next Decade of Urban Education," *The Teachers College Record* 69, no. 6: 517, March 1968.

[24] Dodson, p. 81.

[25] Rhody McCoy, "Why Have an Ocean Hill-Brownsville?" in Nathan Wright, Jr., ed., *What Black Educators Are Saying* (New York: Hawthorn, 1970), p. 254.

[26] Robert H. Salisbury, "Schools and Politics in the Big City," *Harvard Educational Review* 37: 409, Summer 1967.

[27] Christopher Jencks et al., *Inequality: A Reassessment of the Effect of Family and Schooling in America* (New York: Basic Books, 1972), p. 16.

[28] David J. Fox and Valerie Barnes, "School Achievement," *The Encyclopedia of Education*, vol. 9 (New York: Macmillan and Free Press, 1971), p. 387.

[29] Robert E. Herriott and Nancy H. St. John, *Social Class and The Urban School* (New York: Wiley, 1966), pp. 55–83.

[30] B. Othanel Smith, *Teachers for the Real World*, The American Association of Colleges for Teacher Education (Washington, D.C.: 1969), pp. 27–28.

[31] Jencks, p. 109.

[32] Robert Coles, *Children of Crisis: A Study of Courage and Fear* (Boston: Atlantic-Little Brown, 1967).

[33] James S. Coleman et al., *Equality of Educational Opportunity*, vol. 1 (Washington, D.C.: Government Printing Office, 1966), p. 325.

[34] Arthur Jensen, "How Much Can We Boost I.Q. and Scholastic Achievement?" *Harvard Educational Review* 39: 1–123, 1969.

[35] Jerry Hirsch, "Jensenism: The Bankruptcy of 'Science' without Scholarship," *Educational Theory* 25, no. 1: 3–27, 102, Winter, 1975.

[36] Mario D. Fantini, "Participation, Decentralization, and Community Control," *The National Elementary Principal* 48, no. 5: 27, April 1969.

[37] James A. Banks, "Liberating the Black Ghetto: Decision Making and Social Action," in Richard Wisniewski, ed., *Teaching About Life in The City*, 42nd Yearbook of The National Council for the Social Studies (Washington, D.C.: The Council, 1972), p. 164.

[38] Fantini, p. 30.

[39] Havighurst, *Education in Metropolitan Areas*, p. 74.

[40] Coleman, p. 20.

[41] Jencks, p. 31.

CHAPTER 4

Alternatives for Metropolitan Schools

A policy is a settled course of action for a government, institution, organization, group, or individual. School policies are regularly made by school boards, school administrators, state departments of education, and state legislatures. The federal government, though not empowered by the Constitution to control education, also occasionally makes policy decisions for schools. The early law to use the sale of public lands for the support of schools is an example. The existence of a United States Office of Education has many policy implications for schools. More important, perhaps, is the fact that the Supreme Court has made a number of policy decisions that affect every school in the nation. One of these decisions—which, though made over twenty years ago, still is straining the adaptive nature of the educational institution—provides the context for our discussion on alternatives for metropolitan schools.

Desegregation

Racial desegregation has been a policy for public education in the United States since the Supreme Court decision of 1954. Repeatedly, the Supreme Court has reinforced its ruling that racial segregation in the schools must be ended "with all deliberate speed." Districts have been warned not to delay the integration of their schools by either "ingeniously or ingenuously" conceived tactics. In addition, the executive branch of the United States government attempted for a time to hasten the desegregation of schools by threatening to withdraw federal supplementary funds from those schools that were not making significant progress toward compliance with the Supreme Court's ruling. Furthermore, most state departments of education, under pressure from the courts and the federal executive as well as their own state governments, have forced local school boards into compliance by the threat of withdrawal of state aid to schools.

The Supreme Court had taken well over half a century to fashion its policy of desegregation of public education. Prior to its desegregation decision in *Brown* v. *Topeka* (1954), the official policy for public schools was embodied in the Court's "separate but equal" doctrine, applied to schools 58 years earlier in *Plessy* v. *Ferguson* (1896). In 1954 the Supreme Court acknowledged that the grounds for the separate but equal doctrine had narrowed so significantly that it was no longer tenable as a legal premise in United States law. Largely on sociological and psychological grounds, the policy of desegregation was adopted as the favored legal premise applicable to racial discrimination cases in public schools.[1]

Since 1954 there have been several major strategies utilized in the attempt to desegregate the public schools throughout the United States. These have included the pairing of schools, the changing of school district boundary lines, busing, and the clustering of schools on common sites. In many small- and medium-size cities, considerable progress has been made toward the goal of racial integration. However, in the large cities, where the escape hatch to the suburbs is open and where the practice of voluntary residential segregation is most clearly perfected, nearly all attempts to desegregate the schools have been frustrated.

PAIRING SCHOOLS

In the strategy of pairing, two schools of dissimilar racial composition are matched and portions of their student bodies are traded so that each of the buildings becomes desegregated to some degree. The difficulties that arise from pairing schools for "integration" are predictable. If the paired schools are of equal size, one black and one white, decisions must be made on the percentage of each student body that will be transported to the matching school. Each either becomes a 50-50 school or each becomes a majority-minority school with the black to white ratio reversed in the two schools. If the paired schools also reflect different socioeconomic levels, the problems are further aggravated. Further, there is a problem of geographically locating conveniently matchable schools and, given the increasing ratio of blacks to whites in most of our larger cities, there is often a problem of locating enough white schools to match with black schools within the jurisdiction of the city. An effort to accommodate this situation would involve cooperative arrangements between urban and suburban districts. In such cases as Charlotte, North Carolina, Richmond, Virginia, Indianapolis, Indiana, Louisville, Kentucky, and Boston, Massachusetts, orders of federal district courts mandated the "cooperative arrangements."

REDISTRICTING

It was not an unusual practice, at least prior to 1954, for school boundary lines to be shifted periodically in order to follow any changes in the racial residential pattern of the city. Such gerrymandered districts were a common means of maintaining the racial identity of white schools in buffer neighborhoods where the racial composition was changing from white to black. In effect, gerrymandering was used to contain the increasing and spreading black population in black school districts. After 1954, particularly in the late sixties, when the federal executive began to use more powerful mechanisms to hasten integration and the Supreme Court issued more severe rulings relative to the time scheduling for desegregation, gerrymandering has been used as a desegregation tactic. This procedure has worked imperfectly also, because there are too few adjacent black and white neighborhoods that can be gerrymandered into new integrated districts. As a result school authorities have had to seek out nonadjacent pockets of white and black residents as the integrating elements in districts. As with pairing, conveniently positioned suburban communities are beyond the jurisdiction of the urban school authorities as sources of white students to integrate black schools or as the locations of white schools to which the cities' black students can be sent. As we mentioned earlier, however, several federal district judges have mandated in some cases that black, urban students be bused to white, suburban schools, and vice versa.

BUSING FOR RACIAL BALANCE

Both the pairing of schools and the gerrymandering of integrated school districts have required the transportation of large numbers of students from one part of the city to their newly integrated school in another part of the city. The usual means of transporting these students has been by school buses. The practice produced the phrase "busing for racial integration." While the use of buses for transporting school children of all ages to and from schools in the United States predates the automobile (the first buses were horse drawn), this use of buses was met with intense opposition. Opposition has come from groups who basically oppose integration; persons who believe that most instances of busing are subtly discriminatory against blacks, the most often transported group; groups who want to retain the image of the neighborhood school, especially at the elementary level; and persons who believe that busing is wasteful of students' time and dangerous for young children. Some parents and students, both black and white, are among those in opposition. Since the transportation of some students from their own communities to other communities appears to be the only means of integrating many urban schools short of relocating millions of persons in different residential patterns, opposition to busing means opposition to integration. The outcry of those opposing busing was so great that President Nixon was moved to request the federal courts to cease enjoining school boards to use busing to facilitate the integration of their schools. Furthermore, the President promised to seek legislation that would outlaw the use of busing as a means for achieving integration in the public schools. Neither that legislation nor the more ambitious efforts of adamant antibusing groups to persuade Congress to approve a Constitutional amendment that would ban forced busing have succeeded. However, Congress and President Ford have enacted a law that sanctions the use of busing as a means of achieving desegregation only as a last resort.

EDUCATIONAL PARKS

A fourth strategy conceived partially as a means of achieving integration is the massive relocation of all of a city's schools in one or more large educational parks. Educational parks are comprised of clusters of schools on common sites. Presumably each cluster could serve several thousand students from all grade levels in as many or as few buildings as would suit the purposes, conditions, and location. Since an educational park would be designed to serve a very large area of a city, the problem of transporting students could not be avoided. The indictment of discrimination in transportation would be less appropriate, however, since most students would be transported to the school site. Several large cities have tentative plans for the development of educational park systems to replace their existing district schools.

All of the above strategies have as a major impetus the achievement of racial balance in public schools by mixing white students with students of other races and ethnic backgrounds. However, when middle-class families send their children to private schools or move to homogeneous suburbs, integration in the metropolitan area is nearly impossible. When the middle classes evacuate the city and its public schools, the lower-class students who remain are denied association with middle-class students, a premise of a major argument for integration.[2]

It should be recognized, however, that that argument presents a subtly discriminatory concept of desegregation. It suggests that success is dependent on the presence of a majority of middle-class white students. In this concept, it is the blacks primarily who are to be benefited; the middle-class whites are their benefactors.[3]

It is partially on this ground that alternatives to integration have arisen within the last decade. It will be noted, however, as we review some of these alternatives, that not all reject the white racist bias purportedly built into the present concept of desegregation. Some alternatives appear to trade openly on the racial prejudices of the majority of our people.

Alternatives for Metropolitan Schools

A number of alternatives have been proposed as means for improving urban education. Although some of the proposals have a direct bearing on integration, for the most part they attack the problem of urban education from the perspectives of improved curriculum and political management. Our discussion will deal with the range of alternatives under the categories of curriculum adjustments, structural changes, and decentralization.

CURRICULUM ADJUSTMENTS

Proposals for the improvement of urban education by adjustments in the curriculum range from the proposition that nothing special needs to be done, even for so-called disadvantaged youth, to the radical position that the entire curriculum should emerge from the experiences of urban students in their urban environment.

A popular position has been that urban schools, especially those in the inner city, should concentrate on a variety of compensatory programs to help students catch up in skills and knowledge that have been deleteriously affected by their poor experiences. Conclusive evidence on the effectiveness of compensatory education programs, however, is lacking. The existing programs exhibit such wide variations in content and in quality that any general statistical evaluation is precluded. A number of programs pointed at specific testable skills, such as reading, claim positive changes.[4] Jencks, however, claims that his evaluation of available data suggests that neither school personnel nor education experts "know how to raise test scores, even when they have vast resources at their disposal."[5]

A special means proposed as a way to provide a particular training component for an urban school's curriculum is performance contracting. In performance contracting, a university or an educational corporation contracts with a school board to provide a given experience to a group of students and usually to raise their level of performance of a given skill. For example, a performance contract might be issued to raise the reading level by one grade of a group of students performing below their potential. Performance contracting on a much wider scale offers a quick method of creating a competitive alternative to public education in the urban setting. The contract schools would be public, though the management of the schools would be provided by private educational corporations.

Although a promising idea, performance contracting was largely discredited as a quick solution to educational shortcomings when several large-scale experimental contracts failed to achieve their performance goals. The wide use of contracts could also stunt the public's understanding of the meaning of education. Contracts tend to focus on skills but supposedly schools teach more than just skills. Contracts could conceivably reduce the meaning of education in some persons' thinking to the simple transmission of skills. Furthermore, it can be predicted that performance contracting would be no better accepted in the inner city than is the standard public school. Ghetto parents are characteristically suspicious of outsiders, including corporations, universities, and public schools controlled by outsiders. Inner-city residents would prefer to run their own schools.[6]

A far more extensive curriculum proposal suggests that education for metropolitan man should emphasize relevance and participation. In this education, relevance means an immersion in the real metropolis, contact with diverse people, and familiarization with the real problems of life and society. Participation means the testing and validating of one's identity in the metropolitan arena.[7]

A curriculum for such an education would necessarily emphasize immediate experiences. The argument is that the urban alternatives are so great and change is so rapid that the only curriculum that makes much sense would be based on the shared experiences of teachers and students.[8]

Such a curriculum would also emphasize objectives related to respect for cultural differences and problems of identity and powerlessness. The group, the community, and the self become the central content in this curriculum for metropolitan man just as English, mathematics, and science are content.[9] Finally this metropolitan curriculum would be largely interdisciplinary in nature and would offer many opportunities for students to perform socially important work in the process of their learning. Since the curriculum would relate more directly to the experiences of the students themselves, it necessarily would reflect more student choice of what and how to learn.[10]

STRUCTURAL CHANGES

There are many so-called structural changes that could be made to alter the look of the school in its urban setting. Some of the proposals we discussed under the topic of integration could be classified as structural changes. In fact, most decisions on structure are related to the conditions of racial and socioeconomic stratification in the metropolitan area.

A moderate structural change would be involved in the development of a variety of private schools as alternatives to the public school in the urban area. Tuition grants or other direct public grants could be used to support these alternative schools. The legality of such a structural change would be in question, however, if the alternative schools were parochial or were organized to evade racial integration. In the latter case their benefit to the overall education program of the central city would also be in question.[11] Alternative schools are discussed more fully in Chapter 10.

A radical structural approach to the problems in urban education would require a bold effort to reverse the trend toward social and racial stratification by restoring large residential areas in the central city for both middle-class and slum-free, lower-class living. These areas could be adjacent but separate or they could be developed as self-contained, mixed areas in which persons of all races and classes would live together. The attempt would be to stop the flight of middle-class persons from the city by providing attractive, racially and socially balanced communities where they could live and raise their families.

The schools in this socially renewed urban setting would reflect the racial and social class composition of the metropolitan population. While the mixture in the schools would not necessarily exactly reflect the composition of the city, a goal of the present concept of integration, every school would be a mixed one. It is possible that no school should be more than 50 percent black nor more than 70 percent working class. Supposedly, schools with higher percentages of blacks and working class may develop an ethos that is detrimental to learning.[12]

POLITICAL CHANGES

Another set of proposals avoids addressing directly the problems of integration, curriculum, and structure by focusing on the political aspects of metropolitan education. Proposals in this area suggest that the direct political control of the schools, anathema to school professionals, might make them more sensitive to minority groups in the city, more an integral part of the massive problems of the metropolitan area, and more effective agents of change.[13] Earlier we suggested that politicizing the metropolitan school could possibly contribute to its legitimacy. One assumption of this position is that minority groups are more able to exercise political power by their votes in elections than they are to influence school policy as it is presently made. Schools subject to political control would find it difficult to ignore the educational needs of politically potent, minority people.

Another assumption supporting this position is that educational problems cannot be treated separately from the problems of recreation, housing, welfare, and unemployment within the metropolitan area. Therefore, any political leader who intends to improve his city relative to these basic problems must make public education a priority matter.[14] If schools were politically organized, political leaders of large cities could accept a more active educational role on the grounds that the resolution of the complicated problems of urban life must include the effective use of the schools. In this broad context of urban problems, the question is not so much whether political control would lead to more effective urban education, but whether political control would lead to changes in school policy that would make the educational programs more effective in solving the massive and complex community problems.[15]

A proposal for the reorganization of metropolitan education which has gained in popularity in the context of desegregation has wide political implications. Because of these and its educational implications, we will discuss it in some detail.

DECENTRALIZATION AND COMMUNITY CONTROL

A significant trend in urban school reorganization since the 1954 Supreme Court decision has been toward decentralization and increased community participation. A differentiation must be made between administrative decentralization, which is now often the situation in many large cities, and political decentralization with respect to the governance of schools. In the decentralization of governance, the concept involved here, a new relationship between the community and the school is created.[16] The pressure appears to be toward a balancing of community and professional roles in decisions on the conduct of schools. The overall impact of decentralization and increased community control of schools is expected to be a sensitizing of the schools and the formation of more reform-minded school policies.

In theory, at least, decentralization would create more sympathetic and understanding administrators, more sensitive teachers, and more knowledgeable parents. The assumption is that in this improved climate of acceptance and respect, students would be more highly motivated toward higher achievement. The prognosis for this new relationship in the inner city is that when blacks control their own institutions, including their schools, they will develop a sense of cohesion and identity. Once a cohesive identity is developed, the blacks will be more able and better equipped to connect up with the white society.[17] If decentralization achieves its intended ends, the process, while *prima facie* divisive, may eventually facilitate truly metropolitan federations of districts embracing both suburban and urban areas, for limited purposes at least.[18]

There are political implications in decentralization that extend beyond the governance of the schools in a district. As the numbers of community participants increase and their pressure tactics become more sophisticated and disruptive, decentralized public education will become more vulnerable without a radical injection of political energy and power. The prediction from this view is that without political leadership the schools will fly apart. Decentralization may herald the emergence of the mayor as the chief arbiter and policy maker for metropolitan education.[19]

When decentralization begins to occur in a large city, there are expectedly many conflicts between the professional staff and the newly energized community participants. The trend toward community control has been directly countered, for example, by the unionization of teachers and administrators in the city. While these unions have sought improvements by bargaining for smaller classes and lighter loads, they also have tended to support the continuation of the "standard" school. Also, the collective bargaining agreements made with teachers on a citywide basis are often in conflict with the adaptations demanded by the new participants in the local district.[20]

In the Ocean Hill–Brownsville area of New York, community leaders effectively purged the schools of white professional staff by making them feel unwelcome in the mainly black schools of the district. Most white teachers asked for transfers. While black teachers for black students seems appropriate, racial identity alone has not historically been a sufficient condition for the establishment of good schools for black children. The all-black southern schools and the 80 percent black staff in Washington, D.C., are cases in point.[21]

Decentralization may also produce some educational perils for some urban youth. While it presumably would sensitize the schools of a district to the needs of their clientele, it could also lead to increased discontinuities for the highly mobile poor in the cities. Under the present system, a student moving from one school to another in the city does not anticipate a total severance of his program of studies, because programs in different schools are often quite similar. Under decentralization, however a student could not change schools with the same assurances of program continuity, because decentralization presumably could result in the loss of similarity among schools. It is possible, also, that decentralization could reduce the educational choice of students by eliminating some specialized high schools that under the present system are administered under the aegis of the central board and accept students seeking this specialized training from anywhere in the city. Although local control would improve the educational opportunities available to many urban youth, the emergence of an urban educational system comprised of autonomonus districts exercising complete local control would undoubtedly result in vast differences of educational opportunity available to the young people in the city.

Critics of the participatory movement say that it is primarily political in nature and has little to do with what is educationally desirable or what occurs in the school and in the classroom.[22] But a more positive appreciation of the participatory movement in education surfaces when a wider democratic perspective is taken. In this perspective, participation is valued both for the expected increase in the validity of decisions made and for the personal benefits derived by the participants. This view does not deny that cloistered educational experts could, by taking thought, reorganize and reorient the school in desirable and beneficial ways; but if school professionals alone were able to bring about the needed changes in urban education, they would be denying parents and students the opportunity to grow through involvement and participation. Their involvement not only would serve to legitimize the institution but also would increase their understanding of the complexities of teaching and school organization. When this position is taken, it is inappropriate to ask, "What do parents and other nonprofessionals know about curriculum objectives, staffing, and budget?" Rather, the proper question is, "What can these persons learn about the nature of education and schooling in order to participate effectively in decisions on education and schools?"[23]

Some Tentative Judgments

A review of the selected proposals above encourages the following judgments about the improvement of urban education. The proposals that are most feasible are least likely to provide for significant changes in the conditions of urban schools. The technically most easily accomplished strategy, for example, that of busing students from one school to another, has been largely unsuccessful in achieving integration as an initial step in the improvement of urban education. Not only have middle-class whites managed to escape the buses by moving to their suburban bastions, but whites and blacks alike who have remained within the effective range of the buses have raised so vociferous an opposition to the practice that it hardly can be expected to survive as a long-range solution. It is doubtful that all of the more easily accomplished proposals together would significantly improve urban education.

A second judgment is that the proposals that could effect significant changes in urban education are so extremely complex and involved that they are unlikely to be tried. The wholistic reordering of the social and community structure of the city may indeed be a necessity, but its accomplishment may well be preceded by the collapse of most of the social institutions we now depend on to order our lives.

A third judgment is suggested also. While decentralization is hardly the panacea that its advocates tout it to be, it does represent an effort to attack some problems of metropolitan education in a way that could make some useful changes. The initial change it requires is political rather than educational; but its effect is to politicize the schools in a district, broaden their popular support, and sensitize them to the spectrum of voices in the community. The change has a chance to legitimize the school for its clients.

The participatory movement is, of course, a populist approach rather than a professional approach to hard educational problems. That does not seem to fit the practices of a technological society, and may not produce rational solutions to school problems. However, the schools have barely touched the edge of a technology that can produce or predict an intended outcome: "since professional educators do not seem to understand the long-term effects of schooling any better than parents do," says Jencks, "there is no compelling reason why the professional should be empowered to rule out alternatives that appeal to parents, even if they seem educationally 'unsound.' "[24]

Also, while community control does in the short run tend to thwart efforts to desegregate schools racially and socioeconomically, it has a chance of facilitating in the long run more balanced, creative, and productive relationships among experimentally minded school districts.

Our position is that it seems unreasonable to fault a proposal that can generate wide community interest in the schools and develop among teachers, students, administrators, and parents a sensitivity to each other's perspectives and conditions. Community control won't work everywhere; and where it does work, it won't solve many problems in and of itself. But if a community is willing, it is worth trying.

That, however, does not cause us to discontinue our interest in desegregation as a social goal of considerable merit. By itself, desegregation, even if adequately accomplished, is not likely to produce any remarkable educational benefits for anyone in the long run. But it has a chance of enhancing the ability of some blacks and whites to live together. And in the long run, that is a social benefit.

Neither are we rejecting out of hand the potential contributions of alternative schools to the educational life of the metropolis. We discuss that option with some appreciation Chapter 10.

QUESTIONS AND ACTIVITIES

1. What, in your opinion, are the important characteristics of policy? Cite two examples of statements or declarations which you believe to be policy pronouncements.
2. Why weren't the major arguments of the 1954 Brown decision used in the development of educational policy in the decades *prior* to the 1950s?
3. List advantages and disadvantages of attempting to initiate policy at the school district level, the state level, and the federal level.
4. What lessons have been learned in the attempts to desegregate the schools through the four major strategies identified in the text? What are your opinions about these strategies?
5. What are your thoughts about the relative efficacy of the four alternatives that were developed as a partial response to the difficulties the major strategies were experiencing?
6. The authors have arrived at three tentative judgments in their assessments of these strategies and alternatives. What are your reactions to the substance of their judgments? Do you have further thoughts about the various approaches?
7. The authors assert that a meaningful curriculum for metropolitan students would involve shared experiences with their teachers with real problems in the metropolis, probably utilizing an interdisciplinary approach. List some activities that you believe would fulfill these criteria. Justify your belief by showing the connections between the activities and the criteria.
8. If education is a professional function in the society, how can "a balancing of community and professional roles in decisions about the conduct of schools" be justified?
9. How do the insights provided in the study of this chapter assist you in considering the relative merits of the following two approaches to change:
   a. an incremental or piecemeal approach.
   b. a comprehensive, synoptic, or system-wide approach.
10. Identify and investigate at least one school situation where one or more of the alternatives mentioned in this chapter have been tried.
11. What are some alternatives for metropolitan schools not mentioned in this chapter?

NOTES

1 Clark Spurlock, *Education and The Supreme Court* (Urbana: University of Illinois Press, 1955), *passim.*

2 George R. LaNoue, "Political Questions in the Next Decade of Urban Education," *The Teachers College Record* 69, no. 6: 520, March 1968.

3 Mario D. Fantini, "Participation, Decentralization, and Community Control," *The National Elementary Principal* 48: 31, April 1969.

4 U.S. National Advisory Council on the Education of Disadvantaged Children, *Fourth Annual Report* (Washington, D.C.: Government Printing Office, 1969).

5 Christopher Jencks et al., *Inequality: A Reassessment of the Effect of Family and Schooling in America* (New York: Basic Books, 1972), p. 95.

6 Ellis B. Page, "How We All Failed at Performance Contracting," *Phi Delta Kappan* 54, no. 2: 115–117, October 1972; LaNoue, p. 522.

7 Daniel U. Levine, "The Unfinished Identity of Metropolitan Man," in Richard Wisniewski, ed., *Teaching About Life in the City,* 42nd Yearbook of The National Council for the Social Studies (Washington, D.C.: The Council, 1972), p. 39.

8 Richard H. Davis and Pauline H. Tesler, "Social Studies Teachers and the Future," in Richard Wisniewski, ed., *Teaching About Life in the City,* 42nd Yearbook of The National Council for the Social Studies (Washington, D.C.: The Council, 1972), p. 266.

9 Fantini, p. 30.

10 Levine, pp. 41–44.

11 LaNoue, pp. 521–522.

12 Robert J. Havighurst, *Education in Metropolitan Areas* (Boston: Allyn and Bacon, 1966), p. 82.

13 Robert H. Salisbury, "Schools and Politics in the Big City," *Harvard Education Review* 37: 409, Summer 1967.

14 LaNoue, pp. 527–528.

15 Salisbury, pp. 422, 424.

16 Fantini, p. 28.

17 Fantini, pp. 30–31.

18 LaNoue, p. 525.

19 LaNoue, p. 527.

20 Joseph M. Cronin and Julian D. Crocker, Jr., "Principals Under Pressure," *The Urban Review* 3, no. 25: 24–37, 1969.

21 LaNoue, p. 524.

22 Fantini, p. 29.

23 Fantini, p. 31.

24 Jencks, pp. 256–257.

CHAPTER 5

The Developing Adolescent in School

Adolescents are not the majority participants in the public schools, for they are outnumbered by their younger brothers and sisters in the elementary schools; but their presence may be more powerfully felt in their half of the educational institution, the secondary school, because they are bigger in size, more active in demeanor, more variant in their responses, and more interactive in their relationships than are their elementary compatriots. As a result they require more space, bigger equipment, more varied material, and a wider range of adult relationships. As they increasingly encounter experiences beyond the confines of their homes and schools in the wider world of the society, their problems and dilemmas also become more intense.

Some difficulties come about for adolescents because they are glandular interlopers between childhood and adulthood. Their childish habits are no longer acceptable either to them or to those around them and their adultlike actions reflect a kind of ungainly and awkward mimicry. Too often they come off as pubescent and acned monsters who fit comfortably in no world but their own. They are caught awkwardly and painfully between shucking their childishness and accepting their maturity. Eventually they will have no choice but to assume adult roles.

One position has it that adolescents are easily able to accommodate themselves to the norms of the adult society because there is no real break between their childhood and adult roles. Accordingly, adolescents' values are a distorted reflection of the values held by their parents. The so-called adolescent culture is only an immature adult culture.[1]

An alternative analysis suggests that there is a real difference between adults and adolescents. Although they possess some common ideals in the abstract, such as freedom, justice, and respect for life, these terms have different meanings for the two groups. Such differences are particularly evident when value judgments must be made about practical matters. Also, behavioral variations among adolescents can be accounted for largely by peer group influences rather than by models drawn from the adult society.[2]

By either analysis, adolescence is a time of raging inner conflicts, uncertainties, and dilemmas for many persons. An adolescent may have too many selves that have not yet sorted themselves out to know who he is or what he wants in life. As a consequence he often turns to others for decisions about what to be or how to act. He becomes an apt student of what others expect of him.[3]

Adolescents' inner uncertainties also make them vulnerable to the siege of value alternatives in the society. They are impressed with the values fashioned in their own peer culture. At the same time they are pressured to embrace the traditional values of the adult society. They are attracted by the media-proclaimed heroes and their images of *savoir-vivre* and disregard for convention. At the same time they see the wisdom in the standard values of coping and getting along with others. They are torn between hedonistic, fun values and their serious concern for being good and responsible persons.

Adolescent Variability and Similarity

The ideal way to work with people is to treat each one as the totally unique individual that, in fact, he or she is. Ideals notwithstanding, when working with large numbers of persons, it is impossible to characterize each person in a totally unique way. We have neither enough concepts nor a sufficient range of responses to make a "totally unique" approach work. The rational alternative is to develop categories which permit us as people-watchers and responders to group our infinitely variable data. Thus it is useful for a teacher to find ways to characterize adolescents by types. The strategy allows a teacher to attend to similarities among students while acknowledging their variability. The danger is always present, however, that a teacher will develop stereotypic responses to an individual. The antidote to stereotyping is the nurturing of an appreciation of the many factors that affect the personality of an individual.

In this chapter we emphasize only a few of these personality-affecting factors, for example, subculture motivation, intelligence, social class, race, language, sex, and cognitive and moral development, that appear to be important in the success of adolescents in school. In analyzing these factors, we identify and utilize logical categories such as delinquent, academic, and fun subcultures, high and low intelligence, white and black races, and so on.

Adolescent Subcultures

One way to look at adolescents is to examine their general motivations. In most secondary schools important, motive-giving subcultures thrive within the adolescent society. Three common variants are the delinquent, academic, and fun subcultures. Among these, the fun subculture is generally dominant.[4] In most secondary schools the majority of students expend most of their energy and express most of their interests in fun culture activities, for example, sports, entertainment, recreation, and socializing. Most of the prestigious roles and leadership positions in these schools emerge from the fun subculture. The star athlete and the sparkling cheerleader are male and female prestige counterparts in the social life of the secondary school.

The academic subculture claims some devotees in most schools; but it ordinarily is neither the source of leadership, except for special and usually short-term projects, nor the basis for gaining prestige among the great majority of adolescents. Although the majority see the academic subculture as an acceptable alternative, they require its members to participate also in the important activities of the fun subculture in order to "belong."

For most adolescents, the delinquent subculture is the least acceptable alternative. Its membership is drawn disproportionately from the lower socioeconomic class. It tends to be comprised of individuals whose presence and activities are mainly disruptive to the pursuits of the fun majority and to the school in general. Individual members may not be total outcasts, but their general disfavor by the adult management of the school makes their companionship a bit too risky for most fun-loving teenagers. Members of the delinquent subculture tend to be disinterested in many of the activities that preoccupy most adolescents.

Although most adolescents engage in activities that could propel them into the delinquent subculture, their motivation tends to be experimental. They participate in delinquent activities under circumstances that offer considerable protection. For example, alcohol and introductory drugs may be used at parties where a safe return home is assured, but not under higher risk conditions.

These characterizations of adolescent motivations offer a rather simple way of looking at large numbers of young people interacting in a complex social organization such as a school. We continue with other factors that contribute to the variability of adolescent students in school. Primary among these is intelligence.

The Factor of Intelligence

We will take the conceptual position that intelligence is the ability of an individual to profit from experience in both formal and informal conditions. Intelligence is also the ability to deal with abstractions and to think by the use of language and symbols.[5]

As a convenience, psychologists invented the concept of intelligence quotient (IQ) as a means of quantifying intelligence. The modern use of the term IQ refers to a position on an age distribution whose mean (average) is 100. A person's IQ is judged as deviating so many IQ points above or below that mean.

The assumption is that intelligence is normally distributed across any given age population and across the population as a whole. Roughly, normal distribution means that if all the IQ scores for a given population were known and placed in a distribution, the middle, average, and most frequent score would be 100. Half of those remaining would be less than 100 and half would be more than 100. IQ scores of, say, 15 or more points above (IQ 115+) and below (IQ 85−) 100 can be thought of as depicting high and low intelligence.

Although we recognize the dangers in such stereotyping, we offer the following gross characterizations of students with high and low intelligence. These characterizations may provide some understanding of these students by prospective teachers.

THE BLESSINGS OF HIGH INTELLIGENCE

Students with high intelligence are generally favored in schools because most of their behaviors reflect the goals of education. Highly intelligent students learn fast and retain what they learn with little drill. They tend to be naturally and insatiably curious. Such students possess rich vocabularies paralleling their interest in the nature and use of words. They usually have well-developed powers of reasoning and are clear and precise in their thinking. Besides learning fast, highly intelligent students also comprehend quickly, generalize consistently, form relationships, and attend to the logical consistency of their arguments. Their curiosity is evident in their wide knowledge and their appreciation of many realms of phenomena. They are particularly interested in the nature of man and in man's universe. Highly intelligent adolescents ordinarily enjoy being with adults. They fit well in the competitive climate of the middle-class school because of their desire to excel.

Some students with high intelligence do not contribute to the smooth operations of school routines or to the comfort of routinized teachers. Highly intelligent students may be restless and inattentive in classrooms and tend to be disturbing and annoying to their classmates and teachers. Although they read well and maturely and are interested in word usage and derivation, they are apt to be poor in spelling and handwriting and inaccurate in their arithmetical computation. They are likely to be lackadaisical with respect to homework assignments and totally indifferent when they are not interested in the classwork. They also tend to be hypercritical of themselves and others around them. Indeed, some of these characteristics may raise the animosity of teachers.

THE BANE OF LOW INTELLIGENCE

Students of low intelligence present a very different problem for the school. Because their primary inhibition is mental slowness, they typically do not know as much nor have as well-developed skills as their more intelligent colleagues. Although most of them—say, those who are no more than 15 points below the average (IQ 85+)—are capable of learning most of what is taught in the schools, they still tend to fall further and further behind in their achievement because they lack both the time and the perseverance to match the accomplishments of their faster competitors. Classroom instruction is generally paced for moderate to fast learners. They tend also to exhibit less concern for abstraction, relationships, and logical elegance. Partly, this lack of concern reflects their preference for simpler forms of knowledge; partly, it reflects their depressed motivation to grind through the mountains of detailed learning usually prescribed as the appropriate route to the higher cognitive functions. Along this route, their curiosity flags.

Low-ability adolescents are well acquainted with failure both in and out of school, though it is not unusual to find a low-ability and otherwise unsuccessful student enjoying remarkable success in some particular school enterprise, for example, in music or athletics. It is not safe to generalize in this regard, however, for intelligence tends to correlate positively with most human achievements.

Schools are variously disposed to deal with the special difficulties of lower-intelligence students. Given the standard values of most schools and communities, low-ability students are a disturbing element. School achievement averages are depressed by low-ability students while dropout rates are elevated. Special programs, classrooms, and teachers, all of which increase the cost of schools, are often utilized to countervail the effects of lower-ability students. Teachers trained in programs of high academic content usually find working with students of low intelligence unrewarding, especially in homogeneous classrooms where the sparkle of intellectual curiosity is often lacking. Although some low-ability students are diligent to a fault, their progress in academic pursuits seems glacial in comparison to their more capable comrades. Every learning is an effort. Teachers especially suited or specially trained for work with slow learners find the quality of patience a major benefit.

Social Class and Intelligence

One difficulty with our characterizations of students with high and low intelligence is the implication that intelligence is easily and accurately measurable. That simply is not the case. Intelligence, though an extremely important factor in differentiating persons, is an elusive factor. A major reason for the inaccuracy in our measurement of intelligence is the social class bias in intelligence tests.

It is well known that the lower class as a population scores lower on standardized intelligence measures than the middle and upper classes as a population. One possible explanation of this phenomenon is that the upper and middle classes are truly favored with higher proportions of persons with high intelligence, whereas the lower classes have a higher proportion of persons of lower intelligence. But an alternative explanation focuses on the presence of cultural bias in intelligence tests. Analysts have shown that all existing tests of intelligence are loaded to some degree with concepts that favor middle- and upper-class experiences and values. As a result, they disfavor lower-class individuals for whom these experiences and values are foreign. In fact, most standardized measures used in schools, even interest and personality inventories, are biased in favor of middle-class persons. Lower-class students cannot show interest in things they know nothing about.

Beyond the content bias, lower-class students as a group tend to be less test canny than middle-class students; for example, they are more threatened by a timed test or a test administered by an unknown outsider. Black students are particularly threatened by outside, white examiners. Standardized instruments are not only suspect in their ability to measure the achievement, interest, and intelligence of lower-class students but they may also differentiate inaccurately between the more and less able students in the disadvantaged group. The reliability of the tests is reduced because lower-class students produce a narrower spread of scores on standardized tests than do middle-class students.[6]

One can argue, of course, that the scores obtained from intelligence, achievement, and personality instruments have been shown to be reasonably accurate predictors of success and failure in middle-class schools. As such, they determine the degree to which middle-class culture has been assimilated and assess factors related to successful participation in middle-class culture. An implicit value assumption in this argument is that middle-class culture is singularly appropriate to modern life in America.[7]

THE FACTOR OF SOCIAL CLASS

That social class differentiates persons in most parts of our society is both self-evident and well documented by sociological, political, economic, and educational research. Furthermore, social class membership during the plastic years of childhood and youth may indelibly imprint the individual psychologically and characterologically. Lower-social class membership, in particular, drastically affects the participation and success in school of children and youth in our society. Membership in the middle or higher classes also has its profound social, character, and psychological effects on individuals; but these effects more closely parallel the goals and requirements of the schools, which are basically middle-class institutions. Because the lower-class adolescent is specifically and seriously debilitated with respect to his functioning in school, and because few appropriate alternatives to public school are available to him, this discussion will concentrate on the school-related effects of lower-class membership on the adolescent.

THE LOWER-CLASS ADOLESCENT

Compared with his middle-class classmates, an adolescent member of the lower class is likely to be less verbal. His standard English vocabulary is smaller, he speaks standard, school English with less fluency, and he reads the standard, school materials with less facility. He is also more apt to be bilingual, a trait reflecting the fact that Puerto Ricans, Chicanos, and Indians, as well as blacks, are disproportionately represented in the lower class in our society. Bilingualism, often touted as a desirable attribute, is more often a disadvantage to a person in normal schoolwork when his primary language or dialect is not the standard language or dialect of the school.

The lower-class adolescent wants autonomy, but he is likely to have low self-confidence. As a result he is typically more fearful of strangers, some of whom undoubtedly are professionally and personally committed to helping him. Because he perceives in the society and in the school real and imagined threats to himself and to his life hopes, he is also easily anatagonized. He is resentful of rules that deny him control of his destiny.

The lower-class adolescent is less motivated academically and less competitive intellectually than his middle-class compatriot. He probably attends an inferior school, as rated by the criteria of intellectual rigor and academic achievement. His typical isolation in particular urban schools is, of course, well known. When he does attend a predominately middle-class school, he does not conform readily to the traditions of the middle-class-oriented classroom.

In his lower-class environment, he will have learned to like excitement, but he will have enjoyed a limited variety of recreation activities. In a wider sense, he will have had low exposure to the kind of stimulation that would encourage him to want to know about the outside world. As a result he is apt to be less knowledgeable than his middle-class schoolmates about events and issues beyond his immediate contact.[8]

The lower-class adolescent is expected to be tough and, indeed, his culture experience teaches him that this is an appropriate intention. This experience also has taught him to be wary of being outwitted or taken in, especially by an outsider.[9]

One study of the lower-class culture typifies working-class homes as adult-centered; in comparison, middle-class homes are child-centered.[10] One consequence of this class difference is that the discipline standards and methods in lower-class homes are unlike those in the schools. The socializing role of adults is often relinquished to the peer group in the lower-class community. By age nine, a lower-class child is likely to be on the street for the completion of his socialization. His aggressiveness, fatalism, apathy, wariness of authority, and his alleged negative self-concept may well result from the frustrations of this undersocialization. When a lower-class student "acts out" the problems that result from undersocialization, he is likely to be judged by middle-class teachers, counselors, and social workers as having character disorders.[11]

Many investigations have shown that the child-rearing practices in poverty families lead to social and intellectual disability. Lower-class parents are less likely to note the shape, size, color, and place of objects or to talk about them with their children. They tend not to discuss reasons for demands or rules or to provide other rich opportunities for language and number development.[12]

Furthermore, lower-class children display less of the "deferred gratifaction syndrome" than middle-class children.[13] One position has it that preference for delayed gratification over immediate though smaller rewards is related to learning to trust adults. When these children who have learned to opt for the immediate come to school, they move into a society that trades on delayed gratification. The immediate rewards are meager indeed. Little beyond the praise of the teacher is available as an immediate reward in the school setting.[14]

SCHOOL SUCCESS OF ADOLESCENTS FROM THE LOWER CLASS

Most lower-class students know that schools favor upper- and middle-class students over lower-class students. Rules are often enforced differentially and rewards and penalties are often distributed unevenly. More poignantly, these students probably know also that their life chances are restricted by their lower social class background.[15]

This differentiation between social classes continues beyond the high school. Not only are they less likely to go to college, but lower-class adolescents who enter college are also less likely to graduate than their middle- and higher-class classmates.[16]

REMEDIATION RELATED TO SOCIAL CLASS

There have been some efforts within the schools to find remedies for disadvantages attending lower-class membership. The bulk of these remedies have been programs for young children or projects related to the elementary school. Some efforts, for example, Project Head Start, have been organized and financed nationwide through the federal government. Most efforts at the secondary level have been developed in local schools to treat specific disabilities. A notable exception, Upward Bound, is a federally financed, nationwide program to prepare disadvantaged high school students for college matriculation. For the most part, these are compensatory programs designed to develop practical skills that have been found lacking in the target groups. Remedial reading programs are among the most popular.

Very little reliable information is available on the effects of these compensatory programs at the secondary level. What data are available suggest that the results are uneven. Results apparently vary according to the nature of the debility attacked, the unique characteristics of the program, the creativity and talent of the leadership, and most of the other variables that affect all school programs. Compensatory programs in general have not been remarkably successful. Upward Bound is an impressive exception. Two out of three of the students in Upward Bound go on to college.[17]

Most compensatory tactics—for example, direct remediation, smaller classes, and the use of programmed learning, gadgetry, and rewards— do not deal with what some authorities see as the primary problem of the lower-class student, his alleged negative self-image. Some programs tend to aggravate this problem by dramatizing the student's failure through assignment to direct remediation experiences.[18]

Race as a Factor in Understanding Adolescents

An area of some interest to social scientists is the possible relationship between race and psychological and behavioral variances in the population. While some of the evidence supporting such a relationship is persuasive it is not conclusive. And it is unlikely that firm conclusions will ever be possible because of the moral limitations on researchers and the impossibility of isolating the racial and cultural variables involved. Nevertheless, it appears to be generally assumed that there are behavioral differences between black and white students in schools and that these variations are attributable to differences in the racial background of the students.

There is the possibility that some of the behaviors identified as "different" are not nearly as different as they appear to the observer who may be influenced by his own point of view. The fact is that we can never be sure where our objectivity is obscured by the perspective we have acquired from our own cultural experience. From a scientific point of view many so called "racial" differences are understandable only as cultural differences. Thus, much of what we have discussed as social class differences applies also to racial differences. The increasing numbers of middle-class blacks notwithstanding, being black and lower class are commonly related conditions.[19]

THE INTEGRATION EXPERIENCE

Observers of the social relationships in racially mixed schools have noted that students make clear distinctions on the basis of race. Desegregated schools tend to be pluralistic societies. If blacks and whites are evenly proportioned, there are typically two distinct subcultures based on race. In schools with a token number of one race, the majority racial group reigns supreme; the minority group tends to be a nonparticipant. Without special efforts, the desegregation of a school seldom produces an integration of the school society. Rather, subcultures congeal to reinforce socially the racial distinctions.[20]

In Coleman's study, however, the racial mixing of students in schools was concluded to be generally beneficial. The studies reported favorable academic outcomes for blacks integrated in predominantly white schools. At the same time there was no measurable detriment to white students in the receiving classrooms. According to this study, the earlier in their school careers the black students attended desegregated white schools, the more benefit they derived, in terms of higher achievement. The benefits were greatest for blacks who had the longest contact in predominantly white classrooms. Actually, Coleman inferred from the data that the benefit to the blacks from being in integrated classrooms came not from the racial composition per se, but from contact with persons with higher educational backgrounds and aspirations typical of the whites.

The resentment arising from being placed in a situation in which presumably they would have more to gain than to contribute was outweighed by the black students' belief that being in integrated classrooms somehow would increase their own life chances.

Coleman's analysis appeared to show that blacks in white classrooms gained in achievement scores. Black students integrated in white schools from early grades through high school scored close to the national norm on reading comprehension, whereas black students who had never had white classmates scored one to two years below the national average.[21]

Jencks' reassessment of Coleman's and other studies produced less positive conclusions. Jencks found no consistent effect on test scores, school success and retention, or eventual occupation status resulting from desegregated school experiences.[22]

Comparisons of reading scores on standardized tests of reading comprehension consistently show a differentiation between black and white students. When the national median for black students is compared with that for white students, the difference is nearly three years.

A case in point is the 1970–71 report of the reading abilities of elementary and high school students in the city of Chicago. The resultant scores of a standardized reading test "showed that the poorest performances generally occurred in predominantly Black or Spanish-speaking ghetto school districts." The report continues that "all eleven school districts that scored below the city-wide average had predominantly Black or Spanish-speaking enrollments." At the same time, "eight of the ten districts with above-average scores had predominantly white enrollments."[23]

Our examination of social class and race as pertinent variables in understanding adolescents has come to focus, not quite inadvertently, on the factor of language as specifically differentiating whites and blacks and the lower class and the middle and higher classes in our society. Because of the centrality of reading and language ability in the program of the school, we will focus on these variables in the following section. It is our impression that this language dimension is crucial to the understanding of the variations in school achievement among adolescents and in fashioning effective approaches and strategies for working with them in school settings.

Reading and Language Variance in Adolescence

The language of the school is primarily and overwhelmingly middle-class "Anglo-English." One way to look at many of the data and conclusions on the variance in school success among black and white and middle- and lower-class students is with reference to competence in middle-class Anglo-English.

Speech authorities have characterized middle-class speech as "elaborated" speech. It makes use of flexible sentence patterns, many modifiers, and extensive vocabulary.[24] A primary means by which this kind of speech pattern is developed in middle-class children is through verbal interactions with their parents. Middle-class parents tend to repeat, correct, and expand many of their children's utterances from the earliest stages of speech development. When a middle-class child says, "Baby bye-bye car," his mother is likely to respond, "Baby *is going* bye-bye *in the* car." Lower-class parents presumably expand their children's elliptical expressions less often. Also, middle-class children tend to interact verbally with adults. They not only listen to adult speech, but are also listened to and corrected in their language usage. The principle involved is that words learned through hearing alone do not become active mediators in one's thinking, *Sesame Street* notwithstanding. Just hearing speech without interacting verbally and without being corrected results in language deprivation.[25]

Speech authorities characterize lower-class speech as "restricted" speech. Sentence construction is ordinarily simple and vocabulary is limited. This restricted speech lacks the power to symbolize complex logical relations. The consistent employment of restricted speech patterns in the important language development years is believed to preclude the important further development of high conceptual and logical operations.[26] Restricted lower-class language is also presumed in this analysis to match the lower-class outlook on life. The language and the outlook are focused on the immediate, the concrete, the practical, and the necessary. Within this focus there is little opportunity for the creative examination of the future or a logical analysis of the past.[27]

This view suggests that lower-class students are at a disadvantage in schools because they are relatively incompetent in the predominant, middle-class language of the school. Another view of language deprivation must, however, be considered. Linguists have found that inner-city children are highly competent in their own language.[28] In one "Anglo-English"–"Black-English" repetition study, black and white children who heard sentences in the unfamiliar dialect commonly had to translate them to the more familiar dialect in order to repeat them. Both had to translate as the means of gaining conceptual control of the meaning of the sentences. The implication is that black children in middle-class schools are faced with the constant problem of dialect translation in the performance of their schoolwork.[29]

Whatever problems are presented by the dialect differences existing in schools that have black populations, they tend to increase rather than decrease through the high school grades. Speakers of Black-English shift further away from Anglo-English usage as they progress through school. The high point of Black-English usage is with black adolescents in high school, especially if they participate in the street culture. It is only after adolescents leave school that they apparently shift toward Anglo-English usage.[30]

Based on our discussion above, a typology of language deprivation can be fashioned. At the lowest level would be students categorized as verbally destitute. If they have had severe limitations on their opportunities to use language in any situation, they may simply have less language than other children.

In a quite different category would be the students who have full language development, but one that is unlike school language. Persons in this category may be competent in Spanish or in an English dialect such as Black-English; however, they are being asked to perform in school in their second language, Anglo-English, in which they are less competent.

In a third category would be those students who have not learned to conceptualize their experiences because their language is underdeveloped. Such children would lack in their background both school-valued experiences and the occasions to verbalize the meaning of these experiences. As a result both their language and their thinking appear to be impoverished.[31]

Such a typology can at least sensitize teachers to the complexities of the language situation in order to avoid simplistic responses. Teachers should recognize, for example, that current language assessment tests do not reflect dialect differences and therefore are prejudicial to many students. Lower-class black, Puerto Rican, and Chicano students consistently do poorly on reading tests and all other standardized tests employed by the schools. This disability extends also to intelligence tests inasmuch as most intelligence test items tap language abilities.[32] Furthermore, teachers should recognize that the poor success of these students in reading programs and in subjects dependent on reading ability is at least partially attributable to the mismatching of their dialects and the reading material used in the school.[33]

If teachers realize that at least some of what are called intellectual and academic deficiencies proceed from differences in verbal learning, then they may deal more rationally with some of the differences they observe in students. The appropriateness of teaching language skills which are apparently needed for achievement and success in school must be weighed against the possibility that a disadvantaged adolescent will hear, "Your language is inadequate," as, "You are inadequate."[34]

The Factor of Sex

In a number of ways, sex as a significant status and behavioral category may be waning. The expanding role of females and the increasingly passive life-style of males suggest that sex differences are becoming less distinct. Occupations and careers that were once clearly demarcated for one sex have been successfully invaded by the opposite sex. The desexing of the world of work seems to be accelerating.[35] Sex-role diffusion, however, may be something of a social class phenomenon, since sex-role differentiation continues to be more pronounced in the lower class than in the middle class. Lower-class children move toward masculinity or femininity much earlier than do middle-class children.[36]

While most physical sex differences are genetic in origin, it is relatively unknown what behavioral differences between males and females are genetically derived, produced by hormone differences, or simply learned. A major premise of the feminist movement is that many differences in behavior are due to sex role stereotyping which is initiated in the home and reinforced by the school and other social experiences. Girls, for example, are usually verbally superior, whereas boys usually do better on spatial and mechanical reasoning. How much of this difference is due to the encouragement and expectations that the male or female child gets from the environment and how much is biologically determined is simply unknown. Such differences may well be produced by different hormone distributions in males and females.

Some research suggests a difference in the cognitive styles of males and females. Male students have a tendency to be analytic, whereas female students tend to be nonanalytic and impulsive.[37] One hypothesis has it that these differences are a result of the different androgen and estrogen levels in boys and girls.[38]

We do know, of course, that some sex differences are basically cultural, though these also may have some biological content. A pertinent example relates to school. Male and female students have different attitudes toward school, partly because school itself is often thought of as basically feminine and partly because boys and girls are treated differently in school. Teachers are more likely to be biased against males and their "masculine characteristics" of aggressiveness and assertiveness.[39]

It should be reiterated in summary that much of what is known about the differences between male and female characteristics and behavior exists in a causal mix of genetic, hormonal, and environmental factors which cannot be disentwined with our present research capabilities and limitations. For one thing, our present technological capabilities do not permit the identification of specific genes on sex chromosomes, though the sex chromosomes themselves have been identified and photographed. Furthermore, there are appropriate moral deterrents to the kind of human experimentation that would permit a more precise separation of these factors.

The Factor of Development

Adolescents also differ with respect to their development. Development is taken to mean the systematic addition of skills, processes, or abilities that proceeds through a fixed sequence of levels or stages. Physical development is an obvious example, though we have not chosen to include it here. Rather, we have chosen to emphasize cognitive and moral development as specifically related to students' work in schools.

While there are many developmental theories, we have focused on Piaget's and Kohlberg's theories because they appear to represent areas of development most pertinent to the task of the schools. Both theories are biologically based and both also recognize the important effects of the environment on the rate and extent of development.

PIAGET'S GENETIC EPISTEMOLOGY

In Piaget's theory the human organism interacts with its environment for the purpose of achieving a condition of unity. However, this condition is repeatedly disrupted by genetic and environmental changes. The organism must continue to adapt to the new conditions or remain permanently disrupted. Also, after it differentiates itself from the environment, the organism seeks to impose some order on its cognitive structures and on the material environment.

Whereas the pattern of interaction continues throughout the life of the organism, the level of the interaction escalates through a sequence of stages. In general, the stage of development is determined by the degree to which material objects must be present in the environment for the organism to function cognitively.[40] Piaget labels the stages as sensorimotor, preoperational, concrete operations, and formal operations.

In the first stage, *the sensorimotor stage*, the child is wholly involved in acquiring sensorimotor control. At first he has only accidental interactions with the environment caused by his own reflex actions. By the end of this stage, the child is intentionally representing things to himself and interacting with objects that are out of sight.

With these new abilities to control elements within his environment voluntarily through the invention of tactics and the conjuring of "symbolic images," the child is prepared to move to the *preoperational stage* in which he intuitively uses concepts. In this stage, he is able to call to mind a past event by the use of a symbol. Later, these symbols become audible terms understood by his associates.

When the child enters the *stage of concrete operations*, he is fully prepared to operate with representational thought on objects. Concrete operations are real actions on an object in a cognitive rather than a physical sense; but the presence of the object is no longer required.[41] The concrete operator is able to perform such operations as classification, ordering, and elementary logic.[42]

When the *formal operation stage* is achieved, the person attempts to solve problems with abstract thought. Elements of the problem are conceptualized and relationships among concepts are dealt with. At this stage, the person uses the deductive model, propositional reasoning, and analysis in his thinking. The formal operator casts hypotheses verbally and tests them in the abstract before taking action.[43]

Piaget's research has led him to conclude that stage sequence is invariable in the human organism, but the development may occur at different rates for different people. While the formal operations stage is usually reached by age twelve, it may be achieved earlier or much later or perhaps not at all in some individuals. It is also possible for an individual to function at different stages in different areas at one time in his life.[44]

MORAL DEVELOPMENT—KOHLBERG'S THEORY

The above discussion was on cognitive development, but there are also other realms of development. For example, the moral realm is often referred to as being subject to serial development.

A contemporary theory of moral development has emerged from the research of Lawrence Kohlberg. Kohlberg has concluded that individuals progress through moral stages of development that parallel the cognitive stages of Piaget. Kohlberg's typology can be used in understanding differences among adolescents and working with them with respect to their development as fully capacitated persons.

Moral development is given such an emphasis because of the importance of morals and morality in determining the character of the individual. The moral point of view entails deciding what actions to take by considering their effect on other people.

According to Kohlberg the level of one's moral development is revealed not in his behavior per se, but in the reasons he gives for his behavior. Persons of different moral development may do similar things but for different reasons. For example, a person at a low stage of moral development may not steal an unchained bicycle because he has been told not to steal and fears being punished. A person at a higher stage of development may refuse to steal the bicycle because it would earn him the disapproval of his peers. A person at a still higher level of moral development would refuse to steal the bicycle because the act would violate a principle that he has chosen as a criterion for his own behavior.

In Kohlberg's classification, the reasons for moral conduct are categorized into three ascending levels and six developmental stages as follows.

LEVEL I—PREMORAL

Stage 1.—Obedience and punishment orientation. Egocentric deference to superior power or prestige, or a trouble-avoiding set. Objective responsibility.

Stage 2.—Naively egoistic orientation. Right action is that instrumentally satisfying the self's needs and occasionally other's. Awareness of relativism of value to each actor's needs and perspective. Naive egalitarianism and orientation to exchange and reciprocity.

LEVEL II—CONVENTIONAL ROLE CONFORMITY

Stage 3.—Good-boy orientation. Orientation to approval and to pleasing and helping others. Conformity to stereotypical images of majority or natural role behavior and judgment of intentions.

Stage 4.—Authority and social-order-maintaining orientation. Orientation to "doing duty" and to showing respect for authority and maintaining the given social order for its own sake. Regard for earned expectations of others.

LEVEL III—SELF-ACCEPTED MORAL PRINCIPLES

Stage 5.—Contractual legalistic orientation. Recognition of an arbitrary element or starting point in rules or expectations for the sake of agreement. Duty defined in terms of contract, general avoidance of violation of the will or rights of others, and majority will and welfare.

Stage 6.—Conscience or principle orientation. Orientation not only to actually ordained social rules but to principles of choice involving appeal to logical universality and consistency. Orientation to conscience as a directing agent and to mutual respect and trust.[45]

The School and Students' Development

These cognitive and moral developmental factors are important to the secondary school teacher only to the degree that they are useful in understanding and working with adolescents. Teachers sensitized to the characteristics of persons in each of the cognitive and moral stages, for example, their interactions with persons at various stages of development and their reactions to stage-oriented materials and problems, would better understand some very important differences among their students. A teacher may even attempt to move his students to a higher stage of cognitive and moral development.

Adolescents are nearly infinitely variable; and that variability obviously has many sources. In this chapter we have singled out only a few factors, for example, subculture, class, race, intelligence, language, sex, and cognitive and moral development, for our discussion. We have also tended to focus on lower-class, black, and verbally deprived adolescents. Our justification for this emphasis is that in schools, which are mainly middle-class institutions in a thoroughgoing way, there is a tendency to treat such persons as misfits. Teachers in these schools tend also to lack empathy with such students because they do not meet their expectations. We believe that teachers must have a better understanding of these students if they are to organize their classrooms in such a way to provide for their intellectual and social development. Our intention is to provide a starting point for this understanding.

QUESTIONS AND ACTIVITIES

1. What are two of the views or positions that have been advanced about the nature of the period called adolescence? In what ways are these views and the whole concept of adolescence useful to you as an educator? In what ways are they not useful? What conceptual schemes do you have for working with this particular age group?

2. Briefly describe the three adolescent subcultures. Have you identified additional ones? What are they? How would you relate these subcultures to the "hidden curriculum" of the school?

3. What are some of the issues which arise when we begin to attempt classifying people as to their intellectual ability? List arguments to support the categorizing of people according to various characteristics. List arguments against categorizing.

4. Identify some of the characteristics of lower-class adolescents. How would you go about relating this knowledge to the development of curriculum for these students?

5. What are the more significant ways in which race and integration influenced students during the adolescent period?

6. Carefully identify and explain the concepts and facts which you believe to be most useful in the discussion on "Reading and Language Variance in Adolescence." How useful is the typology on language deprivation in understanding the problems faced by adolescent learners?

7. What are some of the more important issues and/or problems associated

with the sex factor in the schools? What suggestions do you have for attempting to minimize some of these problems?

8. In what ways does Piaget's developmental view aid us in the building of curriculum programs?

9. Some recent research efforts in the United States have led some educators to doubt the validity of Piaget's developmental theory. Elementary pupils, for example, have demonstrated a capability for propositional reasoning, a developmental level not ordinarily reached at that age according to Piaget's theory. How would you account for these different findings?

10. How could one use Kohlberg's moral development model in working with high school students in English or social studies classes? How can it be used in teaching mathematics, music, physical education, or foreign language? How could a guidance counselor make use of the Kohlberg model?

11. Kohlberg insists that the school's responsibility in moral education is to advance the moral reasoning level of students. If you had a group of students whose moral reasoning is at *stage three*, that is, a "good boy" orientation, what could you do to hasten their advance to *stage four* and beyond?

12. Develop a questionnaire, interview schedule, or observational check sheet that would produce data which could be used to test some of the assertions made about adolescents in this chapter. Get permission to collect your data in nearby middle, junior high, and high schools.

13. James Coleman and others have identified a group of persons in American society, between adolescence and adulthood, which is largely ignored by the schools. What responsibility might secondary schools assume for the education of this youth group?

NOTES

[1] Frederick Elkin and William Westley, "The Myth of the Adolescent Culture," *American Sociological Review* 20, no. 6: 680–684, 1955.

[2] James S. Coleman, *The Adolescent Society* (New York: Free Press, 1961).

[3] David F. Ricks, "Emotional Conflict in the Pupil," *The Encyclopedia of Education*, vol. 3 (New York: Macmillan and Free Press, 1971), p. 218.

[4] Coleman, *The Adolescent Society*; Calvin Wayne Gordon, *The Social System of the High School* (New York: Free Press, 1957); Abraham J. Tannenbaum, *Adolescent Attitudes Toward Academic Brilliance* (New York: Teachers College Press, 1962).

[5] Harry B. Gilbert, "Intelligence Tests," *The Encyclopedia of Education*, vol. 5 (New York: Macmillan and Free Press, 1971), p. 129.

[6] Joshua A. Fishman, "Testing Special Groups: The Culturally Disadvantaged," *The Encyclopedia of Education*, vol. 9 (New York: Macmillan and Free Press, 1971), pp. 196–201.

[7] James S. Coleman , *Equality of Educational Opportunity* (Washington, D.C.: Government Printing Office, 1966), pp. 20–21.

[8] Martin Deutsch et al., "Guidelines for Testing Minority Group Children," *Journal of Social Issues* 20, no. 2: 127–145, 1964.

[9] Walter B. Miller, "Lower Class Culture as a Generating Milieu of Gang Delinquency," *Journal of Social Issues*, no. 3: 5–19, 1958.

[10] Herbert J. Gans, *The Urban Villagers* (New York: Free Press, 1962).

[11] Thomas S. Langner and Stanley T. Michael, *Life Stress and Mental Health* (New York: Free Press, 1963).

[12] Maxine F. Schoggen, 'The Imprint of Low-income Homes on Young Children," in Susan Gray and J. O. Miller, eds., *Research, Change, and Social Responsibility: An Illustrative Model From Early Education*, Demonstration and Research Center for Early Education Papers and Reports, 2 (3) Nashville, Tenn., George Peabody College for Teachers, 1967; Oscar Lewis, *La Vida: A Puerto Rican Family in the Culture of Poverty, San Juan and New York* (New York: Random House, 1966); Robert D. Hess and Virginia C. Shipman, "Early Experience and Socialization of Cognitive Modes in Children," *Child Development* 36, no. 4: 869–886, 1965; Allison Davis, *Social-Class Influences Upon Learning* (Cambridge, Mass.: Harvard University Press, 1948).

[13] L. Schneider and S. Lysgaard, "The Deferred Gratification Pattern: A Preliminary Study," *American Sociological Review* 18, no. 2: 142–149, 1953.

[14] Walter Mischel, "Preference for Delayed Reinforcement: An Experimental Study of a Cultural Observation," *Journal of Abnormal Social Psychology*, 56, no. 1: 57–61, 1958.

[15] David E. Lavin, *The Prediction of Academic Performance: A Theoretical Analysis and Review of Research* (New York: Russell Sage Foundation, 1965).

[16] William H. Sewell and Vimal P. Shah, "Socioeconomic Status, Intelligence, and the Attainment of Higher Education," *Sociology of Education* 40, no. 1: 1–23, 1967.

[17] Christopher Jencks et al., *Inequality: A Reassessment of the Effect of Family and Schooling in America* (New York: Basic Books, 1972), pp. 150–151.

[18] William F. Johntz, "Mathematics and the Culturally Disadvantaged," in Staten W. Webster, ed., *The Disadvantaged Learner: Knowing, Understanding, Educating* (San Francisco: Chandler, 1966), pp. 573–581.

[19] "America's Rising Black Middle Class," *Time, The Weekly Newsmagazine* 103: 19–28, June 17, 1974.

[20] David Gottlieb and Warren Ten Houten, "The Social Systems of Negro and White Adolescents," Paper read at the 59th annual meeting of the American Sociological Association, September 3, 1964, Montreal; Burton R. Clark, "Sociology of Education," in Robert E. L. Faris, ed., *Handbook of Modern Sociology* (Skokie, Ill.: Rand McNally, 1964), pp. 734–769.

[21] Coleman, 1966, pp. 29, 307, 330–331.

[22] Jencks, pp. 97–103, 153–156, 190–191.

[23] *Chicago Daily News*, November 2, 1974, p. 7.

[24] Basil Bernstein, "Elaborated and Restricted Codes: Their Socil Origins and Some Consequences," *American Anthropologist* 66 no. 6, part 2: 56–57, 63–67, 1964.

[25] Vera P. John and Leo S. Goldstein, "The Social Context of Language Acquisition," *Merrill-Palmer Quarterly* 10, no. 3: 265–276, 1964.

[26] Bernstein, pp. 56–57, 58–63.

[27] Walter D. Loban, "Language Ability in the Elementary School: Implications of Findings Pertaining to the Culturally Disadvantaged," in Arno Jewett, Joseph Mersand, and Doris Gunderson, eds., *Improving English Skills of Culturally Different Youth in Large Cities*. Excerpts of speeches given at a conference, May 31–June 2, 1962. U.S. Office of Education, Bulletin No. 5 (Washington, D.C.: The Office, 1964), pp. 62–68.

[28] Herbert L. Foster, "Dialect-Lexicon and Listening Comprehension," Ed. D. dissertation (New York: Teachers College, Columbia University, 1969).

[29] Joan C. Baratz, "A Bi-dialectal Task for Determining Language Proficiency in Economically Disadvantaged Negro Children," *Child Development* 40, no. 3: 889–901, 1969.

[30] Walter A. Wolfram, *Detroit Negro Speech* (Washington, D.C.: Center for Applied Linguistics, 1969), pp. 122–126, 205–206, 215; Winton H. Manning, "The Measurement of Intellectual Capacity and Performance," *Journal of Negro Education* 37, no. 3: 258–267, 1968.

[31] Alexander Frazier, "A Research Proposal to Develop the Language Skills of Children with Poor Backgrounds," in Arno Jewett, Joseph Mersand, and Doris Gunderson, eds., *Improving English Skills of Culturally Different Youth in Large Cities.* Excerpts of speeches, given at a conference, May 31–June 2, 1962. U.S. Office of Education, Bulletin No. 5 (Washington, D.C.: The Office, 1964), pp. 69–79.

[32] Deutsch et al., p. 142.

[33] Roger Shuy, "Some Conditions for Developing Beginning Reading Materials for Ghetto Children," in Doris Gunderson, ed., *Language and Reading: An Interdisciplinary Approach* (Washington, D.C.: Center for Applied Linguistics, 1970), pp. 88–97.

[34] K. Goodman, "Dialect Barriers to Reading Comprehension," in Joan C. Baratz and R. W. Shuy, eds., *Teaching Black Children to Read* (Washington, D.C.: Center for Applied Linguistics, 1969), pp. 14–28.

[35] Brian Sutton-Smith, B. G. Rosenberg, and E. F. Morgan, "Development of Sex Differences in Play Choices During Preadolescence," *Child Development* 34, no. 1: 119–126, 1963; Ruth E. Hartley, "A Developmental View of Female Sex-Role Definition and Identification," *Merrill-Palmer Quarterly*, no. 1: 3–16, 1964.

[36] Marjorie Hall and Robert Keith, "Sex Role Preference Among Children in Upper and Lower Social Classes," *Journal of Social Psychology* 62: 101–110, 1964.

[37] Jerome Kagan, Howard A. Moss, and Irving E. Siegel, "Psychological Significance of Styles of Conceptualization," Monograph of The Society for Research in Child Development, Serial No. 86.

[38] Donald M. Broverman et al., "Roles of Activation and Inhibition in Sex Differences in Cognitive Abilities," *Psychological Review* 75, no. 1: 24, 42, January 1968.

[39] Ibid., pp. 24, 42.

[40] J. Carson McGuire and G. Thomas Rowland, "Jean Piaget: Theories," *The Encyclopedia of Education*, vol. 7 (New York: Macmillan and Free Press, 1971), pp. 143–145.

[41] Ibid. p. 149.

[42] Richard Ripple and V. N. Rockcastle, eds., *Piaget Rediscovered*, a report on the Conference on Cognitive Studies and Curriculum Development (Ithaca, N.Y.: Cornell University Press, 1964), p. 9.

[43] McGuire and Rowland, p. 150.

[44] McGuire and Rowland, p. 145.

[45] Lawrence Kohlberg, "Moral Education," *The School Review* 74, no. 1: 7, Spring 1966.

CHAPTER 6

The Rights of Students

There are only two public institutions in the United States which steadfastly deny that the Bill of Rights applies to them. One is the military and the other is the public schools. Both are compulsory. Taken together, they are the chief socializing institutions of our society. Everyone goes to our schools. What they learn—not from what they are formally taught but from the way the institution is organized to treat them—is that authority is more important than freedom, order more precious than liberty, and discipline a higher value than individual expression. That is a lesson which is inappropriate to a free society—and certainly inappropriate to its schools.[1]

In Chapter 5, various adolescent traits were conceptualized that appear to have a bearing on students' success in schools. Students possessing certain favored traits were depicted as satisfied, adjusted, and relatively secure with respect to their goals and potentials. Those with other traits, however, were viewed as disaffected; they have grown to distrust and fear and have rejected the values the schools are promoting.

The school itself is a bureaucratic institution. It is characterized by a division of labor, defined staff roles, a hierarchial ordering of offices, and set procedural rules.[2] In a bureaucracy, efficiency in achieving specified goals of the institution is of the utmost importance. Power flows from the top down, and various procedures are developed to protect the organization. It is difficult for schools to operate efficiently as bureaucracies because the goals of the institution are almost never stated in clear and specific terms.[3] Nevertheless, there are norms and those members of the institution who conform to expected norms are rewarded. Those who do not conform are denied rewards or are threatened with denial.[4] In order to function, administrators are in positions of maximum control of power, and the teachers hold a subordinate position in the hierarchy. In the system the students are powerless.

Within the bureaucratic structure of the secondary school, those students who adapt and conform to the expectations of the institution are quite successful within the structure. There are others, however, whose learned and natural traits do not lead to conformity. They are the "troublemakers." These are the culprits upon whom pressure is exerted in order to cause them to conform to the expectations of the institution. They, along with militant teachers, threaten and frustrate the bureaucratic system. Without these individuals this chapter would be a very brief one.

The events of the past decade have demonstrated rather clearly that activist students will not be easily suppressed. It is our intent to examine instances of pupil dissent in the schools, the institutional response to this dissent, and the evolving nature of legal judgments related to this general problem. The data in this chapter are the legal decisions of the various federal and state courts that have considered cases related to freedom of speech, student dress, and other student demands for a more active role in the governance of school affairs.

Dimensions of Student Dissent

In retrospect, secondary school officials had easy going during the first fifty years of the existence of high schools with respect to the willingness of students to conform to the norms demanded by the school. And secondary school administrators in the late fifties and early sixties were still rather comfortable at a time when universities were beset by violence, sit-ins, and the general disruption created by "hippies," "pinkos," the SDS, and others. As recently as 1968 Lawrence M. Brammer was able to write of "The Coming Revolt of High School Students."[5] Although student rebellion in the secondary schools was still an infrequent occurrence in the mid-1960s, by that date it was clear that extensive and organized dissent was not to be the lot of the university alone. Student activism in the secondary schools took many forms. And, while there were few schools that experienced all or most of the forms of activism, a general pattern of activist activities across the secondary schools of the nation was clearly discernable by 1969.

Precisely what triggered the student revolt in the universities and eventually in the secondary schools is a matter of considerable discussion. Many of the general causes were alluded to in the earlier chapters of this text. The society was undergoing a reexamination of traditional values. Emergent values were competing with the generally accepted values of the society. There were many broad issues vying for solution, for example, the war in Vietnam, increased civil rights, unemployment, freedom of speech, sexual freedom, and drug use. Much of the early dissent had its roots in the civil rights movement; and minority groups, especially the blacks and Chicanos, were quick to extend their struggle for civil rights into the educational establishment. At base, the dissent could be classified as political; that is, a struggle to extend the rights and privileges of the democratic society to students, low-income groups, and anyone who might fall in the general category of "have not" where political power was concerned.

Swirling from this tempestuous period in our history, a number of issues roared to center focus in secondary schools across the country. In a very short space of time the schools saw it all: boycotts, riots, sit-ins, armbands and buttons for one cause or another, assaults, underground publications, increased vandalism, violence, and many other forms of student militancy. As the schools moved to contain disruptions, they were frequently accused of violating basic civil rights of their students. Many of these accusations were eventually considered by the courts as cases related to the fundamental rights of people. These cases can be classified within the general rubric of *student rights* as they relate to basic rights of all American citizens; that is, the right of due process, freedom of expression and of the press, freedom of assembly, and the right to privacy.

The struggle to extend these rights to secondary school students has involved considerable strife in and around schools and extensive judicial proceedings, even in the United States Supreme Court. *It is clear at this point that the courts have determined that secondary school students shall have the same rights and privileges as other citizens of this democracy, and that they do not leave these rights at the schoolhouse door upon entering.*

In the process many individuals, notably school-age youth, have made personal sacrifices. School administrators and teachers have had to reexamine their values and practices as they relate to secondary school students. Some have decided that the necessary adjustments were too great for them to remain in the profession. Others continue to perform as educators apparently unaffected, even oblivious, to the problem. But many have internalized the spirit of student rights and are working to modify the schools further.

In Loco Parentis

Historically, school officials have had virtually the same power over students enrolled in their schools as have the parents in the home. The concept of *in loco parentis* is translated simply as *in the place of the parent*; that is, the administrator exercised the rights of a parent toward a child. This concept of school authority is consistent with the puritan morality in which the seeds of our public education system were planted. Over the years the procedures and judgments of school officials in dealing with student problems or problem students have been reinforced by court decisions in their favor. Until rather recently it was usually a foregone conclusion that in any civil case brought by a student or parent in the name of a student against a school official, the school official would be vindicated. In those cases that were decided in favor of the plaintiff, the actions of the school official were usually found to be capricious or arbitrary.

The twentieth century has seen a slow but steady extension of civil liberties to an increasingly large number of individuals and groups within this society. In the quotation at the opening of this chapter, Glasser contends that only two institutions have insulated themselves from this trend: the military and the schools.[6] Today both of these establishments are feeling the efforts of their members to gain more rights and greater liberties. A major obstacle to this move in the schools has been the concept of *in loco parentis*. Many of the civil suits brought by students and parents in recent years have hit directly at this principle.

Social reformers of the early twentieth century had succeeded in removing the child from the jurisdiction of criminal courts. It was believed that the protected environment of the juvenile court could provide the child with a more understanding and humanistic consideration of his problem or offense. This move toward a juvenile court system in fact removed the child from the procedural protection of the legal system.[7] Under the "protection" of the juvenile court system many juvenile cases were resolved without formal hearings. Despite the good intentions of the court, the result was that the child was often denied due process. School officials and teachers and officers of the juvenile court responded similarly. The child was often denied the rights to speak in his own defense, to be confronted by his accuser, or to be represented by counsel. Juvenile court judges and school administrators were also mutually reinforcing in that cases involving offenses of school-age youth were frequently resolved via cooperative efforts of representatives of the school and the juvenile court.

Today's legal trend is clearly to ensure that *due process* is extended to the child on all legal questions. The years since 1960 have involved more court proceedings on matters of student rights than were seen in all the previous years of the existence of our public school system. The decisions of the courts have the effect of moving away from the concept of *in loco parentis* by supporting rights and privileges of citizenship for juveniles.

Freedom of Speech, Press, and Assembly

The First Amendment to the Constitution of the United States provides that Congress will make no laws abridging the individual's right to freedom of speech, press, or assembly for the purpose of petitioning for the redress of grievances. A number of cases have come before the courts during the past decade for the purpose of considering the appropriateness of these freedoms for secondary school students. Among these cases were those dealing with students' wearing of buttons and armbands, student publication of newspapers not sponsored by the school, school dress codes, searching of student lockers, student demonstrations, and, most recently, student suspension and expulsion. Several of these cases will be reviewed below.

STUDENT PROTESTS

Students have worn armbands or buttons protesting involvement in the Vietnam war, or related to the civil rights movement; and they have attempted to boycott certain school activities and to hold silent vigils of protest related to a variety of causes. Typically school officials have prevented such behavior. Their reasons often included the following: student boycotts are not conducive to the maintenance of an orderly school program; the wearing of armbands may cause disruptions or endanger the wearer; any out-of-the-ordinary behavior may be disruptive to the school program, even though a small number of individuals may be involved.

Students who do not follow the admonishments of school officials are liable to sanctions. They can be physically punished, suspended, placed in detention during or after school hours, or expelled. These usual punishments available to school officials have been used to punish protesting students. Since 1965 a number of court cases dealing with the question whether protest is a form of free speech have been heard. The courts have ruled that such behavior is a form of expression, and that freedom of speech not only guarantees freedom of the spoken word but also protects such symbolic expressions as the wearing of an armband or a button and even silent vigils.

In the mid-1960s black students in a Mississippi high school were suspended by school officials for wearing buttons that carried the inscription "Freedom Now." When the case of the suspension was brought before a federal court (*Burnside* v. *Byars*), the students were reinstated. Their reinstatement was based on the grounds that there had been no significant disruption of the educational process as a result of the wearing of the buttons and that the rule prohibiting freedom buttons was an infringement on the students' right of free expression.[8] On the same day the same federal court rendered a judgment on another case that was also related to the wearing and distributing of freedom buttons (*Blackwell* v. *Issaquena County Board of Education*). This judgment provided a criterion that was to prove useful in subsequent cases considering infringement on freedom of speech. In this case the suspension of students by school officials was upheld because there was evidence that the students wearing and distributing the buttons had caused substantial disturbance. The court stated, "In this case the reprehensible conduct described above was so inexorably tied to the wearing of the buttons that the two are not separable. In these circumstances, we consider the rule of the school authorities reasonable."[9] In these two cases the court attempted to restrict the power of school officials in preventing free expression, but at the same time it upheld the power of school officials to regulate disruptive conduct. This action is significant in that the court provided a standard that requires school officials to provide conclusive evidence of substantial interference with the educative functioning before they may prevent or interfere with freedom of expression on the part of students.[10]

LANDMARK CASES

Cases are never identical; they happen in different schools under different circumstances and in different sections of the country. Thus until a large number of legal decisions related to the same or similar principles are accumulated, numerous cases will have to be heard by the courts. Nevertheless, under our system of law certain cases tend to be landmark cases that set precedents that may be applied in subsequent cases. A case in point is that of *Tinker* v. *Des Moines, Independent Community School District*.[11] This case is related to those described previously. School officials in Des Moines learned of a planned protest by students against the Vietnam war. The board adopted a policy that students who wear black armbands to school and who refuse to remove the armbands when requested by school officials would be suspended. Five students were suspended when they took part in a silent protest against the war. They sought an injunction in federal district court restraining school officials from disciplining them. The district court upheld the suspensions and the U.S. Court of Appeals for the Eighth Circuit affirmed the decision of the district court. Eventually, the Supreme Court reviewed the case. The district court had determined that although there was no evidence of disruption at the school which could be attributed to the activities of the students who wore the armbands, the suspensions were reasonable because school authorities *feared a disturbance.* The Supreme Court stated that "fear or apprehension of disturbance is not enough to overcome the right to freedom of expression." In reversing the decisions of the lower courts the Supreme Court went on to point out:

> School authorities do not possess absolute authority over their students. Students in school as well as out of school are "persons" under our Constitution. They are possessed of fundamental rights which the State must respect, just as they themselves must respect their obligations to the State. In our system, students may not be regarded as closed-circuit recipients of only that which the State chooses to communicate. They may not be confined to expression of those sentiments that are officially approved. In the absence of a specific showing of constitutionally valid reasons to regulate their speech, students are entitled to freedom of expression of their views.[12]

The *Tinker* case is significant on several grounds. It reaffirms the principles developed in the *Blackwell* and *Burnside* cases. The wearing of armbands or buttons for the purpose of expressing views is symbolic speech and is clearly within the protection afforded citizens by the First Amendment. Students are entitled to the protection of the First Amendment. The fear that a disturbance might occur as a result of wearing armbands or buttons is not sufficient reason to deny an individual his constitutional rights. Before a school official may prohibit such an expression of views, he must demonstrate that the exercise of the right by the individual would "materially and substantially interfere with the requirements of appropriate discipline in the operation of the school."[13]

PRINTED MATERIALS

Another dimension of the appropriateness of First Amendment freedoms for secondary school students is that of publication and distribution of unofficial newspapers, pamphlets, and similar materials. Students are increasingly utilizing this medium to air issues, points of view, and distribute information they believe cannot be included in approved school publications. Approved publications, while produced by students, are monitored by a faculty advisor and are published within the framework of a specific editorial policy. The major question related to freedom of the press in secondary schools is the right of students to publish and/or distribute unauthorized publications. In such cases the principles described previously in the *Blackwell, Burnside,* and *Tinker* cases are germane and have been reinforced by the actions of courts that have considered cases dealing with school publications.

One of the most significant cases regarding unauthorized publications is the *Scoville* case.[14] Two high school students alleged that the school had violated their rights under the First and Fourteenth Amendments by expelling them for distributing on school grounds a publication containing an editorial critical of school administrators and school procedures. The publication had urged students to disregard the procedures set forth by the administrators. In reversing a decision of a lower court, the Seventh Circuit Court of Appeals ruled that high school students have a right to speak out in print on issues; may criticize school policies and school personnel; and can distribute literature on school grounds and in school buildings. It underscored the students' right to publish papers free from the censorship of the administration, teachers, or the school board; but made it "subject to the primary concern of the school to maintain order and rules and regulations which are *reasonably* calculated to maintain order."[15]

After studying a number of other court decisions regarding freedom of the press in public schools, one investigator concluded that "the essential factor balancing guaranteed freedoms against the interests of school officials is a substantial and material interference with school activities. In the case of publications or the distribution of literature the disapproval by school officials of content, or anticipated controversy is not sufficient to exclude the publication."[16] While we will not attempt to consider the court cases involved, it seems apparent that the positions and principles stated in the cases described above apply also to questions of students' rights of assembly and petition.

Personal Rights of Students

STUDENT LOCKERS

The question of personal property rights is associated with the Fourth Amendment of the Constitution, that is, provisions related to search and seizure. Do school authorities have the right to investigate the contents of student lockers without the consent of the student? Do school authorities have the right to search student lockers without having the student present? Generally, court decisions have reaffirmed the principles that school authorities have control over the use of student lockers and have the right (even duty) to inspect lockers when the facts and circumstances of a case imply that the lockers are being used in an illegal fashion. Further, school authorities can search students when the circumstances of a situation lead them to conclude that a student has in his possession dangerous or illegal articles.

According to Leone, there are two sides to the locker question. One view is that school officials have supervisory power in such matters. This power extends to the inspection of lockers for reasons of health and safety. A second view is that the student in the public schools is entitled to the protection afforded citizens under the Fourth Amendment, that is, protection against illegal search and seizure, and that a warrant should be required to search a person's private property.[17]

A major question regarding locker search is, "Can school authorities delegate their right to supervise lockers to police on a criminal search?" Perhaps the most notable search case is *Overton* v. *New York*. In this case detectives had obtained a warrant directing the search of two high school students and their lockers. The detectives presented the warrant to the vice-principal of the high school, who called the students to his office. The detectives searched the boys but did not find the evidence. One of the students was taken by two of the detectives to search his locker. The second student was left in the presence of the vice-principal and the third detective. During this time the second student was asked whether he had marijuana in his locker. After repeated inquiry by the detective, the student indicated that he may have. The detective, the vice-principal, the school custodian, and the defendant went to the student's locker. It was opened with a master key and marijuana cigarettes were found in a jacket hanging in the locker.

Later it was held that the warrant was ineffective as it related to the search of the locker. Overton's attorney moved to suppress the use of the cigarettes as evidence because the locker search was illegal. The trial court denied the motion on the grounds that the board of education through the vice-principal had retained supervision over the use of the lockers and that the search was therefore legal. Eventually the Court of Appeals of New York ruled that the action of the vice-principal made it a legal search.

We may expect two key questions to be tested in future court cases: Does the school official by virtue of his supervisory powers have the right to inspect a student's locker? (In *Overton* the courts determined that he had that right.) If the school official does have the right to inspect a student's locker, may he transfer this right to others?

HAIRCUTS AND DRESS CODES

Over the years a common action of school officials has been that of regulating student appearance. This includes both the nature and type of clothing worn and, especially with boys, the length of hair including facial hair such as sideburns and mustaches. As of this writing, the Supreme Court has not heard a case involving dress or hairstyle. Yet, imbedded in the issue is the fundamental problem of students rights that exists in other issues we have considered.

For the most part, student dress codes have reflected middle-class expectations of styling. Many educators apparently perceive a linkage between student dress and behavior. Glasser contends that nothing illustrates the repressiveness of the schools more than the attempt of school officials to regulate dress and personal appearance of students. In the past decade violations of dress codes have been among the most frequent causes of student suspension, even though questions of offensiveness, health, or safety are rarely present.[18]

In their verdicts in the hair and dress code cases prior to the mid-sixties, the courts tended to uphold the power of the school official to regulate student appearance. More recently, the courts have held that personal appearance is a matter of individual taste and is beyond the scope of authority of school officials. The *Tinker* decision and other decisions related to *due process* imply that restrictions on dress or hair are limits on self-expression and thus are subject to successful legal challenge. In *Griffin* v. *Tatum*, an Alabama court stated that "there can be little doubt that the Constitution protects the freedom to determine one's own hairstyle and otherwise to govern one's personal appearance." This decision went on to state that the haircut rule was arbitrary and unreasonable. Suspension of a student for breaking the rule violated the equal protection clause of the Fourteenth Amendment. The court also affirmed that it is the responsibility of school officials to protect a student whose deviant behavior might incite other students to deprive him of his constitutional rights.[19] A review of the court cases dealing with questions of personal appearance stimulated one investigator to conclude that questions of dress or hairstyles are really questions of personal rights and are subject to control only when they are proved disruptive to educational programs or processes, offensive to manners or morals of others, or create problems of health or safety.[20]

PUNISHMENT AND DUE PROCESS

As we have noted previously, school officials have tended to rely on certain standard procedures for handling cases of student discipline. Under the *in loco parentis* concept, school officials have traditionally used physical punishment, detention, suspension, and expulsion for the purpose of maintaining appropriate discipline in the schools. Corporal or physical punishment is specifically prohibited in only the state of New Jersey, and the District of Columbia. Forty-nine states have no specific legislation restricting the use of physical punishment in the schools. In the majority of states, policies on the use of corporal punishment are determined by the local school boards. There is no way to determine precisely how much physical punishment is being administered in the schools of the nation. Undoubtedly there is some, but only infrequently are such cases brought before the court. As a rule, the courts have not interfered with the administration of physical force as a disciplinary measure except when bodily injury or maliciousness on the part of the individual administering the punishment is evident. Thus the concept of *in loco parentis* seems to have given the schools a free hand historically in administering corporal or physical punishment. N. Hentoff, in preparing a report commissioned by the American Civil Liberties Union, expressed astonishment at the incidence of the use of physical punishment by school authorities. Carolyn Schumacher of the Committee for the Abolishment of Corporal Punishment in Pittsburgh suggests that the continued use of physical punishment, including paddling, in the schools serves to teach violence as a solution to problems.[21]

Under the concept of *in loco parentis*, the teacher in fact has legal status similar to that of a parent. In order to ensure proper discipline in the school (and the courts recognize that orderly discipline is essential to good education), punishment may be administered within certain limits; that is, punishment must be reasonable, not cruel or in some unusual form; it must not be excessive; it must not be administered in anger or for purpose of seeking revenge; and must be administered in a manner that is consistent with the preservation of the dignity of the individual. Needless to say, a final condition is that the offense must have been a violation of a rule that is reasonable in the first place.

Suspension and expulsion are commonly used by school officials who do not believe in physical punishment or when physical punishment is not sufficient. Suspension is the process of removing a student from school activities and restricting his return for a specified period of time or until certain conditions are met. Most school administrators have the power to suspend students. Expulsion has the effect of terminating or delaying for a long period of time a student's education in a particular school system. Expulsion is generally considered a power of the school board, but may be delegated to other school officials. The expulsion of a student is a very serious form of disciplinary action. Opponents contend that such action is a violation of the student's basic rights. While the courts have not interfered with the school's right to suspend or expel students, they have required that school officials follow *due process* procedures by granting the student a proper hearing. (*Goss* v. *Lopez* 1975[22]). Prior to *Goss*, judgments in court cases dealing with suspension and expulsion tended to focus on the nature of the violation and the justification of the school rule which the student allegedly violated. Future court cases will undoubtedly involve the question of *due process* as well.

In a landmark case, *West Virginia* v. *Barnett* 1943,[23] it was ruled that a student could not be expelled for exercising his right of free speech; in *Burnside* the suspension of students was found to be unconstitutional because they created no disturbance; and in the *Tinker* case students suspended because of the button violations were reinstated because their right to free speech was violated. A multitude of such decisions illustrates that it is the rule that is supposedly broken in a suspension or expulsion case that is most carefully examined by the court. If the rule violates the student's constitutional rights, then the suspension or expulsion is not upheld by the court. This is not to imply that the courts always find in favor of the student. For instance, in the *Blackwell* case suspensions were upheld because the students created a disturbance in attempting to force other students to wear buttons. The courts have affirmed the judgment that regulations are unconstitutional when they are unreasonable, unclear, or arbitrary. When reasonable and necessary rules are broken by students, the test of "material and/or substantial disruption" is utilized as a criterion.[24]

The concept of *due processes* has been a major concern of the courts in examining cases dealing with student rights and disciplinary sanctions. Essentially there are two considerations a court must make in adjudicating cases that involve the rights of students in the schools: Was there an abridgement of the rights of the individual in view of the guarantees of the United States Constitution? Were the basic processes of law followed in determining guilt or innocence? In considering the first question, the courts must determine whether the action of the school authorities or the rule under question is consistent with the constitutional guarantees of freedom of speech, press, religion, assembly, and so on. In the second question the issue of *due process* is raised; that is, were all sides of the questions considered; did all the individuals involved in the case have the opportunity to be heard; did the accused have the opportunity to be represented by counsel; was there adequate time to prepare an appropriate defense?

Although it did not concern the schools directly, a major case dealing with procedural issues in juvenile cases is *in re Gault.*[25] In this case parents of a juvenile alleged that they had not received proper notice, were not informed of their right to counsel or of their right to give sworn testimony, and did not know what the consequences of the case might be. The parents contended that the proceedings of the juvenile court violated the child's right of *due process.* The court had committed the juvenile Gault to the State Industrial School and, furthermore, had retained jurisdiction over him until he reached the age of 21. The original offense was one which if committed by an adult would have been punishable by imprisonment of two months or by a fine of no more than $50. The juvenile court decision amounted to a six-year sentence for the juvenile.[26] The United States Supreme Court reversed the decisions of three lower courts in what has been called the "Magna Charta for Students."[27] The Court determined that juveniles are entitled to constitutionally guaranteed procedures and due process. These include written notice, the right to counsel, the right to face witnesses, the freedom from self-incrimination, and the right to cross-examine witnesses. This decision significantly weakened the historically accepted concept of *in loco parentis* which had denied juveniles the right of due process. In making this momentous decision the Court stated, "Whatever may be their precise impact, neither the Fourteenth Amendment nor the Bill of Rights is for adults alone."[28]

In early 1975, the Supreme Court of the United States handed down two cases which are certain to lead to more *due process* in the schools and increased litigation as well. The *Goss* v. *Lopez* case mentioned earlier requires school officials in suspension cases to provide a statement of charges of the alleged wrong doing, to provide evidence upon request to support the charges, and to afford the student the opportunity to present his side of the problem. While hearing the Goss case, the Supreme Court was also hearing a second case which in the long run may have an even greater impact upon the care exercised by school officials in disciplining students. In February, 1975, in *Wood* v. *Strickland*[29] the Court decreed that school officials are liable if they abridge the civil rights of students. The practical effect of this decision is that school board members and school administrators can be assessed monetary damages if the plantiff can substantiate that his civil rights were violated by the disciplinary action of the school official.

Unfortunately, it is possible that the Wood case could cause many responsible and successful citizens to avoid service as school board members and thereby deprive the schools of some outstanding lay-leadership. Likewise it could have a negative effect when school administrators choose to ignore disciplinary problems or seek ways of avoiding the principles involved without breaking the law. And it is unlikely that school board members or school administrators will consciously place themselves in positions which may jeopardize personal monetary resources.

ACCESS TO STUDENT RECORDS

Record keeping is virtually a way of life in our society. Insurance companies, finance companies, governmental agencies and educational institutions are among the many organiztaions which accumulate data about the private and public affairs of individuals. With the coming of the computer it became possible to assimulate and retrieve bits and pieces of data about individuals much of which formerly may have been tucked away in remote files. This information thus became available to persons or organizations which had entre to the data bank.

Initially this was viewed as a valuable system of record keeping and information retrieval but it became increasingly evident that the system, unregulated, was also a vehicle for stripping the individual of the right of personal privacy. The individual usually was unaware of the existence or the use of such records. Further, incorrect data in the files remained unchallenged with a potential for causing damage. In the late 1960's and early 1970's, increasing concern for this problem resulted in the development of new policies and laws which were designed to protect the individual by controlling and governing the maintenance and use of such files. Among this legislation was the Family Educational Rights and Privacy Act[30] which became operative in November, 1974. The Act stipulates that federal funds are to be denied to any educational institution or agency which has a policy that prevents the parents of students who are or have been in attendance at the institution the right to inspect and review the educational records of their children.[31] This effectively opens to parents and students over 18 years of age their children's or their personal cumulative records of the schools including test scores, interest inventories, health data, teacher and counselor ratings, records of alleged misbehavior, etc. When the content of the records is challenged by the parent or student a hearing for this purpose must be held.

School officials generally have responded to the law in two ways. First, they have proceeded to purge from the files personal and irrelevant materials and items which are potentially libelous or questionable. Second, they have set up new procedures for maintaining the files, making them available for inspection, and informing parents of their right to inspect and review the data in the files.

This legislation undoubtedly is causing considerable inconvenience and difficulty for school officials who need to maintain a longitudinal record which depicts the growth and development of children as they progress up the educational ladder. However, the inconvenience must be weighed against the desirability of preserving and protecting the right of an individual to be represented fairly by his records.

Problems in Adjusting to the Change

The preponderance of decisions of state and federal courts in the past decade has clearly indicated that the rights guaranteed by the Constitution of the United States, particularly the Bill of Rights and the Fourteenth Amendment, apply as much to adolescents as they do to adults. The traditionally accepted concept of *in loco parentis* must give way to *due process* in settling problems related to pupil violations in the schools. Nevertheless, generations of school officials and teachers, many of whom now occupy leadership positions in education, are finding it difficult to adjust to a new way of perceiving students. Although school boards, principals' associations, and various groups interested in student rights have published guidelines for dealing with students justly, it is difficult to change behavior followed over such a long period of time. Some school boards and administrators in high schools are working more cooperatively with students in developing dress codes, codes of student conduct, and mechanisms for review into which are built procedures consistent with the concept of due process.

Nevertheless, some educators are reluctant to extend to students the freedoms the courts have determined rightfully are theirs. For instance, there are indications that equal freedoms are not provided to students engaged in extracurricular activities. A student athlete was forbidden to participate as a member of his high school basketball team following an accusation by a teenage girl that he was the parent of her unborn child. The school took the action without holding a hearing of any sort. In another situation a student who was president of the school glee club was prohibited from appearing with the glee club in public because he was married. Students have been prohibited from participating in school activities for a variety of reasons; for example, hair length, dress, low grades, marriage, and so on. We are sure that many similar cases can be found in schools throughout the country.

It is not a question of merely changing behavior. Teachers and administrators appear to value such practices and regulations for the purpose of controlling students. We have learned to *expect* that students will conform to the standards set forth for them by their parents and by those in charge of their education.

Robert Ackerly, the attorney for the National Association for Secondary School Principals (NASSP), has made a number of observations regarding the behavior of school administrators with respect to legislated change. He states that principals are not well equipped to compete in the legal arena and that their record in court cases is a poor one. Many principals continue to be dogmatic, arbitrary, and arrogant toward students and their rights. When called upon to do so they have not been able to provide reasonable justification for many of their decisions. Ackerly further contends that principals are primarily responsive to elected school boards and legislatures, to the community, and to public opinion, not to the student and his rights. In his opinion, principals have spent little time in providing leadership in the community regarding a reexamination of values related to the rights of students.[32] The school principal is a "man in the middle." It is not an enviable position. He must maintain a positive relationship with his students, his faculty, and the community including the school board. Here is a clear example of how an individual in a position of leadership can be trapped by the conflict between traditional and emergent values, which were described in an earlier chapter.

In part the problem may be one of education. The National Association of Secondary School Principals has made considerable effort to inform school administrators of the nature and significance of recent judicial decisions and to provide them with some suggestions for implementing programs consistent with these decisions. In 1969 the organization published a booklet entitled *The Reasonable Exercise of Authority*.[33] This publication explained to the principals the concept of due process, gave summary positions on ten basic issues of student rights, and provided annotations of major judicial decisions. In 1970 the same organization conducted a study on disruption in urban secondary schools.[34] This study provided the administrator with data on the nature and extent of disruption, explained some of the causes of student disruption, and suggested strategies that the administrator might utilize in getting at the causes of disruption. It also considered school practices that tend to make matters worse. Among these practices direct punitive measures such as suspension, expulsion, police arrest, and in-school detention were described as "unimaginative and traditional control devices" which seem to "produce perverse and contraproductive results."[35]

The NASSP has attempted to inform its members by publishing special issues of its *Bulletin* focused on the problem of student rights. It has devoted numerous sessions to the topic at its annual and regional conferences, and has sponsored special seminars for the purpose of both informing principals of the law and suggesting alternative procedures for protecting the rights of students.

Apparently neither school officials nor students as a group have understood the point of judicial decisions that support basic democratic rights for students. The fact that many school problems today are related to dress codes, hair length, skirt length, and similar problems of a superficial nature indicates that these groups have not faced up to the court's judgments that students should be treated as persons with rights and responsibilities. Further, it appears that some school administrators are making efforts to circumvent the principle of increased student rights. They are reluctant to give their clients the rights that the Constitution says are theirs. If school procedures were designed to treat students as individuals with all the rights guaranteed under the Constitution, there would be no reason why principals must appear before judicial tribunals to defend the practices they are following in their schools.[36]

Students do not necessarily behave in a manner conducive to the preservation of the rights of their peers. For instance, a Louisville, Kentucky, principal asked the school attorney for a legal opinion on whether all members of a graduating class had to wear the formal attire which the senior class had agreed upon for commencement. Ten seniors had previously questioned whether they had to abide by the class decision. The attorney responded, "It is our opinion that neither the board of education, yourself, or members of the senior class have the right to impose this requirement on those participating in the graduation ceremonies." A large number of the graduating class voiced opposition to the ruling.[37] In this case they adhered to the lawyer's opinion, but it was evident that a great deal of pressure was being placed on those students who did not wish to conform. Although the case described here is not significant in terms of its infringement on student rights, it is evident that a majority of students can exert great influence upon the rights of a minority via other than direct confrontation. Peer pressure of a subtle nature may have more impact on student behavior than direct administrative action.

Although it is impossible to determine just how much effort is being expended by school systems to develop policies and procedures that are conducive to the protection of student rights, there is evidence that some school systems are making an attempt. For instance, the school board of Evanston, Illinois, Township High School has adopted a policy on student expression. The policy "acknowledges the rights of students to personal expression while seeking to define a rational position between freedom and order." The aim of the policy is "to give the board a workable position somewhere between students' demands for rights and the need for organizational control of the school by administrators and board members."[38] Therefore, the provisions of the policy include limitations on students but also on school administrators. Students may place notices on school bulletin boards or engage in other forms of communication *without* prior approval of school officials, but the students must put their names on the notices. If an administrator believes that the subject of the posted notice is outside the domain of "protected activities," he may remove it, but he must explain to the student why he took such action. The student may appeal the action all the way to the board. Students' rights to wear buttons, signs, badges, armbands, and so on, on school property are protected by the policy. They may distribute leaflets, newspapers, notices, and so forth; but there are criteria established for "protected activities." Administrators may designate the times for distributing handbills and leaflets if such limitations are necessary to prevent interference with the school program.

Prince Georges County, Maryland, has established a course entitled *Teenagers Rights and Responsibilities.* The course is part of the curriculum for all eighth grade students and is designed to assist the students in examining alternatives available to them in dealing with issues within the system. It also purports to teach practical skills that would be useful in dealing with frustrating social and legal problems.[39]

In 1970 the New York City Board of Education published *Resolution Stating Rights and Responsibilities of Senior High School Students.* The following are provided for in the system-wide policy: an elective and representative student government in each high school; a specific statement of powers of the student government; the establishment of a parent–student–faculty consulting council to discuss matters relating to the high school; specifications related to official school publications which should "reflect the policy and judgment of the student editors;" provisions that students may exercise their constitutionally protected rights of free speech and assembly as long as they do not interfere with the operations of the regular school programs; a provision that students have the right to determine their own dress except where such dress is dangerous or clearly distractive to the learning and teaching process; provision for hearings that must be held within five school days of any suspension; a statement regarding responsibilities, mentioning particularly that students do not have the right to interfere with the education of fellow students.[40]

The American Civil Liberties Union (ACLU) has provided a detailed set of guidelines for school officials interested in developing a school environment consistent with the judgments of the federal courts. In its publication entitled *Academic Freedom in the Secondary Schools,* the organization explains in a concise fashion the basic principles that are involved in the extension of democratic rights to secondary school students.[41] There are three "fundamental principles" which the ACLU believes must be accepted to guard against the elimination of "legitimate controversy and legitimate freedom."

1. A recognition that freedom implies the right to make mistakes and that students must therefore sometimes be permitted to act in ways which are predictably unwise so long as the consequences of their acts are not dangerous to life and property, and do not seriously disrupt the academic process.
2. A recognition that students in their schools should have the right to live under the principle of 'rule by law' as opposed to 'rule by personality.' To protect this right, rules and regulations should be in writing. Students have the right to know the extent and limits of the

faculty's authority and, therefore, the powers that are reserved for the students and the responsibilities that they should accept. Their rights should not be compromised by faculty members who while ostensibly acting as consultants or counselors, are, in fact, exercising authority to censor student expression and inquiry.

3. A recognition that deviation from the opinions and standards deemed desirable by the faculty is not *ipso facto* a danger to the educational process.[42]

The ACLU statement is one that every school administrator and school teacher should study with great care. It provides guidelines that are basic to the creation of an educational environment which not only preserves the freedoms of students and teachers alike but which also helps the students develop skill and sensitivity regarding the many responsibilities that these freedoms place upon all of us. The design and maintenance of such an atmosphere in our schools will not be an easy task.

Some Conclusions

In this chapter it has been demonstrated that the traditional procedures that schools have used in disciplining and restricting students are no longer suitable. Decisions in the courts have established that students are entitled to the guarantees of freedom of the United States Constitution. With these freedoms are accompanying responsibilities; it is an important part of the task of the school to educate a student both as to his rights and to his responsibilities.

QUESTIONS AND ACTIVITIES

1. Identify the important characteristics of the high school as a bureaucratic institution. Does the bureaucratic nature of the institution aid or impede the attainment of important educational goals? Explain.

2. Using the two general categories of students described by the authors (conformists and noncomformists), analyze a problematic situation found in the high school setting. Do students have a tendency to behave fairly consistently within the parameters of one or the other of the two categories or do they have a tendency to shift frequently as school issues and problems change? Cite examples to support your opinions.

3. What student issues of the late 1960s are still with us today in both precollegiate and collegiate education? What resolutions took place with those which no longer appear important?

4. Briefly summarize the development of the concept *in loco parentis* and indicate the impact the explosive sixties had on the concept.

5. What are your reactions to the influence the recent court decisions have had on the basic freedoms (freedom of speech, press, and assembly) within the context of the school community? Can school officials protect these freedoms for the individual and still run an effective educational program?

6. Do the court decisions in the area of personal rights of students find reinforcement in the communities of which the school's are a part? What factors would affect the degree of reinforcement received?

7. In your estimation what are the advantages and disadvantages of the provisions of the Family Rights and Privacy Act?

8. What are some important inservice teacher education or professional development concerns which have arisen as a result of the expanding view of student rights held by the courts?

9. Work up a description of one "rights" problem with which you have a considerable familiarity. Use it as a basis for further class discussion and study of ways in which schools may respond to protect the rights of the individual.

10. Invite a school administrator to discuss with your class his views on the influence which court decisions have had on school management.

11. Secure student handbooks from two or three schools and compare the manner in which these handbooks approach student conduct, dress codes, suspension, and so on.

NOTES

[1] Ira Glasser, "Schools for Scandal—The Bill of Rights and Public Education," *Phi Delta Kappan*, Volume LI, No. 4, December 1969, p. 190.

[2] Frederick R. Smith, and James A. Mackey, "Creating an Appropriate Social Setting for Inquiry," *Phi Delta Kappan*, Volume L, No. 8, April 1969, pp. 462–465.

[3] Donald Arnstine, "Freedom and Bureaucracy in the Schools," chap. 1, p. 50, in *Freedom, Bureaucracy and Schooling*, 1971 Yearbook, ASCD, 1971.

[4] Smith and Mackey, p. 463.

[5] Lawrence M. Brammer, "The Coming Revolt of High School Students," The *Bulletin* of the National Association of Secondary School Principals, Vol. 52, No. 329, September 1968, pp. 13–21.

[6] Glasser, p. 190.

[7] David A. Washburn, "The Development of Law Concerning Pupil Conduct and Discipline: Constitutional Rights and Procedural Guarantees in Public School Systems," unpublished doctoral dissertation, University of Illinois, 1972, p. 6.

[8] *Burnside v. Byars*, 363 F. 2d. 744 (Mississippi, 1966).

[9] *Blackwell v. Issaquena County Board of Education*, 363 F. 2d 749 (Mississippi, 1966).

[10] Glasser, p. 10.

[11] *Tinker v. Des Moines, Independent Community School District*, 393 U.S. 503 (Iowa, 1969).

[12] *Tinker v. Des Moines*.

[13] Glasser, p. 193.

[14] *Scoville* v. *Board of Education of Joliet Township High School District 204,* 415 F. 2d. 860. Reversed F. 2d. 10 (Seventh Cir., April 1, 1970).

[15] Andrew A. Leone, "Legal Aspects in Secondary Education," Indiana University, Bloomington, Indiana, July 1970, p. 4. (Mimeo)

[16] Washburn, p. 98.

[17] Leone, p. 10.

[18] Glasser, p. 193.

[19] *Griffin* v. *Tatum,* 300 F. Supp. 60 (M. D. Alabama, N. D., 1969).

[20] Washburn, p. 108.

[21] Nat Hentoff, "Why Students Want Their Constitutional Rights," *Saturday Review,* May 22, 1971, p. 63.

[22] *Goss* v. *Strickland,* 419 U.S. 565 (1975).

[23] *West Virginia Board of Education* v. *Barnette,* 319 W. S. 624 (1943).

[24] Washburn, pp. 114–127, *passim.*

[25] *In re Gault,* 387 U.S. 1 (1967).

[26] Washburn, p. 128.

[27] Washburn, p. 128; and Robert L. Ackerly, *The Reasonable Exercise of Authority,* (Washington, D.C.: National Association of Secondary School Principals, 1969).

[28] Washburn, p. 128.

[29] *Wood* v. *Strickland,* 420 U.S. 308 (1975).

[30] General Education Provisions Act, PL93-568, Section 438, Family Educational Rights and Privacy Act. 1974.

[31] Ibid.

[32] Robert L. Ackerly, *The Reasonable Exercise of Authority* (Washington, D.C.: National Association of Secondary School Principals, 1969), p. 2.

[33] Ibid.

[34] Steven J. Bailey, *Disruption in Urban Public Secondary Schools,* (Washington, D.C.: National Association of Secondary School Principals, 1970), 66 pp.

[35] Ibid., p. 34.

[36] Ackerly, p. 6.

[37] *The Courier-Journal,* Louisville, Kentucky, Friday, June 2, 1972, Section A, p. 21.

[38] "One School Board's Policy on Student Dissent," *School Management,* August 1969, pp. 43–44.

[39] Barnard L. Collier, "Learning to Cope in Prince Georges County," *Saturday Review,* May 22, 1971, pp. 64–65, 75.

[40] "New York City Board of Education Resolution Stating Rights and Responsibilities of Senior High School Students," *New York University Education Quarterly,* Summer 1970, pp. 23–24.

[41] American Civil Liberties Union, *Academic Freedom in the Secondary Schools,* ACLU, 156 Fifth Avenue, New York, New York, 1968.

[42] Ibid.

CHAPTER 7

Teachers and Their Emergent Professional Power

This chapter focuses on teachers. Today's teachers represent an interesting transition between the traditional concept of educator as public servant and educator as an aggressive proponent of organizational strengths with a high potential for political power. After exploring some general characteristics of teachers, the teacher's place in the hierarchy of the public school system will be examined. Also considered are some major problems and issues that confront the profession today—particularly the acquisition and use of political power, organizational unification, and collective bargaining.

The Gargantuan Enterprise

There are approximately 2.5 million teachers in the United States. The largest number of these is employed in public elementary and secondary schools, with elementary teachers outnumbering secondary school teachers by a small margin. There are over 14,000 school superintendents directing the school corporations in which these teachers are employed, and 120,000 principals and supervisors who provide direct administrative and supervisory services to faculty members.

There are more than 30 million children enrolled in the elementary schools and almost 15 million students enrolled in the secondary schools in this nation. And more than 55 billion dollars per year are expended in educating these children.[1] Education, one of the biggest business enterprises in the nation, is financed almost completely by dollars acquired through local, state, and national taxation. These funds collected by the various levels of government are reallocated to general public works—education demanding and receiving a large share. Teachers and administrators are public employees paid with tax dollars and employed in public schools under the jurisdiction of lay boards of education. This results in a situation in which the profession historically has been unable to control, even if it had wanted to, many factors that must be controlled if professional status is to be attained. Only recently have educators begun to acquire and flex the organizational muscle necessary for the acquisition of professional self-determination. This development will be discussed later in this chapter.

Is Education a Profession?

The question of the professional status of education has been hotly debated in every conceivable situation from the theoretical seminars in teacher education institutions to the teachers' smoking area behind the boiler in the high school basement. By what criteria may a profession be judged? Is it sufficient that those inside the group view themselves as professionals or must those *outside* confer professional status upon the group? Myron Lieberman's book, *Education as a Profession*, which examined many of the major professional questions and problems facing teachers, is perhaps the most comprehensive work on the professionalization of teaching. Lieberman identified "a complex of characteristics which distinguishes professions from other occupations." These are

1. A unique, definite, and essential social service.
2. An emphasis upon intellectual techniques in performing its services.
3. A long period of specialized training.
4. A broad range of autonomy for both the individual practitioners and for the occupational group as a whole.
5. An acceptance by the practitioners of broad personal responsibility for judgments made and acts performed within the scope of professional autonomy.
6. An emphasis upon the service to be rendered, rather than the economic gain to the practitioners, as the basis for the organization and performance of the social service delegated to the occupational group.
7. A comprehensive self-governing organization of practitioners.
8. A code of ethics which has been clarified and interpreted at ambiguous and doubtful points by concrete cases.[2]

Lieberman viewed the list of eight characteristics not as a "fool proof set of specifications" but as a starting point for discussion. His writing conveyed the impression that Education in 1956 was not a profession and that teachers could not "expect to achieve professional status until the teachers themselves participate in the drive toward professionalism."[3]

The two decades since Lieberman's book was published have seen tremendous changes in the behavior of teachers. Teachers have become more aggressive in seeking improved economic benefits and better working conditions through the process of collective bargaining. Teachers' unions and associations, which have demonstrated some movement toward joining forces, do not as yet provide a united front for teachers. Nevertheless, they have provided leadership in organizing teacher groups which speak not merely to safe, mundane, issues as in the past, but to the nitty-gritty questions of economics and teacher rights. The timid, compromising, passive teacher is following the five-cent cup of coffee and the hornbook into the pages of history. That, at least, is what appears to be happening if one examines the militant behavior of teachers as they function in organized groups. The reader is challenged to consider the professional status of teaching in this new context.

Factors Related to the Image of Teachers

Literature and the popular media create certain pictures or stereotypes of teachers which may provide clues to the image of the profession as viewed by outsiders.

FACES OF THE PROFESSIONAL

An early literary description of teachers was the bumbling schoolmaster, Ichabod Crane, of Washington Irving's *Legend of Sleepy Hollow*. Popular television programs in the past portrayed teachers as the mild-mannered Mr. Peepers or the zany Miss Brooks. More recently teachers have been represented on television by the masculine, handsome Mr. Novak, admired for his courage, wisdom, and personalized approach to educational problems. *To Sir, With Love* and *Conrack* have portrayed teachers as insightful, humane, and scholarly professionals, loved by students and admired by parents but misunderstood by their colleagues. Teachers in the media once viewed as absentminded, slightly odd, and not overly competent are now intelligent, suave, humane, and sophisticated professionals.

One can only guess whether the entertainment media mirror a concept of teachers which is held by the public in general. But at best, public opinion is a capricious indicator of professional status. Notwithstanding, an improved public image might well be an aid to increased status.

If we assume that the media aim to reflect public perceptions of teachers, and further, that the media are accurate, then the public must see teachers as apolitical. They are seldom if ever crusaders or activists in the community. The assumption is that the public does not see teachers involved in political or social situations outside the school. In the media they are viewed only as functioning in the educational arena. The image of teachers portrayed by literature and the entertainment media is neither powerful nor particularly prestigious. There is some comfort in the fact that teachers are portrayed less negatively today than in the past, but there is much progress to be made if teaching is to be viewed as a potent profession. The pertinent question is whether the media accurately reflects the public image of teachers.

The character of the public image holds implications for both the recruitment of new teachers and the expected professional behavior of teachers. If teachers are perceived as apolitical, they may not find public support for their more militant activities. Neither will the profession be attractive to politicized young people.

RESEARCH ON TEACHER CHARACTERISTICS AND POLITICAL BEHAVIOR

Hard data gained through systematic investigation provide a firmer and more reliable base for identifying teacher characteristics. Harmon Zeigler has compiled considerable research data on teacher characteristics and political behavior. The National Education Association (NEA) also provides general demographic data in its annual research reports. The following discussion draws heavily on materials from these two sources.

Teaching is traditionally a feminine profession. Elementary schools have always had a predominance of female teachers and until the 1950s, the high schools were largely staffed by women. Zeigler contends that the post–World War II recruitment of male teachers into the secondary schools did not make teaching a masculine occupation; rather it led to the assumption of a feminine role by men. He argues that laymen view teaching as a woman's job, and that individuals performing in this occupation are perceived as playing a feminine role. Men in this situation establish male authority only with difficulty. He argues further that the males in this role tend to behave politically in a manner similar to women.[4]

ECONOMIC REWARDS, SOCIAL MOBILITY, AND JOB SATISFACTION

Historically a serious consequence of the feminine image of teaching has been the low salaries of teachers. Economic and other types of discrimination against women in education and other fields are well documented by leaders in the women's movement of the present day. While female high school teachers are economically rewarded at a higher level than most women holding other jobs, male high school teachers earn less money than males in other occupations. Thus it is not merely the case that males are functioning in a traditionally female area, but they are also receiving female wages. This economic perception of teaching as a feminine occupation is helpful in understanding some other characteristics of teachers. Women who are married and raising families find teaching an attractive occupation that enables them to function as professionals while earning supplementary family income. When the demand for teachers is high, married women can move in and out of the profession. Males are not so flexible, even though teaching for them is not so economically attractive as it is for females. Moreover, males tend to see the classroom as a stepping-stone to higher-paying positions as administrators or supervisors.[5]

Traditionally, administrative roles in education have been occupied by men. A recent report indicated that 89 percent of elementary and secondary school teachers report to a male principal. In the secondary schools alone, 99 percent of teachers have a male principal.[6] Despite the obvious advantaged position of males with respect to upward mobility in the profession, there are not sufficient administrative positions to accommodate all. Consequently, many males in teaching (52 percent) augment their salaries with additional employment during the school year, and three-fourths (76 percent) work at other jobs during the school year or summer. Females constitute 66 percent of the teaching force and approximately three-fourths of these are married. Eighty-nine percent of the married female teachers have working husbands.[7] Thus there is a greater percentage of male teachers who are financially disadvantaged in comparison to women teachers. They hold more than one job and are apt to become dissatisfied with the inadequate financial rewards from teaching. Furthermore, most will be unable to acquire the higher-paying administrative positions. One can anticipate that their frustration will only increase.

Zeigler, in fact, found that there is considerable job dissatisfaction among male teachers, while most female teachers indicated that they would choose teaching again for a career. Undoubtedly, job satisfaction is tied in with the economic situation described above, but it also is related to the class origin of teachers.

Teaching is generally classified as a middle-class occupation. A majority of male secondary school teachers come from lower-class homes, whereas a large number of female teachers tend to come from a middle- or upper-class background. Thus for the beginning male teacher a career in education offers an upward change in class status, whereas for the typical female teacher it does not. The satisfaction that the male gained from his class change is soon lost by staying in a female profession. Although young males do not tend to think of themselves as remaining in the classroom, many do become career teachers. Those who anticipated moving to administrative positions but could not are most apt to experience frustration—especially as they realize that their options for moving are lessening. This hypothesis is supported by research that shows that job satisfaction among beginning male teachers is considerably higher than that of experienced male teachers. On the other hand, female teachers tend to demonstrate increased job satisfaction as their income and expertise increase. Zeigler believes that male job dissatisfaction may be explained in part by the fact that men and women are paid equally in education—a situation well established in schools but not replicated in most employment categories. If male teachers perceive female teachers as earning supplementary family incomes while they perceive themselves as the major bread winners for their families, feelings of job dissatisfaction will continue regardless of future increases in wage levels.[8] This situation may offer in part an explanation for the active role that many males are assuming in the teachers' movement toward greater militancy. Zeigler analyzes teachers' attitudes toward education with an extremely strong statement that may provide a clue to the increased militancy of teachers. "That male teachers should develop anti-establishment attitudes is understandable, but this has resulted in high schools staffed with teachers who do not like their work, who espouse an ideology of discontent, and who reject the educational orthodoxy of the educational establishment."[9]

The solution to this discontent may lie more in the legitimacy that only the society can extend to the profession than in the increased benefits that males may obtain from the educational system itself. This is an interesting and provocative thesis that draws heavily upon the psychological crunch that Zeigler contends impacts upon males employed in a female profession. Presumably the society is not of its own accord going to grant the profession the desired legitimacy. Thus the profession will have to take the appropriate steps to force legitimacy. The acquisition of power and influence as well as increased economic benefits seems to be the course the profession is following.

Societal Attitudes toward Teaching

An important dimension of the professional image of teachers is the view the society holds toward teaching. Teaching is easily accessible to both males and females with a college education and an appropriate sequence of professional courses. The cost of securing teaching credentials is about equal to that of securing a bachelor's degree in any major university. A teaching credential does not require an additional major commitment of funds for those students who were going to attend college anyway. Neither is there an excessive period of professional preparation involved in fulfilling requirements for certification in most teaching areas. Education, therefore, is perhaps the most accessible of the professions. Lower-class parents, particularly, perceive teaching as a major avenue of upward mobility for their children. Studies of social attitudes toward teaching show that rural and village dwellers would encourage children of either sex to enter the profession (daughters 83 percent, and sons 77 percent). Town and urban parents would give encouragement to daughters (78 percent town, and 83 percent urban) but would not encourage sons (36 percent town, and 43 percent urban). Of all the adults sampled in two studies, more than 80 percent would encourage daughters to teach, but less than 50 percent would encouarge a son.

Community origins of teachers provide further evidence that education is a profession that is viewed as a source of upward social mobility. A disproportionate percentage of teachers are of farm origin (about 20 percent). This is nearly twice the percentage one would expect, given the present farm population. Further, approximately two-thirds of the male teachers and more than half of the female teacher are of blue-collar origin.[10]

There is some evidence that school counselors have a perception of teaching as a career that has some parallels with data cited earlier. One hundred counselors were asked how they would advise teacher aspirants who varied in scholastic ability, finances, race, ethnic group, and social class. The counselors were 24 times more likely to encourage students of average ability, limited finances, minority race, and lower social class to attend a teachers college rather than a liberal arts college.[11]

It seems evident that teaching as a career is stereotyped as easily accessible, more suitable for women than men, and a potential avenue of upward social mobility for individuals in the lower socioeconomic class. The practical effect of this stereotype is the denial to education of a large portion of talented young people who are being directed into other professions by educator and community bias that is transmitted in both formal and informal ways.

Extending the Scope of Professional Power

LAY CONTROL

Teachers are public employees who, as a group, have been largely removed from the process of determining policies under which they must function. Traditionally they have had very limited power to influence salaries, working conditions, standards for professional certification, and other matters relevant to their professional status.

Educators have been expected to serve as exemplars of academic excellence and models of good citizenship—performing their assigned tasks of instructing youth to the best of their ability without complaint, regardless of the difficulties involved. But the situation is changing, and school administrators, school trustees, and school patrons are shaking their heads in disbelief. Teachers are seeking and finding power. They are directing this new-found power to the acquisition of those ends they perceive as necessary and justifiable for maintaining a higher quality of personal and professional life.

In order to understand the current situation, it is necessary to review briefly some of the circumstances under which public education developed and functioned in this country. Education is a responsibility of the states. State constitutions include provisions for the establishment of a public school system. It is the responsibility of the state legislatures to finance this system. State legislatures also specify procedures by which the educational system may be governed. In effect, public education in this country has been controlled by laymen. At the state level, lay boards of education develop general policies under which the schools in the state will function. Such boards generally have broad powers delimited only by practical considerations and laws affecting public education which are passed by the state legislatures. Under these arrangements the certification of teachers is under the control of appointed or elected lay boards. Thus the control of entry into the profession is in the hands of laymen rather than professionals. This violates a basic criterion for a profession: that the group set standards for admission and exert control over its membership. Surprisingly, the National Education Association supported this situation for many years.[12]

Although education is the responsibility of the state, most of the control and responsibility for public education has been delegated to local school districts by the state legislature. Although in theory an appointed professional educator administers the schools, a lay board of education determines the policies for the school system. Thus professional educators perform their tasks of administration, supervision, and teaching in a context of control that is external to the profession. It seems evident that if teachers are to have full professional status, there must be major modifications in the system.

FINANCING PUBLIC EDUCATION

Because it is in the economic sector that educational organizations seem to be most militant, it is appropriate to examine the manner in which the schools are financed. State governments are responsible for financing public education; thus "The financial problems of education are largely the result of the failure of states to create and maintain school support programs which assure equal educational opportunities and an adequate level of support for all children."[13] In most states the primary source of school revenue is local property taxes.[14] Unfortunately tremendous differences in per pupil wealth among school districts lead to inequities in funding educational programs. Because the largest portion of a district's budget is for instruction, the inequities critically affect the ability to employ and reward teachers.

There are many variables that influence the district's ability to finance education. Especially critical are the property tax base and population. A suburban school system may have mostly modest homes in which many young families reside. Although each of these homes may contribute two or three children to be educated, it would not produce property tax revenues commensurate with the costs of educating these children. On the other hand, a school district with several large industries may derive extensive income from property taxes paid by these industries but have few children to educate, as many of the workers may reside in other school districts. Conditions such as these cause school finance specialists to conclude that the property tax is an inadequate basis for financing the schools.

It is not proper to convey the impression that schools are funded entirely on the local level. Approximately forty states have some sort of formula by which state funds are allocated to local districts to guarantee a *minimum* revenue per child. These formulas, however, "have not equalized tax levy rates among districts within a state, nor have they addressed themselves to the problems of varying costs for equivalent educational services, or the differences in the educational needs of pupils which require different levels of expenditure to bring about equal opportunity."[15]

The federal government also allocates some funds for public education. These vary from year to year, but in no year from 1962 to 1972 did federal funds exceed 8.8 percent of the combined revenues received by the schools from federal, state, and local sources. Funds received by public schools in that decade averaged 54 percent from local sources, 40 percent from state government, and 7 percent from federal government. Since 1961 there has been a tendency to increase the percentage of revenues for public schools from state and national sources; nevertheless, the local community continues to provide the largest percentage of funds.[16]

The limit of the amount of revenue that can be allocated to public education in the future is unknown. Additional taxes on sales, income, and selected items such as alcoholic beverages and tobacco can be levied or increased. It is evident that overreliance on locally levied property taxes and continued low levels of state and federal support not only places the burden for financing schools on the shoulders of the property owner but also leads to educational inequities for children and economic inequities for educators.[17]

The financial structure of public education has major implications for educators as they seek to make more demands on local school districts. With few exceptions these demands have economic implications. Salary increases and improved fringe benefits are costly; but so are a more favorable teacher–pupil ratio, improved instructional arrangements, and an increase in the number of days for in-service education. Without a change in the present limited revenue base of most school systems, it is impossible to acquire the dollars necessary to improve public education. If the financial system were modified to draw more heavily on state and federal taxes, both equalization and quality could be promoted; but public education would have to learn how to compete for the tax dollar with higher education, welfare, highways, and other agencies funded with state and federal revenues.[18] The financial situation is such that the increased involvement of education and educators in the political arena appears inevitable. Politically aggressive teacher organizations are necessary in this competitive situation. A merger of the American Federation of Teachers (AFT) and the National Education Association could result in a superorganization with awesome political power.

EDUCATION AND POLITICS

Traditionally education in our society has been viewed as being above politics. For example, school boards are considered nonpartisan, and teachers' involvement in political activities has been discouraged if not forbidden. For many years professional associations acted in a nonpolitical manner even to the point of avoiding pronouncements on significant social issues.

According to Guthrie and Craig, apolitical education is a myth. Schooling always has been tied closely to the political process. Educational decisions fall within a comprehensive definition of politics—"the distribution of values within a society that are legitimized through governmental action."[19] Such questions as Who shall attend school? Who shall teach? What shall be taught? and Who shall finance education? demonstrate the ties between education and politics. Furthermore, education has expanded political overtones as a consequence of its greater visibility, and the increased demand for expenditures involving competition with other public sector activities.[20] In recent years there has been an overt recognition on the part of teachers that they are involved in politics. Many have been elected to public office. It is also common for teacher groups including the NEA and the AFT to make major statements on public issues and to support political candidates actively.

TEACHERS' ORGANIZATIONS AND TEACHER POWER

If teachers continue to increase their involvement in politics in the realization that education must compete for the tax dollar with other governmental agencies if schools are to be funded equitably and adequately, the more than 3 million teachers in the United States will emerge as one of the largest and most powerful special interest groups in this country. It is estimated that through organizational dues and assessments, teachers' groups could generate some 500 million dollars each year for use in election campaigns, lobbying activities, precinct organization, and other components of the political system. The political worker potential of 3.5 million teachers is immense. It is conceivable that teacher organizations can equal or exceed the political clout of any other interest group in our society.[21]

Myron Lieberman brings this potential "to life" in a scenario of the Democratic Convention in 1980. Prior to the seventh ballot in the deadlocked convention, a presidential hopeful pledges, if elected, to work toward the assumption by the federal government of one-half the costs of public education from elementary schools through the university. On the seventh ballot 125 delegates switch to support this candidate. Among these delegates switching are 85 classroom teachers, 26 college professors, and 14 officials of local affiliates of the NEA. On the eighth ballot these delegates are joined by others including delegates "beholden to the Public Employment Department of the AFL–CIO." When the candidate is nominated, he names a state governor who has had close association with the NEA as his vice presidential nominee. Subsequently the NEA political education fund of 35 million dollars is committed to the campaign and the ticket is elected.[22]

Lieberman's scenario is only possible with a politically militant and unified educational organization. In the past the NEA, with a membership of over one million, and the AFT, with approximately 250,000 members, have approached educators as organizational competitors.

A major point of division and dissension between the two organizations has been the concept of the labor union. The founders of the NEA in 1870 simply did not conceive of it as a teachers' union. As a coalition of earlier formed teacher and administrator groups, the NEA accepted all educators, including administrators, for membership. Collective bargaining, strikes, and militancy did not suit its philosophy as a professional association. The AFT, on the other hand, organized in 1916 as a coalition of local teachers' unions, has maintained a belief in labor union principles as well as an affiliation with organized labor. As a result its membership, which excludes administrators, is largely in urban areas where labor unions are strong and where teachers have felt comfortable with union militancy.

According to Lieberman the NEA affiliates have been "forced" to assume the "substance as well as the form of unionization in order to compete for members." As a consequence differences between the two organizations are slowly disappearing. In fact the current questioning of education and the financial problems facing schools in this country seem to be bringing these organizations together.[23]

The movement toward merger began in a modest way in Flint, Michigan, in 1969. In 1970 the Los Angeles Association of Classroom Teachers and AFT Local 201 combined their 14,000 members into The United Teachers of California. The merger of the New York State Teachers Association (NEA) and the United Teachers of New York (AFT) in June 1972 produced the largest state public employees' organization in the country.[24] Movements toward merger at the state or local levels are also in process in Rhode Island, Illinois, Louisiana, and Florida.

Although there are still significant obstacles to a national merger of the NEA and AFT, the differences between the two organizations are less of a barrier today then ever before.[25] Despite pronouncements to the contrary, it appears to be only a matter of time until the two groups can arrive at some compromise about or at least accommodation of differences in philosophy, eligibility for membership, tactics, and leadership.

UNIONS AND PROFESSIONALISM

As suggested above, a major issue separating the NEA and the AFT is the alleged unprofessional nature of unions. Supposedly teachers lose professional status by joining unions. Lieberman reasons that the real test of the professionalism of an organization rests not in its name but in its power, prestige, and activities. Indicators of lower status of teachers belonging to unions would be lower salaries, lower prestige among laymen, and less teaching freedom. He concludes that since teaching salaries and working conditions in large cities and suburban areas, where most teachers are, are generally superior to those in rural areas and small communities, unionization does not lower professional status. He further points out that members of many other professions are members of national labor unions and that some of these—for example, airline pilots, symphony orchestra conductors, some engineers, doctors, lawyers, and even presidents of some learned societies—have higher professional status than teachers. He contends that one does not suddenly lose professional status by joining a union: "The professionalism of union teachers is not something that can be settled by so *defining* unions that their members cannot be professional."[26]

STRIKES AND WORK STOPPAGES

Cited as evidence that the AFT is unprofessional is the advocacy and use of strikes by teachers' unions. The concept of the teacher as public servant dictates that it is wrong to take action that denies children their right to education. Thus strikes violate the public servant concept and are unworthy of a professional. Many states also have laws prohibiting strikes by public employees, presumably including teachers.

In contrast to the common belief about the AFT's predisposition to strike, several early conventions of the AFT in the late forties and early fifties adopted and reaffirmed a no-strike policy. The NEA, on the other hand, apparently had no written policy on strikes at that time.[27] The fact of the matter is that between 1904 and 1954 there were a number of work stoppages by locals of both the AFT and NEA. Whether these were strikes is perhaps academic. The result was the same: school children were without teachers.

The withholding of services by teachers has become a frequently used procedure. Between 1955 and 1966 there were 35 teacher strikes in the United States. In 1967–68 there were 114 strikes in 21 states and in 1968–69 there were 131 strikes involving almost twice the number of lost man-days as in the previous year. By 1971–72 the number of strikes had dropped to 89 and the loss in man-days was significantly less than the year before. In 1974, however, the number of teacher strikes was back up to 106 for the year. At the onset of the 1975 school year, the NEA predicted the likelihood of some 200 strikes before the end of the year. As the fall semester of 1975 got underway, full-blown teacher strikes in some fifty cities extended the summer vacation for over two million elementary and secondary students. The bulk of this number was in New York City and Chicago where in two of the nation's largest school systems, more than 100,000 striking teachers kept more than 1500 schools closed.[28]

During the period of increased strike activity from 1965 to 1975, there was a significant rise in the number of negotiated agreements between teachers and school boards. There were also significant gains in teacher salaries. Guthrie and Craig, using data from the *Digest of Educational Statistics,* compared the average annual salaries of teachers with those of full-time employees in all industries. During the period of 1952–1968, teachers' salaries increased 128.6 percent as compared with an increase in per capita income of 94.7 percent and an average increase per employee of 94.1 percent. When dollars were adjusted to 1970–1971 levels teachers' salaries had risen by 36 percent, whereas that of full-time industrial employees had increased by 24 percent.[29] Although one cannot claim a direct cause-effect relationship between the strikes and the salary increases, it appears that some relationship existed between the two. In addition one might conclude that the years 1967–1969 during which there were approximately 245 teacher strikes firmly established the strike as a potent and available source of professional power. Considering the number of instances when services have been withheld in recent years, the professionalism of striking teachers does not appear to be a question of importance to teachers today.

THE ADVANCE TOWARD COLLECTIVE BARGAINING

We have cited a number of factors that tended to inhibit the movement of teachers toward a position of strength as a professional group. Among these were the tendency of teacher associations to assume a soft posture toward welfare issues, the feminine character of the profession, the lay control of professional certification and policy matters, and the division among professional organizations. In the past fifteen years the situation has changed, and teachers have demonstrated a steady move toward increased aggressiveness. Much of this transformation occurred in the 1960s, a period characterized by the increased militancy of many groups. Minority groups, particularly racial and ethnic minorities, as well as young Americans on college campuses, repeatedly tested the effectiveness of militant behavior and civil strife in seeking social and polotical justice. Further, labor unions had for years demonstrated that collective bargaining could bring significant economic benefits and improved working conditions. Unionized teachers in the cities likewise had demonstrated that militancy yields dividends. The United Federation of Teachers (UFT) in New York City in 1963 defied both state law and a court injunction to win a major victory. Even the nonunionized Utah Education Association (UEA) threatened to close down the state's schools unless state appropriations for schools were increased. Although the NEA lagged in its support of the UEA, the NEA affiliated Department of Classroom Teachers, representing some 90 percent of the NEA membership, stood squarely behind the Utah teachers.[30] Teachers observed and learned their lessons well.

The increased aggressiveness of teachers may be explained in part by the increase in the numbers of males in education. We cannot conclude this for certain, of course, but there are some generalizations that seem to support such a hypothesis. Male teachers are, for the most part, the primary wage earners in their families. They find themselves more and more economically bound to the profession as they invest years of service in teaching. Today approximately 50 percent of the teachers in the United States are male, a much higher percentage than in the earlier years of the century. It is not surprising, then, that many male teachers, in an era characterized by militancy and aggressiveness, have assumed a militant posture and assumed a more active role in teacher organizations.[31]

The militancy was predictable in view of Ziegler's analysis of the situation in 1967. He perceived the associations as attracting "those teachers who have the fewest complaints about the educational establishment, and largely representing conservative orientations of comfortably satisfied teachers." A typical local teachers' association had an active minority of high-income females with a lengthy history of participation in the association. Males who believed they could not achieve their goals through teachers' associations tended to dominate the union movement.[32] He concluded that teacher associations could probably draw more support from males in the future if they became more militant and moved from their opposition to union methods.[33] This appears to be what has happened.

Today it is often impossible to differentiate between teachers' unions and teacher associations by examining their goals and activities. Both provide opportunities for aggressive leadership by teachers who perceive these organizations as vehicles for improving the quality of life for career educators.

COLLECTIVE BARGAINING

Until a few years ago teachers waited apprehensively to receive their contracts from the school board each spring. These contracts specified the salaries the teachers would receive and the number of days they would teach during the following year. Typically a teacher had little or no involvement in the determination of that salary; his options were generally, "Take it or leave it." In some communities there were prior discussions of the economics of the situation between school boards and teacher association salary committees, but a salary committee's findings and suggestions were generally only advisory. In some rural communities salaries were parceled out by school trustees who made the decisions by processes known only to themselves. In urban school corporations, however, it was becoming more common for contracted salary scales to be produced through a process of collective bargaining. The teachers' agent was almost always a teachers' union.

Today, in increasing numbers of school corporations, teachers' organizations and school boards are negotiating contracts through collective bargaining. This process entails the negotiation in good faith by representatives of each party meeting at reasonable times to execute a written contract which may be ratified by the governing body of the school corporation and the teachers' bargaining unit. Although neither legislated nor voluntary collective bargaining includes the · obligation of either party to agree to a proposal of the other or to make concessions to the other, agreements reached through negotiation and agreed to by each group are binding as a contract.

Collective bargaining agreements, which generally deal with salary schedules and working conditions, are gradually being extended to include matters more closely identified with curriculum and instruction. Included among the items that have been negotiated through collective bargaining are class size, teacher transfer, assignment to noninstructional duties, teaching hours, teacher–pupil ratios, committee assignments, use of bulletin boards and school mail by teachers' groups, organization dues collection, parking arrangements, clerical services, and procedures in announcing and filling administrative and instructional vacancies.

LEGISLATION

In 1962 President Kennedy signed an executive order giving federal employees the right of collective bargaining. Since then more than half of the states have passed legislation providing bargaining rights to public employees, and many of these statutes include teachers. Nonetheless, two-fifths of the states have not passed bargaining legislation, and to date there is little uniformity in the bargaining rights of public employees from one state to another. This situation will likely change. Some state legislators, in anticipation of a more powerful teacher lobby resulting from the merger of the NEA and the AFT, are trying to improve their records by supporting legislation they believe teachers want.[34]

An example of state collective bargaining legislation is Public Law 217, Acts of 1973 of the Indiana State Legislature. This law specifically states that

> a school employer shall bargain collectively with the exclusive representative on the following: salary, wages, hours and salary- and wage-related fringe benefits. A contract may also contain a grievance procedure culminating in final and binding arbitration of unresolved grievances, but such binding arbitration of unresolved grievances shall have no power to amend, add to, subtract from or supplement provisions of the contract.

The law further states that certain subjects *may be* discussed and *may be* bargained collectively, but the employer

> shall not be required to bargain collectively, negotiate or enter into a written contract concerning or be subject to or enter into impasse procedures on the following matters: working conditions, other than those provided in Section 4; curriculum development and revision; textbook selection; teaching methods; selection, assignment or promotion of personnel; student discipline; expulsion or supervision of students; pupil–teacher ratio; class size or budget appropriations.[35]

The Indiana law is typical of state legislation governing collective bargaining in that it specifies what must and what may be negotiated, provides for mediation in event of an impasse, and bans strikes.

> It shall be unlawful for any school employee, school employee organization, or any affiliate, including but not limited to state or national affiliates thereof, to take part in or assist in a strike against a school employer or school corporation.[36]

It also provides for the development of a grievance procedure by which alleged violations of a contract may be adjudicated and it allows for binding arbitration. Although some teachers' groups have had extensive experience in negotiations, there are relatively few educators who are sufficiently expert to meet the increased demand for skilled negotiators. Many teacher leaders are engaged in learning the process in workshops designed especially for them. Administrators and board members likewise are attending special workshops designed to train them in the art of negotiation from a management perspective. Legal firms, consulting firms, labor unions, and state teachers' assosications frequently supply negotiation specialists to school corporations and local teacher organizations on a contractual basis. Some larger school corporations are now employing labor specialists as regular staff appointees; likewise, some of the larger teacher groups employ individuals as legal counsel to represent them in contract negotiations and subsequent functioning under the contract.

THE USES OF POWER

The growing power of teachers raises new questions. What directions will collective bargaining take in addition to salary and related economic matters? How many and which of the substantive instructional concerns will be included in future negotiations? In view of the present limitations on local school systems for financing public education, will teacher economic demands result in changes in the manner in which schools are financed? Will contract negotiations be carried out by some regional or state agency? If regional or state agencies take over, what are the implications for local control of the public schools? What is the limit of teacher power which society is willing to tolerate before other groups organize to counterbalance this power? If the NEA–AFT merger is consummated, how will this new "superorganization" function in relationship to matters of public education and the political, economic, and social dimensions of the society?

QUESTIONS AND ACTIVITIES

1. In your view is teaching a profession? What reasoning supports your response?
2. Do others in the community view teaching as a profession? Construct a short questionnaire about teaching as a profession. Ask other students in your college or university, public school teachers, and laymen to respond to these questions. Compare the results of your survey with those obtained by other members of your class.
3. Do you believe it is necessary that teachers improve their professional status and image? How could this be accomplished?
4. Is it preferable for a teacher to join the NEA or the AFT? Why? Does it make any difference?
5. If a school board member asked for your ideas on how the financial condition of the schools could be improved, what would you recommend?
6. Do you believe that the certification of teachers should be administered by a lay board? Why or why not? Do you have an alternative plan to suggest?
7. Do you believe that teachers should become involved in partisan politics? Should they campaign for candidates for the school board? Should they be eligible to serve on the school board in the school system in which they teach? Would that comprise a conflict of interest?
8. What are the five most important "demands" which teachers should argue for in negotiations with the board of education? If you had to drop three of these demands, which ones would you drop?
9. Do you believe that teachers have the right to strike under certain conditions? In your opinion what, if any, conditions justify a teacher strike?
10. Do you have any idea how parents view teachers and/or selected professional issues? Interview some parents with children in school in the community to learn of their perceptions of teachers or of professional issues which you have identified as being important.
11. Interview some junior and senior high school students to learn more about their perceptions of teachers.
12. Invite school board members, teachers, or administrators to your class to learn more of their ideas on the professionalization of teachers.

13. The executive secretary of the teachers' union and the executive secretary of the state education association are valuable resource people. Invite them to speak to your class about the ways teachers can strengthen themselves professionally.

NOTES

[1] "The Magnitude of the American Educational Establishment, 1971–1972," *Saturday Review*, December 18, 1971. Figures based on estimates from USOE and NEA. Numbers have been rounded off for ease in reading.

[2] Myron Lieberman, *Education as a Profession* (Englewood Cliffs, N.J.: Prentice-Hall, 1956), pp. 2–6.

[3] Ibid., p. 13.

[4] Harmon Zeigler, *The Political Life of American Teachers* (Englewood Cliffs, N.J.: Prentice-Hall, 1967), pp. 11–12.

[5] Ibid, pp. 15–17, *passim*.

[6] *ISBA Journal*, Indiana School Boards' Association, Vol. 18, No. 5, September–October, 1972, p. 22.

[7] National Education Association, *Status of the American Public School Teacher 1970–71* (Washington, D.C.: Research Division N.E.A., 1972).

[8] Zeigler, pp. 16–21.

[9] Zeigler, p. 27.

[10] Ricrard L. Turner, "An Overview of Research in Teacher Education," *Forum*, Vol. 2, No. 4. Division of Teacher Education, Indiana University, Bloomington, Indiana, 1974. Mimeo, pp. 9–12.

[11] Sidney J. Drumheller, "The Image of Teacher's College as Seen by High School Counselors." (Doctoral Thesis, Columbia University, 1961). Reported in Turner, p. 11.

[12] Robert J. Havighurst and Bernice L. Neugarten, *Society and Education*, Third Edition (Boston: Allyn and Bacon, 1967), pp. 498–499.

[13] Phi Delta Kappa Commission on Alternative Designs for Funding Education, *Financing Public Schools—A Search for Equality*, Phi Delta Kappa, Bloomington, Indiana, 1974, p. 13.

[14] Ibid., p. 17.

[15] Ibid., p. 18.

[16] Ibid., p. 35.

[17] Ibid., p. 37.

[18] Ibid., p. 35.

[19] James W. Guthrie and Patricia A. Craig, *Teachers and Politics*, Fastback No. 21, Phi Delta Kappa Educational Foundation, Bloomington, Indiana, 1973, p. 6.

[20] Ibid., pp. 7–8.

[21] Ibid., p. 10.

[22] Myron Leiberman, "The Union Merger Movement: Will 3,500,000 Teachers Put It All Together?" *Saturday Review*, June 24, 1972, pp. 50–51.

[23] Ibid.

[24] Guthrie and Craig, p. 12.

[25] Lieberman, "The Union Merger Movement," p. 52.

[26] Lieberman, *Education as a Profession*, pp. 307–308.

[27] Ibid., p. 309.

[28] "Teachers: In a Striking Mood," *Time*, September 22, 1975, pp. 16–18.

[29] Guthrie and Craig, pp. 12–14.

[30] John Scanlon, "Strikes, Sanctions, and Schools," *Saturday Review*, October 1963, *passim*.

[31] Guthrie and Craig, pp. 15–16.

[32] Zeigler, pp. 61–62.

[33] Zeigler, pp. 90–91.

[34] Lieberman, "The Union Merger Movement," p. 56.

[35] Public Law 217, Amending IC, 1971, Title 20, Acts of 1973, The State of Indiana, p. 4.

[36] Ibid., p. 11.

CHAPTER **8**

Developing the School Curriculum

The school curriculum consists of all of the planned educational experiences that the learner has under the direction of the school. This is a common definition reflecting the general pragmatic orientation of professional educators. This definition frequently is encountered in educational literature. Curriculum, broadly defined, embraces four major categories: *the program of studies* including both general and specialized education, *student activities* sometimes referred to as co-curricular activities, *student services*, and *instruction*.

Major Categories of the Curriculum

PROGRAM OF STUDIES

The program of studies, that is, courses and sequences of courses, comprise the formal portion of the students' educational program and is ordinarily described as having two components: general education and specialized education. The largest of these components is prescribed as the *general education* dimension of curriculum. This required sequence of courses and experiences, designed to provide essential skills and knowledge, generally includes basic experiences in communication, the study of society, computation, health and safety, and so on. The student will also select a number of experiences or courses that constitute his *major* or *specialized area* of interest, sometimes called curriculum, program, or track. There may be a business curriculum or track, a college preparatory curriculum, a vocational or industrial education track, and so on. Within each curriculum or track, various courses or sequences are specified. The college preparatory program may require a sequence in mathematics, science, English, and foreign language. The business education curriculum may require sequences in skill subjects such as typing, shorthand, or bookkeeping.

STUDENT ACTIVITIES

Under the comprehensive definition of curriculum, such activities as dramatics, clubs, athletics, dances, and intramural sports are called *student* or *co-curricular activities.* Student activities are designed to develop cognitive, affective, and psychomotor behaviors that cannot be learned as well in formal classroom settings. Thus the oft-used label "extracurricular activities" is not appropriate to describe these activities believed to be essential to the pupils' education. The activities program also provides opportunities to practice skills that can only be verbalized in the formal classroom setting. For instance, a social studies class may study theories and characteristics of a democratic system while student government, democratically organized clubs, and other student activities provide situations in which skills of democratic participation may be employed and refined.

STUDENT SERVICES

A third dimension of curriculum is *student services.* This dimension includes instructional support activities and services related to the physical and psychological well-being of students.

Instructional support activities include the services the library staff provides in extending the formal program of studies. For instance, they assist students in conducting individualized research projects by providing guidance in the location of resource materials. Some schools have expanded their libraries into learning resource centers, containing printed materials, multimedia materials and equipment, and artifacts.

A comprehensive student services program monitors student physical growth and development and identifies health problems, physical deficiencies, and psychological disturbances that may influence the pupils' education. In addition to regular school staff, such a program generally involves nurses, doctors, dietitions, and other specialists.

Individual and group counseling is perhaps the best-known aspect of student services. Besides counseling, the guidance program tests for aptitude and achievement, compiles pupil records, maintains files on occupations, and provides post-high school educational information.

INSTRUCTION

The fourth component of curriculum is *instruction*. Instruction is defined as the interactions between teacher and learner, the physical setting in which instruction takes place, and the manner in which the school day is structured. The character of the interaction between the teacher and learner includes the method of instruction, the intellectual and emotional climate in the classroom, the teacher's attitudes toward the learner, and teaching techniques used. The physical setting refers to the use of classrooms, laboratories, individual study carrels, learning resource centers, or any other facility in which instruction may be carried out. School days may be structured according to standard periods of time or by flexible modules that can be arranged to satisfy needs of specific activities.

When the learner is viewed as the central figure in the educational process, the four components of curriculum are seen as interrelated. In its own distinct way, each affects the learners' ability to function in the school and each contributes to the welfare of students as human beings. Students draw from these components according to their different needs and interests. A school with this wholistic view of curriculum will be engaged in a continuous effort to increase the quality, efficiency, and accessibility of these activities for all of its students.

Making Decisions about Curriculum

In Chapter 2 we suggested that a rationale for secondary education must consider normative conceptions of the social world, empirical descriptions of the social world, the nature of knowledge, the nature of thinking, and the nature of learners. Decisions on these elements were presented as necessary to the choice of purposes for the schools. Further, we suggested that decisions about the activities in schools emerge from the choices of purposes (see Figure 1, p. 25).

In the preceding sections we categorized these school activities as the program of studies, student activities, student services, and instruction. Presumably, the activities selected for use in the schools would be related to one or more of these four curriculum components.

In the following section we will concentrate on the way schools are organized to deal with curriculum decisions and how a teacher operates within the organization to make decisions about his own classroom.

Curriculum decisions by school committees and classroom teachers are made in the context of the influence of state legislatures and agencies, professional organizations, and special interest groups. This influence ranges across legislation on school offerings, state curriculum guidelines, standards used by accrediting agencies or specialized professional organizations, and the pressures of special interest groups in the community, state, and nation. These will be discussed in Chapter 9.

Curriculum decisions that will have a widespread impact on the schools are more apt to occur when they have their origins in a critical mass of professional and community support. It follows that curriculum change has the greatest opportunity for success when it is in response to a felt need on the part of the community and when the desire for change has strong administrative and teacher support.

Individual teachers or groups of teachers have almost constant opportunity to modify the curriculum within specific sectors. For instance, a creative, imaginative teacher may reorganize specific units or an entire course. Or several teachers within a department may make major changes in the course offerings and/or the instructional strategies and materials in that department.

CURRICULUM DEVELOPMENT—A COOPERATIVE EFFORT

In contrast to the older notion of curriculum development as a product of small-group work or administrative fiat, the contemporary view is that curriculum is best improved by a cooperative effort of individuals, groups, and agencies.[1] Potential participants in the process fall into five categories: the teacher, the learner, the public, the administration, and the consultant. Theoretically, representation from each of these five categories provides opportunity for input into curriculum planning by individuals and agencies with relevant interests, talents, responsibilities, and points of view. Further, the process of participating in curriculum planning should engender in the actors an attitude of psychological ownership of the final product. Perhaps most important, however, in the cooperative approach to curriculum development are the democratic principles upon which this approach is based. By involving representatives of various groups who will be affected by the curriculum, one is faithful to the principle that those who must live by a decision should have a share in its making.[2]

To ensure that curriculum improvement functions democratically, many school systems have established procedures and structures that provide for representation and cooperation. Since the nature of these arrangements varies from community to community, it is impossible to identify a single or most efficient arrangement. In large cities such as

New York or Philadelphia there may be a centralized curriculum bureau or office staffed with full-time personnel with expertise in many dimensions of curriculum planning. Medium-sized school districts tend to utilize systemwide coordinating committees. The membership of these committees is largely individuals with full-time instructional, supervisory, or administrative responsibilities but may include some full-time curriculum personnel. Smaller school systems may not have a centralized curriculum group. Centralized curriculum agencies or committees deal with policy development, communication, arbitration of disagreements, the assignment of tasks to subgroups, and other problems of curriculum planning and evaluation. The sophistication and complexity of the curriculum development superstructure vary considerably with the number of subunits in the school system. In general, there are components on at least two levels—some sort of agency, bureau, or committee that governs, guides, coordinates, or oversees, and groups at a more localized level that carry out specific tasks or functions. Because the widespread involvement of individuals and groups requires specific organizational patterns and procedures, the democratic, cooperative approach to curriculum development results in a bureaucratic organizational structure.

Within this structure the teacher will have limited opportunity for significant impact on the curriculum as a whole during his initial years with a school system. As he gains experience and acceptance by colleagues, his professional judgment will carry more weight. He will be in a better position to exert influence on significant curriculum decisions by representing his department on systemwide committees and by providing input into curriculum decisions on the school or task force level.

The remainder of this chapter will focus on the teacher as he exerts influence on curriculum in the classroom he controls. The considerations that the teacher makes in approaching curriculum decisions within a given classroom are not significantly different from those that curriculum committees must make with respect to the total school curriculum.

THE TEACHER AND CURRICULUM

The teacher in planning instruction is determining curriculum for the students enrolled in his classes. Once the classroom door is closed, the curriculum becomes a reality for both students and teacher. In the process of determining curriculum, the teacher sets goals for a course and develops specific objectives for instruction. The general goals serve as guides in selecting appropriate instructional objectives, teaching strategies, and evaluation procedures. Before teachers can make specific plans about instruction, however, they must consider the general curriculum guidelines, the course outline, and the characteristics, needs, and interests of the students enrolled.

The teacher may receive a curriculum guide and a course outline as part of his general orientation to the position. Most departments will stipulate the objectives and content for the course. In most cases a textbook or other instructional materials will be available. A first task for the teacher then is familiarization with the course, considering its fit with the general offerings of the department and the school curriculum as a whole. Course outlines, curriculum guides, discussions with other faculty and with students, and material assessments are possible sources of useful information.

A second consideration in planning for instruction is student characteristics. While the school's student population represents a certain distribution of socioeconomic classes, minority groups, intellectual characteristics, and so on, the membership of an instructional group may vary from the general profile of the student body. Some schools utilize "grouping" in assigning students to classes, for example, by reading level, achievement, and intellectual abilities. If such a system is utilized, it is important that the teacher know about the grouping process and the profile of a particular class. Some classes may be affected by scheduling practices that group students unintentionally. For instance, if only one section of physics is offered or if the school band rehearses at a specific hour, the other classes offered at the same hour may have fewer scientifically or musically inclined students. These students, however, may be disproportionately represented in other classes.

Whether a course is required or is an elective affects the profile of a class. If a course is required, the students may have little interest or motivation. In this case it is especially important that the teacher knows the profile of the class and has an understanding of the relation of the course objectives to the general curriculum plan of the school.

It is obviously important to know whether a course is introductory or advanced. Prior learning is generally assumed in advanced courses. Teachers of advanced courses in foreign language and mathematics, for example, assume that students have attained certain objectives in earlier courses. When a hierarchy of objectives is not specified in a curriculum area, however, teachers of advanced courses cannot make such assumptions about prior learning.

Although there are official channels for learning about students, for example, records and interviews with counselors, the students themselves are potentially the most valuable source of information. "Rap sessions," small-group discussions, simulations, and student essays can provide information about student interests and concerns. Pretests in the subject area may reveal the level of knowledge a student possesses. It is appropriate that the teacher plan his instruction in terms of what he has learned about his students. His is a special perspective not available to schoolwide curriculum groups. Unfortunately, many teachers seem to avoid plumbing this perspective.

Broad Goals and Instructional Objectives

Although general goals are important for curriculum planning, they are of limited value in determining the precise nature of instruction in a given class. A teacher uses instructional objectives to clarify what is to be achieved in each lesson. These objectives should constitute an integrated whole that fulfills the goals for the course. Instructional objectives, derived through an analysis of general goals, are the teacher's working translation of these goals.

Theorists who contend that learning occurs when there is changed behavior on the part of the student advise teachers to focus on the desired change in student behavior. When instructional objectives are stated in terms of the behaviors that students are expected to demonstrate *after* instruction has taken place, the teacher presumably can select appropriate learning experiences and judge whether pupils have achieved the behavior. Thus instructional objectives help in identifying learning experiences, in communicating to students what is expected of them, and in providing standards for evaluating progress.[3]

Classifying Instructional Objectives

THE COGNITIVE DOMAIN

Instructional objectives commonly deal with the recall of knowledge and the application of intellectual skills. Objectives of this type are called cognitive. In 1956 Benjamin Bloom and associates developed a taxonomy for classifying cognitive objectives.[4] The classes of objectives within the cognitive domain are arranged in a hierarchical order as shown in Figure 3.

In general the levels of the taxonomy move from simple (1.00 level) to complex (6.00). The arrangement of categories also tends to represent a concrete to abstract continuum. In this hierarchy the behaviors included in a given class build on and make use of behaviors found in lower classes in the list.[5] The taxonomy is an interdependent system in which the simple and less complex levels are part of the more complex and abstract classifications. Thus as one moves up the taxonomy, be-

Figure 3

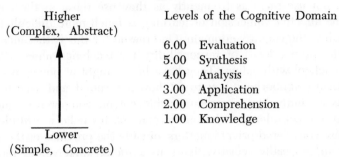

Higher
(Complex, Abstract)

Levels of the Cognitive Domain

6.00   Evaluation
5.00   Synthesis
4.00   Analysis
3.00   Application
2.00   Comprehension
1.00   Knowledge

Lower
(Simple, Concrete)

haviors at a more sophisticated level include the lower or less complicated behaviors.

The application of the cognitive taxonomy can improve course planning. The teacher may utilize it either as a reference for writing cognitive objectives or as a yardstick for measuring the emphasis being placed upon objectives at various levels of sophistication.

THE AFFECTIVE DOMAIN

Statements of curriculum goals and instructional objectives are not limited to cognitive matters. Frequently statements of objectives entail beliefs, attitudes, and values—for example, an appreciation of good music, or art; preference for the democratic way of life; tolerance toward those who are different; respect for the rights of others. Krathwohl, Bloom, and Masia, who developed a taxonomy for the affective domain of educational objectives, define the domain as dealing with "objectives which emphasize a feeling, tone, an emotion, or a degree of acceptance or rejection."[6]

Affective objectives are generally stated as interests, attitudes, appreciations, values, biases, and emotional sets. They range from the simple level of attending to a complex level of characterization by a value.[7] Like the cognitive taxonomy, the affective taxonomy is arranged in a hierarchy (Figure 4).

Figure 4

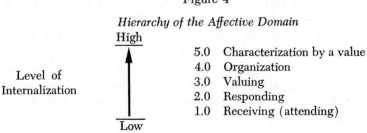

Hierarchy of the Affective Domain
High

Level of
Internalization

5.0   Characterization by a value
4.0   Organization
3.0   Valuing
2.0   Responding
1.0   Receiving (attending)

Low

Although teachers like to *express* affective instructional objectives, they do not *use* them as frequently as they use those in the cognitive area. The affective dimension of learning is much more difficult to deal with than is the cognitive domain. One reason for this is the uncertainty about the proper locus of responsibility for teaching values. Children come to school with values. They have been taught at home, at church, and in their neighborhood how to act, how to respond, and what to value. Whereas an individual's academic achievement, competence, and productivity are considered to be public matters, his beliefs, attitudes, and values are considered private matters, outside the province of the school. This is an especially sensitive issue in a society that values pluralism and freedom of choice.[8] Furthermore, some contend that the teacher is not immune to his own affect. He may have biases or inhibitions that may compromise his objectivity. Community attitudes and beliefs also may inhibit the teacher's willingness to deal with certain emotionally loaded value issues or problems. In addition, the results of teaching in the affective area are not easy to measure. There is a paucity of evaluation instruments designed to measure affective outcomes.

Although the division of behaviors into domains is artificial, they are useful tools for the analysis of instruction and evaluation. Nevertheless, in reality the domains are interrelated. Broad curriculum goals often cut across the domains. Also, objectives that are classified in one domain may have implications in the other. Individuals logically maneuver between the domains in resolving problems. Krathwohl illustrates the relationship between the cognitive and the affective domains:

> In the cognitive domain we are concerned that the student shall be able to do a task when requested. In the affective domain we are more concerned that he *does do* it when it is appropriate after he has learned that he can do it. Even though the whole school system rewards the student more on a *can do* than on a *does do* basis, it is the latter that every instructor seeks. By emphasizing this aspect of the affective components, the affective domain brings to light an extremely important and often missing element in cognitive objectives.[9]

In designing goals and instructional objectives, teachers must deal with both cognitive and affective behaviors. Many teachers do this intuitively; but the taxonomies provide a systematic, hierarchical framework that may be utilized in assessing the degree of cognitive and affective emphasis in instruction. Nevertheless, the teacher should not be tied to the sequencing pattern of the taxonomies. Nor should he assume that the two domains are necessarily balanced in "proper" instruction.

Summary

We have defined curriculum as including the program of studies, student activities, student services, and instruction. The learner is viewed as the central figure in the educational process. Each component of the curriculum makes a unique contribution to the growth of the learner as a human being.

The contemporary notion of curriculum planning is a cooperative effort of individuals, groups, and agencies that represent various interests, talents, responsibilities, and points of view. School systems differ in their organizational and procedural arrangements for curriculum study, evaluation, and modification. Because of their professional training and instructional responsibilities, teachers play a key role in curriculum development. The individual teacher can make the greatest impact on curriculum within his own classroom by understanding the relationship of his courses to the general curriculum and by learning more about his students. By carefully monitoring his instructional objectives, the teacher may determine how his course relates to the general goals of the school and the interests, needs, and abilities of his students. The cognitive and affective domains offer the teacher a systematic way of assessing instruction.

QUESTIONS AND ACTIVITIES

1. Identify the four major categories of the school curriculum. Using your own criteria, rank order them in terms of their relative importance to the mission of the schools. Be prepared to explain your criteria for the ranking.
2. Which of the curriculum categories identified in this chapter is most in need of change or improvement? How would you change it?
3. In speaking of curriculum development, the authors have identified five categories of potential participants. Rank these in order of importance in the development of past curriculum programs. Do you see any need for changing this pattern of involvement? If so, in what way?
4. From your own observations and/or classroom experiences, what considerations appear to be most important as the teacher engages in the process of curriculum planning?
5. Identify the many factors which might be used in analyzing individual learners. How could this information about these factors be used in curricular decision making? What are some problems which arise when attempting to apply this knowledge in curriculum planning settings?
6. Brainstorm with other members of your class the strategies which can be used by teachers in obtaining various kinds of feedback from students.
7. Develop lists of both the advantages and disadvantages which can accrue from the stating of instructional objectives in behavioral terms. Are there areas of the curriculum where behaviorally stated objectives might be inappropriate? Explain.

8. Activity on objectives: Identify a short lesson plan of one to two days' duration. Develop a set of behaviorally stated cognitive and affective objectives for the lesson. Once this has been accomplished, answer the following questions:

   8.1 How beneficial was the experience for you in deciding which instructional activities might be used in teaching the class? If you actually use these objectives in a classroom setting, you might apply the question to the students.

   8.2 On what levels of Bloom's taxonomy does the emphasis of the lesson focus?

   8.3 What problems, if any, did you encounter in determining specificity?

   8.4 Approximately how long did it take to write the objectives? Assuming that once you have acquired more skill in developing objectives the time needed would be reduced, then how much time would you set aside for developing objectives for a week; for a semester-long course?

9. Write out your response to the following statement. "Developing specific instructional objectives and planning daily lessons is a lot of busy work. Good teachers instinctively know what to do when they walk into the classroom." Review your response—does it give evidence that teaching is a profession?

NOTES

[1] Albert I. Oliver, *Curriculum Improvement: A Guide to Problems, Principles, and Procedures* (New York: Dodd, Mead, 1965), pp. 47–48.

[2] Ibid., p. 49.

[3] Julie S. Vargas, *Writing Worthwhile Behavioral Objectives* (New York: Harper & Row, 1972), p. 3.

[4] Benjamin S. Bloom, ed., *Taxonomy of Educational Objectives: Handbook One: Cognitive Domain* (New York: McKay, 1956).

[5] Ibid., p. 18.

[6] David R. Krathwohl, Benjamin S. Bloom, and Bertram B. Masia, *Taxonomy of Educational Objectives: The Classification of Educational Goals, Handbook Two: Affective Domain* (New York: McKay, 1956), p. 7.

[7] Ibid.

[8] Ibid., pp. 17–18.

[9] Ibid. p. 60.

CHAPTER 9

Forces Affecting the Curriculum

Curriculum decisions are not made in a vacuum. Numerous agencies, organizations, and interest groups influence curriculum in a variety of ways and through many channels. Some of these agencies, organizations, and groups possess considerable power as a result of their legalistic or professional status; others are powerful because of their relationship to significant issues during a particular period in history; and others derive their strength from their proximity to the school itself. Individuals who are involved in the process of curriculum development should be cognizant of these forces and the influences they exert.

Higher Education

Colleges and universities have had a tremendous influence upon public education in the United States. In Chapter 1 we noted that the Committee of Ten in 1894 assumed that the best education for all youth is a college preparatory type of program. Many of the recommendations made by that committee are evident in the secondary school curriculum of today. They are also reflected in college programs designed to prepare teachers for the secondary school. Most teacher education programs include an emphasis in the liberal arts and a major in a given area of study, for example, history, English, science, or mathematics. High school curriculums designed along disciplinary lines provide a ready source of employment for discipline-oriented teachers. Since colleges and universities do not offer alternative preparatory programs, teachers are not prepared to deviate from the present method of organizing the curriculum.

Colleges and universities also reinforce the present curriculum through the method of instruction commonly utilized in college classes. The usual method of instruction is the lecture where students sit "at the foot" of a scholar absorbing his reservoir of knowledge. They are evaluated on their ability to recall the data, interpretations, and conclusions presented by the professor. It is, of course, erroneous to characterize all college instruction in this manner, but professors who make use of a variety of teaching strategies are too uncommon. The prospective teacher learns to teach largely by example. Some of his finest and most revered university professors and high school teachers have used the lecture, recitation, and examination approach to teaching. Teachers accustomed to these instructional practices tend to emulate this model. Moreover, teacher educators who merely lecture about good teaching reinforce the traditional instructional model.

College entrance requirements and college entrance examinations also influence the secondary school curriculum. Although college entrance requirements are more general and flexible today than in the past, certain courses continue to be recommended by colleges as desirable for students preparing for higher education. Such recommendations are often viewed in secondary schools as requirements.

College entrance and other standardized examinations, such as the Scholastic Aptitude Test (SAT), also influence the secondary school curriculum. Many colleges and universities utilize results of standardized tests as one criterion for admission. Consequently, some high schools "prep" their students for the examinations by altering course content, offering special tutoring seminars, and by administering practice examinations. It is not unusual for similar procedures to be utilized in assisting students in competing for scholarships, medals, and certificates for scholastic attainment. Even though a modest percentage of students in the school may win these honors, some individuals perceive this as indicative of the high quality of the school's program for all students.

Instructional Materials

Materials used in instruction wield influence on the curriculum. Despite the technological advances of recent years, printed materials are still the primary vehicle of instruction in most classrooms and shall be the focus of our discussion. Although texts may be written for a number of reasons, the profit motive is a major concern. A primary consideration of authors and publishers in the development of new materials, or in revising existing materials, is marketability. Will it sell? Materials of instruction that differ radically from those that have been utilized in the past will have little appeal for textbook selection committees. Regardless of the promising theoretical underpinning of new materials, a publishing house must make a careful assessment of the material's suitability for the prospective market. Even the most imaginative and substantial materials may not be purchased if they do not "fit" in the present curriculum, or match the educators' perception of new directions in curriculum development. As a result textbooks change slowly in design and content.

The publishing industry is capable of making changes when it appears to be necessary and desirable. For instance, today's materials contain more information on blacks, women, Spanish-Americans, American Indians, and other minority groups, drugs, sex, and social conflict. The approach, however, is still a cautious one; controversial topics are treated in an "acceptable" manner. For instance, when the war in Vietnam was a hot issue, it was examined from a historical perspective. Only when the issue became less emotional were the major pros and cons of the U.S. involvement in Vietnam explored.

Some publishers have made efforts to be more innovative with their textbooks. Many publishers displayed an immediate interest in the new approaches to curriculum which were developed by the various national curriculum projects in the 1960s. Once the publishing houses were convinced which of the project alternatives would be attractive to public school teachers, there was a great rush to make the new materials available commercially. Materials from the Mathematics Curriculum Study Projects, the CHem Study Project, and the Carnegie-Mellon Project in social studies were published within a short time after they had been placed in the public domain. To the extent that the materials and content produced by the national curriculum projects differed from traditional materials and content they have brought about some change in the secondary school curriculum. In general, however, textbooks published in recent years have tended to reinforce traditional concepts of curriculum much more than they influenced change and innovation. Book publishers cannot be faulted alone in this regard, however. Textbooks that deviate significantly in content or format do not do well in the secondary school market. Apparently teachers not only prefer the traditional content, but they also prefer that it be packaged in a traditional manner.

TEXTBOOK SELECTION

Textbook commissions and local textbook committees influence curriculum. There has been some reluctance to allow teachers freedom in selecting instructional materials for use in their classes. A significant number of states control the range of options in textbook selection through a state-approved list. Several states have a state textbook commission that oversees the process of examining materials that are candidates for adoption. These commissions generally make use of appointed subcommittees of teachers, administrators, and laymen that evaluate texts submitted by teachers, publishers, or other designated sources. The process produces a list of several approved books for each grade level or course. Textbook selection committees are subject to pressure by publishers' representatives who want their books on the state-approved list; by professional organizations of teachers who believe that certain materials are better than others; and by organized lay groups that support or oppose certain titles. Most teachers oppose the system of state textbook adoptions. Local materials selection committees are viewed in a more positive way. These committees comprised of groups of teachers are recognized as performing a professional service for their colleagues. Nevertheless, some teachers would prefer to be completely free to determine what materials their students use. In many classrooms, that preference results in a "show shelf" of adopted texts and "use shelves" of preferred materials.

Legislated Curriculum

State legislatures have considerable influence on the school curriculum. Under the Constitution of the United States, education became a function of the states because it was not a reserved power of the federal government or prohibited to the states. States have assumed the responsibility for educating their citizens; state legislatures have developed organizational, fiscal, and substantive guidelines for public education. An obvious influence of the legislature on curriculum is the specification of basic educational requirements for all children. These requirements are in the area of curriculum which we earlier described as *general education*. Although basic educational requirements for secondary schools vary among states, they usually include two or three units of English-language arts, one or two units in mathematics, one or two units in social studies including American history and government, and other general requirements such as physical education. On occasion a state legislature will become more specific in prescribing curriculum. For instance, during the height of the "cold war" in the late 1950s and the early 1960s, a number of state legislatures considered bills that would require that the secondary schools teach courses in anticommunism. Two states passed such legislation. This type of prescriptive legislation in the opinion of many educators constitutes an unwarranted intrusion upon the professional rights of teachers and local educational authorities.

Leadership at the State Level

State departments of education also exert considerable influence on curriculum. Most state departments of education employ curriculum and technical consultants in the various subject areas, school administration, finance, pupil personnel, special education, and other areas of public education. In many states, consultants in the subject areas are responsible for the development of state curriculum guides. Although these curriculum guides are intended to provide general guidelines for curriculum development at the various grade levels, the fact that they are published by state departments of education carries an aura of official approval. Local curriculums frequently adhere closely to the guidelines. An aggressive state consultant can have significant influence on schools by encouraging certain practices and withholding approval of others.

In recent years the federal government has distributed an increasing amount of its financial aid to public secondary schools via state departments of education. The responsibility of distributing federal funds has given state departments of education even more power over the schools.

A recent trend in the states is the change of the office of state superintendent of education from an elected to an appointed position. Many state superintendents of public instruction were formerly elected for two- or four-year terms. Since these were partisan elections, state superintendents had to remain in the good graces of the party. They had to avoid endorsing educational legislation or policies that were politically unacceptable. Because of this involvement in politics, a number of patronage positions in state departments of education changed hands with each new superintendent. Consequently, many state departments of education, weakened by personnel turnover, could not maintain continuity in programs. It is assumed that the appointment of state superintendents of public instruction will result in the staffing of state departments of education with more qualified career educators who will provide increased leadership and assistance to the public schools. While the professionalization of the state education office counts as a good trend in education, it must be weighed against the likely loss of political clout by the superintendent, a matter of no small concern in our society.

Accrediting Associations

Secondary schools may be accredited by state departments of education, state universities, and regional accrediting associations. Although accreditation by any of these agencies is important, many schools perceive membership in one of the six regional accreditation associations as being most prestigious.* A secondary school may apply for accreditation by the association in its region of the country. The associations specify standards on institutional purpose, organization, administration and control, instructional program, professional staff, student activities, and financial support which schools must meet if they are to be accredited.[1] A school seeking accreditation initiates a year of self-study of its program, facilities, and instructional staff. The regional association requires the use of an instrument such as the *Evaluative Criteria* of the National Study of Secondary School Evaluation as a guide for intensive self-evaluation by the school.[2] After the self-study is completed, the association appoints a committee comprised of school principals, classroom teachers, and university professors to assist the school in the process of self-evaluation. This committee responds to the same criteria utilized in the self-study. During a three- or four-day visit at the school, the visiting committee develops a report that is submitted to the association. When approved for membership, schools must engage in a self-study and reexamination approximately every ten years.

One advantage of membership in an accrediting association is psychological. Faculty, students, and community members believe that accreditation is indicative of the high quality of the school. Another advantage of membership is the recognition by colleges and universities that the school's graduates have completed a program of acceptable quality for college matriculation.

Although the evaluation procedure is not intended to force schools to conform to some preconceived notion of a good school, schools feel pressure to meet the standards of the association and try to implement the recommendations of the visiting committee. The committee report, reflecting an application of standards, identifies both strengths and deficiencies of the school. A committee's recommendations for remedying deficiencies can be used advantageously by a school in securing community support, especially for an increase in school taxes or a bond referendum.

Local Influences on the Curriculum

A traditional view has it that the control of education should be local. An assumption underlying local control is that the community under-

---

* These agencies are the New England Association (6 states), the Middle States Association (5 states and the District of Columbia), Southern Association (11 states), North Central Association (19 states), Northwest Association (8 states), Western Association (California).

stands the needs of its youth and, therefore, is in the best position to make appropriate educational decisions. While "lip service" is given to local control, many of the forces that are discussed in this chapter have eroded the influence that communities may exert over the educational program. Nevertheless, those closest to the scene are in an advantageous position to influence the specific character of curriculum either indirectly through the school board or directly through the school faculty.

Organized groups, as compared to individual patrons, have a greater potential for influencing the curriculum. Such groups as the Parent-Teacher Association, the Daughters of the American Revolution, the John Birch Society, the Chamber of Commerce, and the League of Women Voters, as well as local band parents clubs, athletic boosters clubs, and historical societies, are examples of organizations that may have curriculum interests. Few groups take a wholistic view of the school and tend to exert pressure in a single area, for example, instruction, facilities, finances, or student services. School officials, who have a responsibility to maintain a wholistic view of education, must work with these groups to preserve the integrity of the program.

Sometimes organizations get "out of hand." In one community the band boosters were able to finance appearances of the band at several prestigious, out-of-state events. Although warned that the school would lose its accreditation, the boosters persisted and the band participated in these events. The school was placed on probation by its accrediting association.

The existence of meritorious programs, especially ones that result in public displays or appearances, appeals to the community's desire for excellence in its school. Championships, outstanding dramatic or musical presentations, and academic awards build community support for the school. While community support for education is crucial, it is also necessary to maintain a perspective on individual activities and the nature of their contribution to the school program and the goals the program is designed to achieve.

Some groups are organized to redress what they perceive as injustices in the schools. Pressure exerted by black parents and students forced many schools to add courses in Afro-American studies to the curriculum. Bicultural education has become more evident in the schools as a result of pressure by Latino and Chicano groups. Parents from lower-income families who believe that their children are being forced into vocational education tracks have organized to demand more equitable treatment for their children.

Pressure groups may utilize existing agencies, for example, NAACP, ACLU, and community action groups, to represent them. Some groups raise funds in order to hire an attorney to present their case to the school board and sometimes to the court. Petitions from organized groups carry more weight in the political system than requests from individuals. Interest groups that represent the business sector of the community will invariably have their opinions on school matters carefully considered. Businessmen provide opportunities for on-the-job training in distributive education, secretarial positions, apprenticeships, and so forth, all of which are important components of school vocational programs. Business also provides jobs for high school graduates. Businessmen are successful and powerful men in any community. They are active in many civic groups; they influence community opinion, are frequently members of school boards and pay a large portion of the taxes that support the schools.

We stated earlier that the control over schools by local educational officials has eroded. This situation is not altogether undesirable. Although proximity may give local leaders a better grasp of the educational situation, it may also hinder objectivity and contribute to the maintenance of parochialism. Although local communities are not completely free to decide who can teach and what will be taught, they can exercise considerable control in these matters. Some observers contend that it is this sort of control that enables communities to deny their children the education necessary for the real world. They can protect them from "noxious" topics like sex, evolution, and the United Nations.

National Commissions and Reports

Much of the impetus for modification in the public school curriculum has been generated by reports of commissions studying particular dimensions of public education in the United States. In Chapter 1, where a historical perspective was drawn, we noted some important earlier reports on education. Several major reports have been made in the years since World War II.

The Conant Report. In the mid-1950s, James B. Conant, a former president of Harvard University and U.S. High Commissioner in Germany, was commissioned by the Carnegie Corporation to examine high schools in the United States and to make recommendations for their improvement. As a result of his study, which included visits to a number of secondary schools in the United States, a report entitled *The American High School Today* was published.[3] The report was received enthusiastically by educators throughout the nation who studied their schools to determine how they fared with respect to the 21 recommendations in the Conant Report.

The report defined the *comprehensive* high school as "a high school whose programs correspond to the educational needs of all the youth of the community."[4] A comprehensive high school should have three primary objectives: (1) to provide a general education for all the future citizens, (2) to provide good elective programs for those who wish to use their acquired skills immediately upon graduation, (3) to provide satisfactory programs to those whose vocations depend on subsequent education in a college or university.[5]

Many of the recommendations in the report,—for example, emphasis on the education of the academically talented, the individualization of programs, ability grouping, and special help for slow readers—had been practiced in some schools for years. However, the Conant report gave impetus and legitimacy to many of these developing practices.

Clearly this report was, for educators, one of the most exciting to appear in the early postwar period. It dealt with both academic offerings and organizational concepts in the public high school. It had the stamp of authority and authenticity of both the Carnegie Corporation and an important American educator. While there is no way of measuring the impact of the report, it was used in many high schools as a yardstick for program evaluation and improvement.

The most critical reaction to the report came from educators who supported educational programs organized around the needs and interests of learners. The Conant report seemed to them to reinforce the dominance of the academic disciplines in education.

The Educational Policies Commission (EPC). Over the years various national educational committees have produced influential statements on public education. *The Cardinal Principles of American Education*[6] in 1918 and *The Purposes of Education in American Democracy*[7] in 1938, discussed in Chapter 1, are significant examples. A more recent statement by the Educational Policies Commission of the N.E.A. in 1961, *The Central Purpose of American Education*,[8] served to legitimize American education's post *sputnik* hysteria aimed at matching Russia's space technology. A burst of interest in science followed. The 1961 statement of the EPC and the Conant report are consistent in that they stress the development of the child's education from an academic or intellectual perspective. The EPC report states that the central purpose of American education is the development of the student's rational powers.

The Trump Report. In 1956 the National Association of Secondary School Principals established a commission to explore ways of improving education during a period of acute teacher shortage. Financed by the Fund for the Advancement of Education and the Ford Foundation, the commission studied a number of innovative approaches to education in junior and senior high schools. A report entitled *Guide to Better Schools: Focus on Change* was published in 1961.[9]

The report stressed the development of more economical ways of utilizing financial and human resources. It emphasized several new organizational concepts: team teaching, flexible grouping of students, large groups, small groups, and individual study. Innovations suggested in the Trump Report are evident in some form in many secondary schools today. The Trump Report presented a challenge to school administrators and teachers to reexamine the traditional instructional organization of the school as a first step in curriculum modification.

The Coleman Report. In the early 1960s the society became painfully aware of the many inequalities that existed within it. With regard to education there were tremendous differences in the resources that various states and communities could devote to the education of youth. In 1964 the United States Commissioner of Education undertook an extensive survey to determine the extent of inequality of educational opportunity nationwide. The study was designed to yield data on racial and ethnic segregation, inequality in the school resources among racial and ethnic groups, achievement test performance of pupils of different backgrounds, and the relationship between school and student characteristics and student achievement. Data were gathered from 3,100 schools. In 1966 an extensive report entitled *Equality of Educational Opportunity* was published.[10]

It was not the intent of the Coleman Report to prescribe ways to eliminate inequality in education. The report was concerned with collecting data regarding the nature and extent of inequality. Nevertheless, a number of generalizations or implications were drawn from the data. The following generalizations from the report appeared to generate the most discussion and concern:

1. There was little relationship found between per pupil expenditures, books in the library, quality of facilities, curriculum measures, and achievement if the social background and attitudes of the individual students and their schoolmates are held constant.[11]
2. The effect of a student's peers on his achievement level seems to be more important than any other school influence.[12]
3. There is a small positive effect of school integration on the reading and mathematics achievement of Negro pupils after differences in the socioeconomic background of students are accounted for.[13]

Today, a decade after the Coleman Report, the lack of success in equalizing educational opportunity has made it evident that balancing student population in terms of color or/and socioeconomic status is an extremely complex and difficult task. Although many communities are busing students to achieve racial balance in schools, the logistics of such arrangements are costly in both dollars and human emotions. Even as the schools struggle to achieve racial balance, the usefulness of this solution is being questioned.[14] As recently as the fall of 1975, antibusing factions were demonstrating in near riot conditions in Louisville, Kentucky, and Boston, Massachusetts, where court-ordered busing plans were being implemented in order to racially balance the schools.

Summary

Many groups and agencies representing various interests attempt to pull the curriculum in one direction or another. There are supervisory and support agencies that condone and condemn, assist and obstruct. There are accrediting associations, publishers, legislatures, and textbook committees that perform in periods of crisis, periods of plenty, and periods of scarcity. Educators attempt to plan educational programs that respond to the needs of the individual and to the needs of society amidst technological and scientific changes, and changes in what man knows, what he believes, and what he feels. Somehow the school and its teachers must put it all together in a meaningful pattern.

QUESTIONS AND ACTIVITIES

1. In discussing and developing various curriculum programs most people have at least a general notion of a model or gestalt for the curriculum building process. Diagram or rough out, as well as you can, your current view of the process of curriculum building.
2. Brainstorm ways and means for influencing fellow professionals to decrease their reliance on the lecture, recitation, and examinations as the primary teaching/learning strategies.
3. Are there strategies/approaches which high school students and/or college/university students can use in influencing their teachers away from such heavy reliance on the more traditional teaching/learning approaches? How would you react if one of your students suggested that you consider an alternative teaching style?
4. Briefly survey dictionaries and other references on the meanings of *effective* and *efficient*. How might you use these two concepts in discussing the ways in which one might resolve educational problems?
5. Research the meaning of "the hidden curriculum." Then identify the various elements of the hidden curriculum in both the high school and college settings.
6. The teaching/learning process has been categorized into three major areas: *didactics* (content specific learning), *heuristics* (discovery, inquiry, or problem solving learning), and *philetics* (human relations or affective learning). Using these categories as analytical focal points, how do you view the relative importance of each in the *contemporary* school setting (the *what is*)? Next speculate as to their relative importance to education

in the *future* (the *what should be*). Finally, make some estimates as to the magnitude of the discrepancy between the *what is* and the *what ought to be*. How do you account for this discrepancy?

7. Among the many forces which may influence the school curriculum which do you see as most helpful, most deserving of professional attention? Which do you view as most threatening or potentially dangerous to the development of a desirable school curriculum? What is the rationale upon which you have made this judgment?

NOTES

[1] North Central Association of Colleges and Secondary Schools, *Policies and Standards for the Approval of Secondary Schools, 1972–73*, Commission on Secondary Schools, 5454 South Shore Drive, Chicago, Illinois, p. 54.

[2] National Study of Secondary-School Evaluation, *Evaluative Criteria*, (Washington, D.C.: National Study of Secondary-School Evaluation, 1969).

[3] James B. Conant, *The American High School Today* (New York: McGraw-Hill, 1959).

[4] Ibid., p. 12.

[5] Ibid., p. 17.

[6] Commission on the Reorganization of Secondary Education, *Cardinal Principles of Secondary Education* (Washington, D.C.: United States Office of Education), No. 35, 1918.

[7] Educational Policies Commission, *The Purposes of Education in American Democracy* (Washington, D.C.: National Education Association, 1938).

[8] Educational Policies Commission, *The Central Purpose of American Education* (Washington, D.C.: National Education Association, 1961).

[9] J. Lloyd Trump and Baynham Dorsey, *Guide to Better Schools: Focus on Change* (Skokie, Ill.: Rand McNally, 1961).

[10] James S. Coleman, et al, *Equality of Educational Opportunity*, (Washington, D.C.: Office of Education, 1966).

[11] Ibid., p. 325.

[12] Ibid.

[13] Ibid., pp. 29–30.

[14] Christopher Jencks, et al., *Inequality: A Reassessment of the Effect of Family and Schooling in America* (New York: Basic Books, 1972).

CHAPTER 10

Innovative Organizational Patterns

In this chapter we shall consider proposals and procedures for organizing the school for more effective instruction under two general topics: (1) establishment of criteria for judging proposed organizational models; (2) description of the general aspects of a number of organizational patterns, with emphases on the major innovative approaches.

Stress on Change and Innovation

We live in a highly complex, rapidly developing technological world. Even individuals of minimum voting age have lived through an era of change. Improved methods of communication enable us to watch "live" the signing of an agreement 10,000 miles away via satellite-relayed television. Men have gone to the moon and returned; they have even lived in space capsules for months. Development of wonder drugs continues; living tissues and organs are successfully transplanted from one person to another. The list of scientific and technological achievements is long. Society likewise has experienced many changes—some simple, some complex, many accompanied by violent conflict. In this book we have considered several situations in which the school has had to adapt to changes. Once again the educational bureaucracy has to demonstrate that it has the flexibility to adjust quickly and efficiently because educators throughout the country are forced into a preoccupation with change and innovation.

The pressure on the schools to present the image of a relevant, viable, alert, modern educational institution has forced the profession to abandon its traditional preference for evolutionary change in favor of rapid solutions to problems. Desire for innovation has become a major driving force.

Designs for innovative buildings, new organizational formats, and up-to-date instructional approaches are commonplace in the literature. Certain school systems, schools, and even departments within schools, which have acquired reputations as being innovative, are the subject of much discussion, envy, and emulation. This "bandwagon" effect often means that new designs are adopted by large numbers of schools that have varying degrees of readiness. Generalizing about the problems of premature adoption of innovations, one observer has written:

> Scratch the surface of what a high school principal tells you is an innovation and you are likely to find a hard core of conventional practices. I can report to you that there is a lot of superficial, off-the-top-of-the-head, half-baked, under-planned, under-organized, under-financed and under-staffed innovation going on.[1]

Similarly another critic cautions against underestimating the schools' ability "to make a new map fit old territory." He explains:

> This is most commonly done by calling an existing practice by a new or faddish name. Lately, I have seen the most Buchenwaldish elementary schools called "open" because it is the vogue term and the public blindly accepts the word of school officials who contend that they are up to date.[2]

A third condemns the impatient, often naive innovators who hit and run, who jump from place to place, who create more problems than they solve. His language is vivid: "Their ambition to get ahead and make headlines tends to put them in the class of educational rapists who leave behind them a trail of prostrated communities subdued for personal gain."[3]

We do not propose to slip into the easy role of hostile critic, to view all innovations as "snake oil" and those who propose them as educational hucksters. The point is that in the haste to identify and implement new approaches to organizing a school for improved education, educators often yield to the strong temptation to bypass time-consuming but nevertheless essential steps in studying, evaluating, and preparing for the planned change. Success under such circumstances must be chalked up to chance.

Criteria for the Evaluation of Innovative Organizational Patterns

We believe that essential steps in designing, adopting, and implementing new organizational approaches in today's schools are the identification and application of basic criteria for assessing the innovative approach. We suggest the following primary and secondary criteria.

PRIMARY CRITERIA

To what extent does the innovation

1. Increase the opportunity for the student to develop appropriate intellectual skills, habits, knowledge, and processes?
2. Increase the opportunity for the student to develop evaluative skills and knowledge?
3. Increase the opportunity for growth through human interaction with fellow students and with teachers?
4. Increase the opportunity for developing each student's personal educational goals by providing ways and means for identification and fulfillment of such goals?
5. Increase student access to and encourage his use of resources essential to the achievement of criteria 1 through 4?
6. Provide for the maintenance of an appropriate balance among the total of educational goals of the school?

SECONDARY CRITERIA

To what extent is the innovative design appropriate in terms of

1. Intellectual and personal characteristics of the faculty?
2. Faculty preparation for and attitude toward the plan and their participation in both its adoption and implementation?
3. Community preparation for and attitude toward the plan and their participation in both its adoption and implementation?
4. Learning resources available?
5. Necessary physical facilities including buildings, grounds, flexible space, etc.
6. Available fiscal resources?

The six primary and six secondary criteria are, in our judgment, central in the assessment of any organizational modification. This is not to deny the existence of other criteria, nor does this list imply a fixed hierarchy within the primary or secondary criteria groups. Although the primary criteria are most important in our view, it is entirely realistic to assume that an innovation need not satisfy all our even most of the primary criteria. Nevertheless, it would be difficult to justify an organizational modification that did not satisfy at least one of the primary criteria or that unreasonably *inhibited* acceptable goals that were already being accomplished by the old program.

On the other hand, an innovation meeting the test of primary criteria may not be realistic in terms of secondary criteria. The secondary list is important only in advancing or inhibiting the goals in the primary list. Adoption of organizational arrangements only to satisfy some of the secondary criteria might lead to greater efficiency but not to significant or substantive educational innovation.

Both the primary and secondary criteria are most useful when applied to an innovative plan that is in operation; but they can also be useful in designing an innovative plan for a specific school setting. In this case the primary criteria would have greater use in designing the plan itself, whereas the secondary criteria would be most useful in preparing for the implementation of the plan. In examining general concepts of innovative approaches, such as those presented in this chapter, the primary criteria may have some utility, but their value really depends on the amount of descriptive detail in the concept. The secondary criteria would have no value in the examination of these general concepts because we make no reference to situational data that would make these criteria pertinent.

Organizational Patterns

Aside from curriculum content changes, most current proposals for modifying the organizational structure of the school focus on increased efficiency in meeting traditional educational goals rather than on the development of new goals. This is not surprising in view of the many pressures tending to reinforce a conservative role for public education in our society discussed in earlier chapters.

Much literature deals with new ways of organizing for more effective instruction. In this volume we can only select from the long list of proposed innovations, identifying organizational designs that seem most *comprehensive* in terms of potential for reaching large numbers of students in many schools. A second principle of selection is *longevity*. An innovation has longevity if it is standard practice in a number of schools but has yet to be tried by most schools. A third principle of selection is *currency*. An innovation has currency if it has not been tried in most schools but is an active candidate for future implementation.

In presenting brief descriptions of several formats for improved school organization and practice, we shall attempt to minimize judgmental statements. We believe that any organizational scheme must be evaluated in terms of criteria. Two sets of criteria—primary and secondary—were offered earlier in this chapter. However, the reader should recognize that our vignette descriptions may be so general in many cases that the required details of characteristics to which the criteria may be applied are lacking. Also most of the alternative concepts themselves contain so many options that the specification of characteristics is all but impossible. A person may ask, however, "Under what circumstances would this innovation provide a criterial advantage?"

Flexible Scheduling

FLEXIBILITY OF TIME PERIODS

Flexible scheduling is an attempt to break away from the standard five, six, or seven periods of 70, 50, or 40 minutes each by substituting a greater number of smaller time units, say, 15 or 20 minutes, that can be variously combined for different purposes.

Flexible scheduling is designed to provide maximum opportunity for teacher and student to make decisions about how they will use their own time. The smaller blocks of time than in the traditional school setting or modules allow teachers to arrange shorter or, in multiples, longer periods for instruction, depending upon the activities. Arrangements vary from school to school. One school's day might have 20 modules of 20 minutes each; another, 15 modules of 30 minutes. Thus, for instance, a language arts teacher may take pupils to a museum, having arranged to use all the modules for a full day of English on Monday, with a short one-module follow-up session on Tuesday, and not meeting again until Thursday or Friday. A social studies teacher may use 80 minutes, for example, four 20-minute modules back to back, early in the week to introduce a new subject or to teach the students how to use the library. During the remainder of the week, the social studies class may take only one or two modules a day. Classes may be unscheduled in order to allow students free time to practice their new skills in doing reference work in the library.

Obviously the mere use of a smaller time unit will accomplish little if teachers are unwilling or unable to plan for and teach with flexibility. Administration for effective use of a modular schedule is complex; schools frequently use computers in programming. Furthermore, the system calls for considerable responsibility from both teachers and students. In addition to flexibility of time periods, there are generally four grouping options available to teachers and students in a flexible scheduling program: large-group instructional activities; small-group instructional activities; laboratory work; and individual or independent study.[4] Schools have various procedures for selecting among the four options. In some schools this means planning a fairly set schedule featuring varying period lengths in advance of the semester. Other schools have procedures that enable faculty to plan by the week or modify schedules on very short notice.

TEAM TEACHING, LARGE AND SMALL GROUPS, AND DIFFERENTIAL STAFFING

One cannot discuss flexibility in schools without considering team teaching and its primary management feature, the use of different sized groups for different learning activities. Just as there are differences among children, teachers possess different talents, interests, and personality characteristics. Some have specialized knowledge within their disciplines. Of five or six English teachers, one may be strong in English literature, another in early American literature, a third in contemporary literature, a fourth in linguistics, a fifth in grammar, while yet another is a creative writing buff. Some teachers are superb with large groups, others may have a particular skill or interest in the use of instructional media, and still others may have their finest hours when working with smaller groups of 12 or 15 students or even with single students.

One way of capitalizing on the various talents of faculty is to develop teams or informal groups who cooperatively plan and teach. There are unlimited possibilities. At its simplest, two teachers in the same subject cooperatively teach their two classes that meet at the same hour. At the other extreme a very complex arrangement of six or eight teachers representing several subject areas might cooperatively plan for and instruct 150 students in an interdisciplinary course involving language arts, social studies, art, and music.

Closely related to team teaching is the concept of *differentiated staffing*. We cannot explore the considerable literature available on the topic here. Briefly, differentiation involves recognition of differences in skill, knowledge, and experience among teachers and the commensurate allocation of responsibilities and rewards. Differentiated staffing, when combined with the teaming concept, permits the use of paraprofessional teaching assistants or aides, clerical help, and preservice teacher trainees. These team members can assist the teachers in tasks that do not require fully professional expertise.

The Trump Report (Chapter 9) made one of the earliest moves to question the almost exclusive use in the schools of the standard classroom of 25–35 students.[5] The report emphasizes the relationship between educational purposes and instructional arrangements: the size of the group, the physical facilities, and the time allocated to the activity must be consistent with the purpose. For some purposes it is appropriate to make a presentation to a large group of 150 or more students; and the appropriate setting for this presentation may be a large lecture hall, a gymnasium, or a theater. For other goals it may be more appropriate to have small discussion or laboratory groups of ten or so students. For study or research purposes it may be most appropriate for a student to operate independently at his own rate of progress. Such instruction may call for separate learning carrels, learning resource centers, laboratory facilities, or in some cases mere freedom.

INDEPENDENT STUDY AND INDIVIDUALIZED INSTRUCTION

Although educational literature has for many years stressed the necessity of identifying and adapting to individual differences of learners, the emphasis on individualized instructon in schools is rather recent. It has become increasingly clear over the years that the traditional classroom setting inhibits teachers' freedom to work individually with students. Providing for individual differences in learners was a theoretical goal that was difficult to fulfill in the real world of the public school classroom.

Renewed efforts to provide more appropriate instruction for the individual student occurred in a social milieu that was more sensitive to the individual. The increased emphasis on the rights and freedoms of individuals was translated in schools as an awareness that the traditional classes tend to view children not primarily as individuals but as members of groups. The Trump plan has stressed individualized instruction as a major dimension of the changes that must take place in public schools of the future.[6] Technological advances in teaching, particularly the development of programmed instruction machinery, provided tools for initiating individualized study programs. Individuals who advocated programmed learning called attention to the new capability for assisting the student to progress at his own rate. Proposals for and reports of individualized instruction and independent study programs became commonplace in discussion of educational innovations. In fact, individualization has become a focal point of many innovative programs.

Actually, "individualized instruction" loosely describes a continuum of patterns from teacher-directed study to independent student inquiry with virtually no teacher direction. Alexander, Hines, and Associates clearly differentiate between independent study and individualized instruction. *Individualized instruction* may be a highly directed tutorial that may not increase the learners' ability to function independently at all. In *independent study* the student directs his own learning, referring to a teacher, peers, or other appropriate persons when he needs help. It would appear that the latter is more apt to result in a self-directed or independent learner.[7]

SELF-INSTRUCTIONAL PACKAGES

The move toward individualized instruction has recently spawned the learning package. A learning package contains a combination of readings, pictures, slides, films, recordings, exercises, questions to be answered, experiments to be performed, and so forth. The package is carefully designed to teach specific skills, concepts, or habits. The applications for learning packets are almost limitless. A series of packets may constitute an entire course, a mini-course, a unit, an enrichment activity, or a remedial exercise. Generally the package is for an individual student who follows its study guide and completes assigned activities at his own rate. Learning packages further individualize instruction by utilizing materials specially designed for learners with certain characteristics.

Additional advantages claimed for learning packages are summarized in the following statements:

They provide for continual progress, whatever the learning rate of students.
Students missing school can easily resume study where they left off.
Central themes or concepts can be carefully sequenced from simple to complex.
Students using successive packages can build upon and utilize knowledge which has been gained in earlier packages.[8]

Limited only by the creativity of the developer, learning packages have considerable potential for making learning more interesting for the student. Wisely inserted into standard courses they can enable the teacher to "program" activities with common objectives for the class and remain free to provide individual assistance to students needing special instruction. Poorly designed or unimaginative packages, however, can have an adverse effect, and overuse of the technique may bore students. Furthermore, unwise use of such packages could inhibit the development of social skills and attitudes which can be fostered only by human interaction between teacher and learner and between learner and fellow learner.

Alternative Schools

Since 1960 many schools have been created in response to special needs or concerns of local groups. Called *storefront, new, free,* or whatever, they sprang from the notion that a legitimate educational purpose is not being met by existing schools.[9] "Their founders ranged across a wide spectrum in terms of political beliefs and educational philosophy, just as their location ranged from rural commune to ghetto-storefront."[10]

The schools exist for their own purposes and view themselves as accountable to the particular populations they serve. Most of the early alternative schools were outside the public school system, funded by clients, special interests, or foundations. Frequently theirs was a short and spectacular life. Their leaders saw themselves as reformers in educational goals, structure, and curriculum—but they were not all of the same philosophy. Depending on the school's purpose, the pupils might study anything from weaving and carpentry to rigorous academic subjects.

Concerned people are developing alternative schools parallel to, or increasingly, as part of the local public school system. Their concern may be for more emphasis on intellectual development, creative development, improved teaching methods, pupil self-knowledge, or any number of purposes which they feel conventional schools inadequately fulfill. Gradually alternative schools have been taken over or established by local school boards and financed with public funds. They provide options beyond the standard program of the public school system without infringing on the rights of the mass of clients who are satisfied with the regular program. Several alternative schools (Philadelphia's Parkway School, Chicago's Metro School, and the Brown School in Louisville, Kentucky) have achieved wide acclaim. Some communities have become closely identified with the Alternative School Movement. For instance, the Berkeley (California) Unified School District has developed 25 options in four program categories: multiculture schools, community schools, structured skills-training schools, and schools-without-walls. In the Alum Rock School District in San Jose, California, parents may use vouchers in selecting from among six schools offering at least two alternative programs each. Grand Rapids, Seattle, St. Paul, Minneapolis, New Orleans, Dallas, Denver, and many other cities have alternative schools.[11]

The term *alternatives* embraces a wide variety of educational options. Vernon Smith, one of the founders of the National Consortium on Options in Public Education, located at Indiana University, identifies several types of alternative public schools:

> *Open Schools*—with learning activities individualized around interest centers within the classroom and building.
>
> *Schools without Walls*—with learning activities throughout the community and with much interaction between school and community.
>
> *Magnet schools, Learning Centers, Educational Parks*—with a concentration of learning resources in one center available to all of the students in the community.
>
> *Multicultural Schools, Bilingual Schools, Ethnic Schools*—with emphasis on cultural pluralism and ethnic and racial awareness.

Street Academies, Dropout Centers, Pregnancy-Maternity Centers—with
emphasis on learning programs for students in targeted populations.
Schools-within-a-School—could be any of the above organized as a unit
within a conventional school.
Integration Models—could be any of the above, with a voluntary population that is representative in racial, ethnic, and socioeconomic class
makeup of the total population of the community.
Free Schools—with emphasis on greater freedom for students and teachers.
This term is usually applied to non-public alternatives, but a very few
are operating within public school systems today.[12]

Although there are clearinghouses for the collection and dissemination
of data on the nature and number of alternative schools across the nation,
their unique local characteristics make systematic assembly of data
difficult. Nevertheless, allowing for exceptions, it is possible to describe
some of their common characteristics.

1. They offer options to public education, open to all on a voluntary basis.
2. More than conventional schools, they are committed to some specific local
   need or interest.
3. Their high priority goals tend to be more comprehensive than those of the
   public schools. In addition to basic skills, they also emphasize development
   of individual talents and preparation for various roles in the society.
4. They are flexible and responsive to change.
5. They attempt to eliminate traditional school characteristics which are most
   oppressive to students and teachers, to be less bureaucratic and more humane than traditional schools.[13]

There have always been some alternatives to public education—for
example, private schools, multicultural and ethnic schools, parochial
schools, and so forth—but they have been available to only about 15
percent of American families. Alternatives traditionally offered within
public education—for example, vocational education, special education,
dropout prevention programs, programs for unwed mothers and the like
—usually classified, even stigmatized, their pupils as unfit for normal
education.[14]

Many people who were dissatisfied with the schools saw these traditional alternatives as inadequate and supported new options in public
education. The movement has met with considerable resistance. Educators and those patrons satisfied with the traditional system have tended
to suspect alternative schools, many of which grew out of problems of
urban areas, racial strife, a general dissatisfaction with the condition of
society, and criticism of the programs of the educational establishment.
Thus alternative schools were viewed as radical and revolutionary; in
general, they generated the same type of reactions as did other, more
violent, aspects of the unrest of the 1960s.

As educators began to perceive the nature and possibilities of alternative schools, more prestigious school systems like Newton (Massachusetts), Scarsdale (New York), Great Neck (New York), and Webster Groves (Missouri) developed similar options within their systems. The mainstream then began to see legitimacy in the movement,[15] resulting in the significant growth of alternative schools as components of school systems. Still no one really knows how many alternative schools there are. One source estimated that there are 60 school districts with 15,000 students and 3,000 staff members involved.[16] The National Consortium for Alternatives in Public Education, a voluntary organization, claims 200 members representing over 100 individual public schools and other interested agencies, individuals, or groups.[17] The Directory of Alternative Public Schools lists over 400 schools in the United States, Canada, and several foreign countries.[18]

Although options in public education are clearly increasing and the alternative school today represents a genuine movement in which change is more evolutionary than revolutionary, it is not immune to questions and criticism. One articulate critic is Mortimer Smith, Executive Secretary for the Council for Basic Education, a conservative organization viewing schools existing in society to provide "the essential skills of language, numbers, and orderly thought, and to transmit in a reasoned pattern the intellectual, moral, and aesthetic heritage of civilized man." Smith doubts the validity of the schools. He questions the soundness of the leaders of the movement, some of whom he calls "cultists rather than serious reformers." He views the movement as opposed to book learning and indifferent to basic skills and structure. He further says the alternatives movement falls far short of the realistic reforms that many laymen and educators have been demanding.[19] Evaluation of the Alternative Schools Movement will be extremely difficult. Although the movement is alleged to have some common characteristics—for example, voluntary attendance, commitment to specific needs, responsiveness to change, humaneness, and so forth—the alternative concept has no clear parameters. Even if the concepts, parameters, and characteristics were more clearly defined, data about alternative schools are not generally available. It appears that any application of criteria for assessing alternative schools must focus on particular schools that can be viewed in their functional setting.

Summary

In this chapter we have presented primary and secondary criteria for assessing innovative organizational patterns. The criteria are most useful when applied to functioning innovations or when employed to develop plans for the design and implementation of innovative programs. Flexible scheduling, differentiated staffing, individualized instruction, team teaching, and learning packages were among the innovative approaches described. Alternative schools are emerging as options in many public school systems. While there are no accurate data on the number or forms of these schools, it is apparent that they are increasing in popularity. Innovative organizational patterns appear to share some assumptions about students, teachers, time, and facilities. We add them here as a general set of statements that tend to characterize many of the innovations we have reviewed.

1. The size of a group should be appropriate to its purpose.
2. The composition of a group should be appropriate to its purpose.
3. The time allotments assigned to any group should be appropriate to its purpose.
4. The physical and psychological environment must be appropriate to the activities of the group.
5. The nature of a task assigned to a staff member must be appropriate to his talents and interests.
6. It is possible for students to learn in places other than classrooms in groups which are not classes and with people who are not teachers.[20]

QUESTIONS AND ACTIVITIES

1. Identify one innovation about which you have some knowledge. To what extent does it appear to meet the six major criteria outlined by the authors?
2. To what extent were the criteria beneficial in looking more critically at the innovation? Are there other criteria which you think should be included? What are they? Which, if any, of the authors' criteria would you not use again?
3. Which innovations in the schools do you view as being substantial and significant departures from traditional school practices? Which do you classify as being of little significance, merely "fads"? What criteria did you use in making these judgments?
4. Identify some of the topics or problems in your own subject area which are adaptable to team teaching. Develop a general model of a team approach to one of these topics.
5. Do you see yourself functioning as a member of a teaching team? Explain.
6. Do you feel that you could function effectively as a teacher in a school with a flexible schedule? Explain your answer.
7. Assume that you have been asked to address the PTA on the topic: "Independent Study and Individualized Instruction; There Is a Difference." Give a brief outline of your presentation and the major points that you will stress.
8. Do you believe that the Alternative School Movement will have a lasting impact on the educational system of our nation? Will the system be improved as a result of the movement?

9. If you had the authority to change an entire school or even a specific department within a school, what changes would you seek to implement? Why?
10. At this point do you view yourself as a *traditionalist* or as an *innovator*? How have you arrived at this conclusion?

NOTES

[1] Eugene Howard, "Organizing the High School for Change," *The North Central Association Quarterly*, Spring 1967, p. 293.

[2] Letter from Gerald Unks to Roger L. Williams, Chapel Hill, North Carolina, June 24, 1973, p. 9.

[3] Norman E. Hearn, "The When, Where, and How of Trying Innovations," *Phi Delta Kappan*, February 1972, p. 359.

[4] Eugene R. Howard, "Flexible Scheduling," *The North Central Association Quarterly*, Fall 1965, pp. 208–213. Glenys G. Unruh and William Alexander, *Innovations in Secondary Education* (New York: Holt, Rinehart and Winston, 1970), p. 119.

[5] J. Lloyd Trump and Dorsey Baynham, *Guide to Better Schools: Focus on Change* (Skokie, Ill.: Rand McNally, 1961).

[6] Ibid.

[7] William M. Alexander, Vynce A. Hines, and Associates, *Independent Study in Secondary Schools* (New York: Holt, Rinehart and Winston, 1967), pp. 9–10.

[8] Arthur B. Wolfe and James E. Smith, "Learning Activity Packages," in *The LAP at Nova*, Nova High School, Fort Lauderdale, Florida, Summer 1968. Mimeo, pp. 2–6.

[9] Vernon H. Smith, "Options in Public Education: The Quiet Revolution," *Phi Delta Kappan*, March 1973, p. 434.

[10] Robert C. Riordan, *Alternative Schools in Action*, Phi Delta Kappa Educational Foundation, Bloomington, Indiana, 1972, p. 7.

[11] Mario D. Fantini, "Alternatives Within Public Schools," *Phi Delta Kappan*, March 1973, p. 446.

[12] Vernon H. Smith, pp. 434–435.

[13] Vernon H. Smith, p. 435.

[14] Fantini, "Alternatives Within Public Schools," p. 444.

[15] Fantini, "Alternatives Within Public Schools," pp. 444–445.

[16] Fantini, "Alternative Schools: Do They Promise System Reform," Editorial, *Phi Delta Kappan*, March 19, 1973, p. 433.

[17] Vernon H. Smith, p. 435.

[18] "Directory of Alternative Public Schools," *Changing Schools*, No. 008, 1974, School of Education, Indiana University, Bloomington, Indiana. Lists schools by state and city. Provides addresses.

[19] Mortimer Smith, "CBE Views the Alternatives," *Phi Delta Kappan*, March 1973, pp. 441–442.

[20] Howard, "Flexible Scheduling," p. 209.

CHAPTER 11

Implementing Change

A recurring theme in previous chapters has been the implicit or explicit emphasis on change. Changes proposed or implied include school organization and curriculum and the manner in which professional teachers work with their students. Changse also extend into the realm of finances, governance, and professional associations. It has been emphasized that if the school is to be a relevant, viable institution, it must be capable of adjusting quickly and efficiently to the educational demands of the society by utilizing new technology, new organizational patterns, and by designing curricula that are consistent with the general and specialized educational needs of student clients. In this chapter we propose to deal with the topic of change in education by examining the process from the perspectives of the teacher and of the supervisory and administrative staffs.

Dimensions of Change

Change is making "the form, nature, or content, etc., of something different from what it is or from what it would be if left alone."[1] Things can be substituted for, removed, replaced, altered, or modified. One way of grouping changes in education is by their direct or indirect influence on what and how children are taught. Changes in curriculum, instructional organization, and in-service teacher education programs are direct influences. Changes in the instructional support system such as a new administrative structure for a school system or changes in the budgeting procedures are indirect influences.[2] Because teachers are most involved in, concerned with, and affected by direct changes, this will be the focus of our discussion.

For many years it was assumed that teachers assisted by supervisors and administrators could manage and develop instruction and curriculum. This view held that as changes in standard procedures in teaching and curriculum were necessary, teachers, departments, or perhaps whole faculties could make appropriate alterations utilizing resources that were available to the school system. This concept of evolutionary, "do it yourself," change was challenged in the 1950s and 1960s when funds were allocated by federal agencies and private foundations to groups that proposed to revolutionize curriculum and instruction through organized development efforts. Development groups or teams composed of various combinations of scholars, teachers, and curriculum writers designed courses and units in specific curriculum areas. The courses and materials they produced became labeled as "new math," "new social studies," "new English," and so forth. Because the projects had funds in quantities not generally available to school districts, the materials produced by the projects were viewed by their creators and others interested in changing schools as more comprehensive and substantial than those produced by classroom teachers working by themselves in the limited times when they were not teaching their students. Project funds were utilized in securing full-time workers, and consultant expertise, and for the production of multimedia instructional materials that supplemented the usual written textual materials. Most of the early projects reflected the views of Jerome Bruner and others who proposed a school curriculum based on the inquiry method with content derived from the structure of the scholarly disciplines.

It was assumed by the developers that the new curriculum packages were a functioning machine which could be adopted by a school and inserted *in toto* into the curriculum. It became commonplace for project personnel to conduct workshops designed to train teachers in the use of the new "teacher proof" project materials. Although some schools have adopted and are using project materials today, the diffusion and dissemination of the projects are still a major concern to many educators who believe that the rate and extent of adoption are inadequate.

Roughly parallel to the growth of the curriculum project movement was the emphasis of other reformers who advocated the adoption of innovative organizational patterns for schools such as those described in Chapter 10, for example, team teaching, flexible scheduling, and individualized instruction. Thus there has been a two-pronged movement for change in the school: the curriculum projects which are directly concerned with the substance of curriculum and instruction, and the proposals for new patterns of instruction which deal with the structure of the instructional program.

Publicity on the two major thrusts of proposed educational innovations has increased many educators' sensitivity to the need for reexamining their schools. Nevertheless, strategies designed to increase the rate of the dissemination and diffusion of innovative ideas, materials, and organizational patterns have occupied the attention of impatient reform-oriented educators who perceive that the traditional lines of communication via professional journals and annual conventions were not sufficient to spread the word. Their efforts have contributed to increased efforts to inform educators about innovative alternatives and to assist them in the implementation of these alternatives. Special workshops on innovative approaches for teachers and administrators have been offered; professional associations have emphasized the new materials and approaches to organization at national and regional meetings; commercial houses have published the new materials; field agents in the model of the agricultural extension agent have conducted in-service education programs for teachers and administrators; and universities have offered instruction on the new programs. These several efforts notwithstanding the common belief is that the rate of adoption of new ideas by the schools is woefully slow. Surveys of school practices tend to support this conclusion.

Communication of new ideas is only part of the problem, however. Changing the established practices of individuals or institutions is a complex, difficult, and time-consuming process. Norman E. Hearn offers an interesting analogy.

> Changing people is not an academic exercise that can be accomplished by memoranda. It is a process that tampers with peoples' cherished value systems. As persons and as a group, innovators represent a real threat to the psychological, social, and economic 'health' of many individuals. Innovations are often perceived as foreign bodies in live organisms. Unless the organism is seriously ill, it will resist instinctively all foreign bodies. It will release 'enzymes' to destroy the innovation or to isolate it and eventually reject it from the body politic. In short, the innovation will be met with blind resistance by the system.[3]

Persons experienced in working with people recognize the aptness of Hearn's analogy. Maintenance of the status quo is the line of least resistance: "We have always done it this way" appears to be sufficient justification for some individuals for continuing in old patterns.

Insufficient time, funds, or evidence that the new way is better are also reasons frequently proffered by opponents of change. It is not unreasonable and quite natural to prefer time-tested patterns of behavior in performing professional activities as well as routine tasks. In addition, those who will be affected by the change may be uncertain about what new patterns of response will be expected of them, what knowledge will be required of them, and whether they can successfully meet the challenges of implementing the change.

The successful adoption of any major modification in education always depends on the extent to which those who must implement the new program understand it, accept it, and are willing to work to achieve it. Schools may call themselves "open," "free," or "nongraded"; they may call their programs "individualized," "flexible," or "packaged"; or they may claim to be teaching inquiry in the "new English" or "new math." But the simple adoption of the name of a project or organizational concept, no matter how sophisticated, popular, or educationally justifiable, is meaningless without accompanying changes in the flesh and blood of the educational organism.

The Process of Change

The scholarly study of change has made significant strides in recent years. Whereas early notions of change in the schools seemed to cluster around the teacher, recent literature focuses on systematic approaches to planned change which are initiated from a higher administrative or supervisory level. A number of excellent texts provide extensive theory, and describe organizational procedures for bringing about change in schools and other organizations.[4]

The Systems approach to change appears to represent a "top-down" perspective in which an administrator, supervisor, or change agent plans a strategy which should culminate in a change in the institution. We shall refer to some of this literature in our discussion. It is surprising, however, that the literature places little emphasis on the possibility that change may have its origins in the "grass roots" and develop in a "bottom-up" direction.

There are at least two plausible explanations for change strategies designed to manipulate teachers rather than to accord them a significant active role in planned change. Theorists may have concluded that change cannot be successful unless it has support from higher echelons in the bureaucracy; or it may be assumed that "bottom-up" change is insufficient in scope and frequency and therefore is unproductive as a general approach to change. Since we view the teacher as the central figure in the process of changing instruction and curriculum, our discussion will begin with a look at the innovative teacher drawing upon the literature of planned change as necessary.

A number of studies have described innovative teachers: they are younger than average; they have relatively high status in their group; they are cosmopolite and use impersonal and cosmopolite information sources; and they see themselves as innovators. Other characteristics frequently evidenced by innovative teachers include frequent attendance at professional meetings, extensive travel, high intellectual and verbal ability, individualism, creativity, and enthusiasm.[5] All descriptions are not positive, however; some studies characterize innovators as rebellious, alienated, excessively idealistic, emotionally unstable and prone to resentment.[6] The literature on innovative teachers does not develop a unique profile of innovativeness; moreover the relationship between teacher characteristics and innovative practices remains vague. It remains no more than conjecture that a tendency toward innovativeness and other professional habits are causally related. Does an individual innovate because he attends professional meetings or does he attend professional meetings because he is innovative? We have ample evidence that attendance at professional meetings is not a sufficient condition for innovativeness; we are uncertain whether it is a necessary one.

Research studies on change and systematic strategies for bringing about change stress the importance of appropriate organizational climate. A stable organization that is supportive of innovation and that provides security for the risk taker is very conducive to change. Considerable change may even occur in an organization that tolerates rather than encourages innovation; but little will happen in an environment of overt hostility toward new ideas and practices. Predictably, a teacher who may initiate change or who is at least receptive to change in a positive environment may exhibit quite different behavior in a situation that is not supportive of innovation. This may be especially true for teachers new to a school.

In a recent study of an innovative program in a school, Snavely characterized the school involved and, by implication, most schools as *mechanistic* organizations. Mechanistic organizations display a high degree of formal structure, specialization, and compartmentalization. He contrasts this type of system with *organic* organizations which have less formal structure and are dependent on members who understand the entire structure and are committed to its organizational goals. Organic structures, which tend to be very complex, are particularly conducive to innovative schemes because they emphasize adaptiveness. Mechanistic structures, on the other hand, which tend to be relatively simple and centralized (organizational flow charts are very popular), are less tolerant of innovations because of their inherent emphasis on production and efficiency. While each of these types of organization has its place in the scheme of things, the likelihood that most schools are more mechanistic than organic offers a plausible explanation of why innovations have hard births in the public schools.[7]

The novice teacher in a school may be influenced more by the norms of the institution than the experienced teacher, but both must be sensitive to the mode of behavior expected of them. As we have noted earlier, schools tend to be mechanistic and bureaucratic, with a division of labor, defined staff roles, and a hierarchy of offices; most routine operations have established procedures. Those in the best position to influence change will be supervisors, department chairpersons, or senior teachers. Frequently these people have long tenure in the system and have assimilated the norms of the system. Thus they tend to exhibit and expect others to exhibit behavior consistent with those norms. School systems are characteristically conservative toward change; but in some schools, or in even an entire school system, normative behavior may be oriented toward change and innovation. Whichever the case, the system's momentum is for the maintenance of its norms. In the socialization process the rewards (i.e., verbal reinforcement, acclaim, newspaper releases, improved teaching assignments, merit pay increments, and so on) encourage those who conform. Those who deviate, who do not perform as expected, are liable to withdrawal of rewards, disapproval of colleagues, and perhaps even overt hostility. A teacher who wants to remain in such a situation has relatively little incentive or opportunity for independence. He shapes up or ships out; he adopts the expected profile or leaves.

Factors Related to Change

Too often those advocating change in the schools underestimate the effects of the school's social climate on the teacher's behavior. It seems to be commonly assumed that potentially innovative teachers who are put through in-service or pre-service programs can function as innovators in almost any environment. But most research tends to confirm the systems approach hypothesis that the social climate *within the school* is of critical importance. To effect changes in school organization or curriculum, potentially innovative teachers absolutely must have colleagues who advocate, support, or at least tolerate innovation. Studies indicate that colleague expectations probably have more to do with both the maintenance and modification of an individual's values than any other single factor.[8] Under the right conditions a teacher may not only be innovative but he may also function as a change agent who encourages innovative behavior in others. Hearn[9] suggests that a teacher may increase his opportunities to be innovative by being employed in a school that

Has cosmopolitan staff members. Such a staff has traveled widely, attends many professional meetings outside the state, has had experience in other school districts, and is presumably more amenable to new ideas.

Has a youthful administrative staff. Research indicates that youthful adminis-trators though sometimes impatient and naive, have energy and enthusiasm. Fewer older administrators are "risk takers," but those who are have the experience and maturity to innovate successfully.

It is also important to consider the circumstances in which an inno-vator or change agent best functions. Assuming that one can select his locale, Hearn suggests that the potential innovator should seek a com-munity that

Is "liberal." Such a community often has a politico-social perspective favorable to governmental intervention for social progress and may be more tolerant and supportive of change and new ideas.

Has a high income and educational level. Middle income and lower income groups are less flexible and tend to resist change. The latter group espe-cially seeks attainment of the basic educational objectives which they believe have been enjoyed by the more prosperous.

Is ethnically, religiously, and economically homogeneous. Such communities are less complex and the strategies for introducing new ideas may be fewer and simpler.

Hearn's article allows an interesting image—a prospective innovator surveying school systems arrayed before him and wondering: "Where can I best fulfill my innovative tendencies?" While Hearn's list of com-munity and staff attributes conducive to innovation is consistent with other statements found in the expanding body of literature on change, we find its implications alarming given the present state of affairs in education. Those school systems and communities identifiable as suitable for supporting educational change and innovation usually need it least. They are the wealthy suburban elite—the brahmins of education. Fewer urban or rural schools are likely to possess the specified characteristics, yet the need for program improvement through innovation is typically greatest in such schools.

Administrative support and involvement are crucial to the successful initiation and adoption of major structural innovations such as team teaching, flexible scheduling, large and small group instruction, and other organizational changes. They are also needed for major changes in curriculum such as the addition of new courses, although probably not essential for changes within courses or in methods of instruction. In addition, those in authority can demonstrate a willingness to share responsibility when calculated risks are taken and can give psychological support to the innovator through overt encouragement. Unless psychological support of this nature is offered, it is doubtful that many teachers will be enthusiastic about initiating or assisting in the quest for major changes. Frequently major changes also require extra faculty effort, particularly in the planning and initiating phases. The administrator or supervisor is the "gatekeeper" for additional financial resources, increased staff, or other necessary assistance. By giving or withholding aid, he can be a major factor in change efforts.

There is little question that the administrator is one of the keys to successful organizational change. Administrative reluctance or opposition is often cited by teachers as a primary obstacle to change. Whether adminstrative obstacles are real or not, in the perception of teachers they effectively exist. Some administrators are not innovators and refuse to support divergent programs or practices. Their innovation-oriented subordinates, supervisory or instructional, are bound to be frustrated if their case, however carefully planned and presented, gets no support.

Theorists envision the school administrator as a stimulator of change and leader toward improvement. Ideally the administrator should ask, "How can I create an environment in which teachers can design and maintain the most effective educational program possible for our students?" Some superintendents of schools may attempt to deal directly with change; but, especially in larger school systems, they frequently delegate the task to an assistant superintendent, to building principals, or to systemwide coordinators who work with teachers in specific subject areas. More and more one hears of specially trained "change agents" who, freed of administrative duties, primarily concern themselves with creating an environment in which change can happen. Change agents are usually basic to a school's systematic program for planned change.

Change theorists generally agree that change by "administrative fiat" is the least desirable, and generally the least effective way of proceeding. It is desirable to create an environment in which the individual will discover a need for change. The administrator or change agent can then provide encouragement and support for designing and implementing the change. Lacking the ideal situation, one might *persuade* individuals who will be affected and involved that a change is needed and that they should participate. In any case, the process of changing is time consuming; it requires considerable patience and understanding from all parties. Given the tremendous number of interacting variables, no single ideal model or plan for change will fit every school. However, there are some general guidelines.

A Generalized Model for Change

Whether the "change agent" is an administrator, supervisor, department chairman, or teacher, a successful plan for innovation will approximate five general steps or stages: awareness, interest, evaluation, trial, and adoption.[10] Strategies can be devised to increase the individual's awareness of new ideas, new programs, new methods of teaching, and new curriculum projects. Among these strategies are teacher in-service workshops, consultant help, encouragement to attend and participate in professional meetings, and maintenance of a professional library. Interest in an innovation is most apt to occur when the teacher views the new approach as compatible with and of possible assistance in attaining his goals. The opportunity to observe the innovation in practice at another school, especially when it is being used by another teacher, may remove much of the hesitancy to consider seriously the adoption of a new procedure or process.

Opportunities for limited tryouts of the idea on an experimental or short-term basis may also serve to heighten interest while assisting in the evaluation of the idea. After a limited tryout and study of published research data on the merits and liabilities of an innovation, the teacher may have a desire to participate in a more extensive trial, perhaps for a full semester or even a year. During the trial period psychological support is critical. The practitioner has ventured from the security of tried-and-true practices into unfamiliar territory where the risk of failure is present. At this point some financial resources are usually necessary. If evaluation indicates that the trial was successful, it may be possible to implement the change on a schoolwide or departmental basis. In this case the practices of numerous colleagues can be affected and they must be fully informed about the innovation and likewise convinced of its merits.[11]

When major changes are adopted in a school, there may be other problems. Some affected teachers, for instance, simply may not be able to adjust to or cope with the change. Provisions ought to be made to preserve the personal and professional dignity of these individuals. School patrons likewise may be affected by changes in school curriculum or organizational patterns. A complete change strategy will anticipate this and make some provision for educating the community, particularly parents, about the nature, goals, and anticipated outcomes of the innovation.

There are always some added costs in mounting new educational practices. These costs may be incurred only in the initial stages of implementation, but in some cases, new programs are just more expensive. Sometimes *extra* funds may be obtained by reallocation of other school or departmental funds, by additional appropriations from general school funds, or by a "grant" from state, federal, or private agencies. If a change is to endure as part of the ongoing program of the school, the necessary support funds must become part of the regular budget of the organization. When this is not accomplished, there is a great difficulty in supporting innovative programs, particularly those funded by external grants, over an extended period of time. When the money runs out, the innovation is dropped or modified.

The Teacher as Change Agent

Much of our discussion about the change process has centered on maxi- or major changes at the school or departmental level. Such changes affect others, frequently cost more, and usually require administrative support. We have intended to convey the idea that successful change strategy depends on teachers. It has little likelihood for success without teacher acceptance and involvement.

All changes, however, are not major. Some changes do not involve large groups of people and the expenditure of large sums of money. In Chapter 8, "Developing the School Curriculum," we emphasized the significant role the classroom teacher can play in curriculum development. The innovatively oriented teacher has considerable opportunity to modify instruction and course content by trying "new" methods, arranging course content in various ways, and employing a variety of student learning activities. As an innovator, he can operate as an individual; but he can also seek to develop ties with other innovatively oriented teachers in his department or in other departments. Such relationships can reinforce his own innovative tendencies by providing moral support, serving as a sounding board or a source of new ideas, and providing opportunities for cooperative and innovative teaching arrangements such as team teaching.

Even in a school environment that does not overtly encourage innovation, a teacher can win support for or at least neutralize resistance to new ideas and practices. He can accomplish this by developing rapport with many faculty members, sharing professional concerns with them, listening to their ideas, and by teaching in a manner which may earn the confidence and respect of colleagues. Certain individuals such as principals, supervisors, and department chairpersons hold status because of their administrative roles in the school and can be influential in shaping faculty opinion. In addition, they frequently have access to resources and can facilitate arrangements that add to the effectiveness of innovative efforts. The teacher, by analyzing the roles played by individuals in the school, will have a notion of where and how decisions are made, who controls the resources, and who influences the opinions of the group. When he ascertains who can be of help in his efforts to implement an innovative practice, he should discuss his ideas and possible implementation strategies with these persons.

Although some innovative approaches to instruction and curriculum may not require assistance from individuals outside the teacher's classroom, they could fail because they are flagrant violations of the norms of the school or the community, for example, dealing with emotionally loaded controversial issues. Teachers who have gained the confidence and support of the principal, department chairperson, and opinion leaders may experience some success in carrying out innovative practices that are counter to the norms. Nevertheless, there are times when the innovation may be perceived as too extensive, too radical, too spectacular; in such a situation it may be better to "back off," thereby avoiding a major confrontation, retaining the confidence and support of the administration, and preserving the opportunity to innovate another day. Sometimes, of course, a principle is at stake. In that case, the individual may have to decide whether to violate his conscience or jeopardize his retention on that faculty.

Summary

Changes in schools begin with a knowledge and understanding of the alternatives available in instruction, curriculum content, and new organizational patterns. The adoption of an alternative will be meaningful as it satisfies criteria appropriate to the improvement of the education of youth.

Schools are complex institutions not noted for their rapid response to the changing demands of a society which itself is experiencing significant changes. In order to increase the ability of the school to change, there appears to have been a movement away from sole reliance on the teacher as the center of change to a systematic approach to organizational development through planned change strategies. There seems to be a consensus that the human dimension of change is most important. Hardly any significant modification will be made in the school without the faculty's support, or at least its acquiescence.

Most of the major changes proposed for schools originate in sources external to the school. Regardless of origin, most innovations become a worthwhile reality only when those who must implement the change are willing to give the idea a try. Legislated change of a general regulatory or procedural nature, like the Carnegie unit, compulsory attendance, or minimum age for leaving school allow no choice and are exceptions. There is always the possibility that changes mandated by external or internal authority will never win faculty support and thus produce, at best, a "going through the motions" or, at worst, open rebellion.

A systematic approach to change follows a more or less sequential process: awareness, interest, evaluation, trial, and adoption. Change agents are perceived as facilitating the process. Once adopted, innovations should become part of the regular procedural and budgetary processes of the institution.

Although contemporary literature on planned change emphasizes the overall approach to organizational change, rather than the individual teacher, the classroom teacher still appears to be the most critical element in the process. Innovation is most apt to occur when the faculty agrees that there is a problem or situation which *needs* solution and that a change will help resolve the problem. Faculty members will probably demonstrate more interest in innovations that may result in better working arrangements, more effective instruction, better use of facilities, or improved opportunities for human interaction. Openness and ease in communication, mutual trust and respect, and a general sense of colleagueship must exist if changes are to be expected. The importance of openness cannot be overemphasized. Only in an atmosphere of openness can goals and purposes be honestly debated and the merits and potential of proposals for achieving agreed-on goals be subjected to honest discourse.

The following guidelines designed by James Becker should be useful to educators who want to function as change agents.

1. Success in implementing innovation generally requires careful preparation.
   a. This preparation might take the form of providing the user with opportunities to discuss and try proposed innovations in a non-threatening atmosphere, where there is no pressure to make quick decisions about commitment to the new program.
   b. In introducing innovations to your colleagues, you may find it more productive to emphasize the positive results of an innovation rather than the undesirable situation that it will replace or overcome.
2. It is important to recognize and accept the natural human resistance to change. Ambivalence about the desirability of trying new programs is likely to be widespread.
   a. These sentiments should be brought into the open by encouraging clients to discuss their feelings for and against the innovation.
   b. The personal need for change as a form of self-renewal should be kept in mind as a possible and important motivational factor.
3. Try to provide maximum support at the point of greatest risk taking.
   a. In-service discussions or demonstrations in department meetings to elicit commitment and support are not likely to be as threatening as the first classroom trial. Make sure that everything is in order for initial classroom tryouts.
   b. Keep in mind that the benefits of change may not be instantly apparent. Things may get worse before they get better. Encourage patience and persistence.

4. Tap as many sources as possible in collecting impressions about new programs as a basis for revisions, further trials and evaluation.
   a. Firsthand observation, interviews with students, clues from informal discussions in teachers' lounges and absentee rates all provide useful feedback on classroom innovations.
   b. Sharing information with co-workers and dividing the responsibility for trying to improve additional trial runs or experiments can help build a working team that will lend continuity to the change process.
5. Include in your plans provision for further implementation, continuity and follow-up.
   a. Consider how all the elements in the present system will be affected by the innovation.
   b. Remember that a few trial runs do not make a new program and that new materials do not necessarily bring desired changes in approach or style. Buying a new set of multi-media materials may result in little or no significant change unless further steps are taken to make them a functional part of existing programs.
   c. Integrating the new into existing programs may be facilitated by giving teachers ample opportunities to acquaint themselves with unfamiliar materials and equipment and by providing examples of various ways in which they might be used. Equitable scheduling of projectors and easy access to these and other necessary pieces of equipment may help encourage experimentation by insuring that they are available to all faculty members who want to try them.
   d. A "promotional campaign" may be necessary before the new materials become part of the working system. Developing or adapting a set of guidelines for use by the department could be a good way to get staff members involved and help insure the success of future efforts to introduce change.[12]

QUESTIONS AND ACTIVITIES

1. Make a list of the various skills, characteristics, and types of knowledge which you believe are necessary for a person interested in assuming the role of change agent or innovator. Are positive personality factors as important as intellectual strengths in influencing others to change?
2. Why is it easier to bring about change in some schools than in others? Assuming that you want to be involved in a school where changes are likely to occur, what characteristics will you look for in the school setting before you accept a new position?
3. Brainstorm ways and means by which students can be involved in the curriculum building process. Your focus should range from individual classroom settings to school and district wide settings.
4. Develop a fairly specific outline, with appropriate diagrams, of an inservice training or faculty development program focused on improving participants' abilities to manage change.
5. Investigate the Force Field Analysis technique developed by Kurt Lewin.

Apply the analytical strategy on at least one major problem identified by your class.

6. With a small group, study and develop the ability to use the Analyzing Performance Problems model developed by Robert Mager. It will be found in Mager's book titled *Analyzing Performance Problems: You Really Oughta Wanna.* Introduce this strategy to the members of your class and use a class-identified problem as a focus for its demonstrated use.

7. Organize a small group to study and develop the ability to use The Delphi Method as developed by Norman Dalkey. Introduce it to the class by using the method in a problematic situation of modest proportions.

NOTES

[1] Jesse Stein, ed., *The Random House Dictionary of the English Language* (New York: Random House, 1966), p. 246.

[2] Glen Heathers, "Planned Educational Change in Search of a Research Tradition," p. 9 in *Viewpoints*, Bulletin of the School of Education, Indiana University, Vol. 50, No. 3, May 1974.

[3] Norman E. Hearn, "The When, Where, and How of Trying Innovations," *Phi Delta Kappan*, February 1972, Vol. LII, No. 6, p. 360.

[4] See Warren G. Bennis, Kenneth D. Benne, Robert Chin, and Kenneth E. Corey, *The Planning of Change*, Third Edition in press (New York: Holt, Rinehart and Winston, 1976). See also David S. Bushnell and Donald Rappaport, eds., *Planned Change in Education: A Systems Approach* (New York: Harcourt Brace Jovanovich, 1971).

[5] James S. Dick, "A Study to Determine the Characteristics of Innovative Social Studies Departments in the Secondary Schools of Indiana," Unpublished doctoral dissertation, Indiana University, Bloomington, Indiana, 1974, pp. 34–35.

[6] M. B. Miles, ed., *Innovation in Education* (New York: Bureau of Publications, Teachers College, Columbia University, 1964). Cited in Dick, p. 33.

[7] Robert James Snavely, "A Description and Analysis of the Roles and Structures Created in a University/Public School Cooperative Teacher Education Program (CTEP)," Unpublished doctoral dissertation, University of Illinois, Urbana, Ill., 1975, pages 39–40. See also, Tom Burns and G. M. Stalker, *The Management of Innovation*, Chicago, Quadrangle Books, Inc., 1962, pages 5–7, 119–125.

[8] Frederick R. Smith and James A. Mackey, "Creating an Appropriate Social Setting for Inquiry," *Phi Delta Kappan*, April 1969, pp. 462–465.

[9] Hearn, pp. 358–359.

[10] Everett M. Rogers, *Diffusion of Innovations* (New York: Free Press, 1962), pp. 81–86.

[11] Lee Ehman, Howard Mehlinger, and John Patrick, *Toward Effective Instruction in Social Studies* (Boston: Houghton Mifflin, 1974), pp. 422–424.

[12] James Becker, "Organizing for Change: The Individual in the System," *Social Education*, March 1973, pp. 194–195.

CHAPTER **12**

An Essay on Schools

When we started this book a dozen chapters ago, we promised to withhold our private judgments as much as possible. The intent was to give our readers a chance to think about hard educational questions and make up their own minds. In the last chapter we would like to rescind our promise partially and expose more openly some of our own judgments. We say partially because some of the questions still do not have justifiable answers; we are no more ready than before to make a judgment. Another reason for saying partially is that we do not intend to review every question that was raised nor to treat all questions evenly and equally. That would be overly tedious. Besides, we and our readers may not agree in all cases when a question is actually a question.

In the spirit of inquiry that we have tried to maintain throughout this book, we plead tentativeness on all counts. Today's truths may tarnish by tomorrow. We would prefer not having the lines we draw around these issues seem, on second thought, more like nooses about our necks; but that is the danger of sharing. So, here is our small essay on schools.

Society and School

It does not seem especially noteworthy that schools are under attack in the United States. That simply is the nature of our society. We are pluralistic in such matters and the society seems to be undergoing a shift in preferences in the area of education. While there is no call to be flippant about the condition, there is likely no reason to panic. The schools will continue and, in the long run, will adapt quite adequately to whatever goals they are given and to whatever form or forms seems most useful. Over the next quarter of a century, the two least likely consequences for schools in this crisis period are (1) that the society will purge itself of public education, that is, become deschooled, and (2) that schools will remain just as they are now. Neither of these alternatives would be consistent with our history and our national temperament.

We have noted the most radical school changes in our 340-year experience with organized secondary education from Latin school to academy to high school. Each of these institutional forms reflected important social changes and each represented a move toward educational saturation. In a very general way each also reflected an increased tolerance for variety and alternatives. The series of schools, nonetheless, displays a remarkable continuity of practices, goals, and organizations. The venerable roles remain intact and the basic rules endure.

A third unlikely consequence for the schools is that they will make a serious attempt to reconstruct the society. Though social reconstruction often has been hailed as a useful educational purpose, schools have never really been tooled for this purpose and are unlikely to be so now. Schools are much too sensitive to the whims and desires of their clients to set out to remold them in any radical way. That does not mean, of course, that schools do not change people or that their effect is necessarily reduced to the least common denominator of the whole society. The schools have been especially adept in negotiating among the academic knowledge, the social wisdom, the political power, and the radical alternatives of the society in producing programs that are a cut above stagnation and several cuts below revolution. That makes them conservative institutions on the whole, but able to adapt to social changes when their own survival is at stake.

A decent wager for the next quarter century is that the alternative school movement will continue to expand in many directions. These will provide educators, students, parents, and all other school clients an opportunity for social experimentation with a variety of school forms and practices. Somehow and somewhen the society's preferences and likes will emerge. Gradually and painfully they will be accommodated in school districts throughout the country.

Purposes for Schools

The form of an institution has some kind of relationship to its function. At least, major changes in one often attend changes in the other.

Ordinarily one would expect a change in form to follow a decision to alter function, but that has not always been the case with schools. It did seem so in the transition from Latin schools to academies, but less so in the progressive era of the high schools. Also there is the argument that the high schools were only slightly different from the academies until they found themselves flooded with middle- and lower-class students. The progressives made some change in the purposes for the schools, though the form of the institution did not change radically. It did, of course, become more bureaucratic; that could count as an important change. With the coming of the high school, formal changes were made in schools, for example, coeducation, free tuition, a more comprehensive curriculum. But the changed purposes, including common and general education for all youth, citizenship education, and vocational competence, followed the realization that something ought to be done for the many students who were not going to college.

In the discussion above there is the suggestion that purposes for schools are often not thoughtfully designed. One hesitates to say that they are never so, though a cursory review of the school's history strongly suggests, as we said earlier, that the institution's managers have been more adept at negotiating feasible compromises among social, academic, and political forces than in designing society-bending goals. That does not license teachers to practice pedagogical prostitution, though in retrospect that seems to have been their natural trade. Rather, it argues for a new model of teacher education which can generate teachers with a new configuration of knowledge, attitudes, and skills. The first and most important task for these teachers is to attend to the persistent problems of purposes.

We set out in Chapter 2 a framework for that task. Unfortunately most readers will have passed it by because most persons who are preparing for teaching are not of a mind to worry about such topics. That disinclination notwithstanding, we choose to emphasize it once again. We present it here as a set of framing questions for the development of a rationale for education. Our point is that teachers generally do not care about such questions and do not prepare themselves to deal with them. Before purposes for schools can be dealt with rationally, however, we need teachers who are willing and able to deal with such questions as these:

1. What is the social world like?
2. What ought the social world be like?
3. What is knowledge?
4. What is thinking?
5. What is man?

These questions are not only for teachers. The issues involved are socially pervasive. Everyone ought to be concerned with them. But if teachers aren't, a large part of our hope for the schools is lost.

Metropolis Schools

Not everyone goes to a metropolitan school, and some who read this text will never teach in a metropolitan school. In spite of that, three-fourths of our population and three-fourths of our teachers live in metropolitan areas. Within a few years, 80 percent, perhaps 90 percent, of the persons above the age of five in this country will have gone to school in a metropolis. It seems obvious to us that whatever happens in schools in the next quarter of a century will take place mainly in metropolis schools. That is our primary justification for emphasizing education for metropolitan man in this text.

A major assumption of our treatment of metropolitan schools is that schools, like other institutions, are being subjected to their greatest test in the city. These institutions, which should be helping us to order our lives in ways that provide for the fulfillment of our highest social values, are also the traditional keeps of the very beliefs and outlooks that hinder us from achieving equality and justice for all our people. In a humanized society, all persons have the right to be served by institutions that help them apply the best technology and the most valid knowledge to their problems. The legitimation of our institutions in the lives of all persons in the metropolis is a major social challenge of our times. The challenge extends to the schools.

It would seem a reasonable expectation that a legitimate, humanized school could ameliorate the conditions of environmental inauthenticity and personal identity loss. But for schools to accept this challenge will require them to develop different options than they now display. We have suggested two ways that could facilitate such options. One of these would be the encouragement of experimental alternative schools that would permit the exploration of activities and curriculums that truly reflect the richness and variety of the cityscape. Another would be the further expansion of the participatory movement which would permit the infusion of the life of the community in the life of the school.

Social class and racial segregation have made it nearly impossible for schools to promote the social goals of equality and justice. Segregation, a general condition in our society, is aggravated and magnified in the metropolis. It has resulted in schools that tend to be segregated by class and race. While this is a general condition in our society—for example, historically we legally maintained racially segregated schools—

it is worsened in the city because of the great numbers of persons involved and the political organization of school districts in metropolitan areas. This combination of factors continues to frustrate efforts to desegregate schools.

A major reason for attempting to desegregate schools is that minority groups, especially blacks, our largest racial minority, are denied educational equality and thus life chance equality in segregated schools. Some research has shown also that when black students attend school with white students, the blacks' achievement scores are elevated. Presumably, fully desegrated schools in this country would help to equalize the life chances of all. Some reassessments of the data that support this conclusion have indicated, however, that equalizing education actually would have very little effect on the gross inequalities that exist between races and classes in the United States. Social and family experiences outside of school are so powerful that confidence in the simple manipulation of schools as the sole social remedy is not warranted.

We are not persuaded, therefore, that desegregation for the purposes of equalizing educational opportunity and life opportunity is a valid argument. As a singular approach it is mostly ineffectual on both counts. Nonetheless, there are other grounds for desegregating schools that are compelling. We live in a multiracial and multiclass society and we must live together. Desegregated schools offer one context where we can learn and practice the skills and attitudes needed to make a success of it.

There are no simple answers to the problems of metropolitan education. There is certainly no single solution. It does not even seem probable that any of the major problems of metropolitan education can be settled satisfactorily in isolation from many other metropolitan problems. The metropolis has invalidated the isolation of problems as a strategy; educational problems must be attacked in relationship to the political, aesthetic, economic, legal, intellectual, religious, and moral conditions in the metropolitan area. Partly because of our holistic convictions, we see considerable merit in supporting multiple approaches to hard educational problems.

An old African proverb says, "If you don't understand, it doesn't matter what you do." Our willingness to allow many approaches is based in part on the realization that since many educational problems aren't understood, multiple experimental alternatives must be advanced.

We are willing to press for desegregation wherever it has a chance to develop a truly integrated school society while promoting decentralized but segregated school districts wherever they have a chance to produce truly community-infused schools. Also we are willing to promote the development of alternative schools while continuing to try to improve the common and general educational program in standard schools.

The problems are too great, the situations too diverse, and the technology too uncertain to fault out of hand any plan that gives some promise of fulfilling at least one important educational goal. In this experimental spirit, we must be willing to accept the question of whether some plan or another will achieve or destroy a goal as primarily a researchable question. In the end, we can know which goals are met and which are denied by trying something and examining the consequences.

The Adolescent Student

When we discussed students in this book, we concentrated exclusively on the American adolescent. That, in itself, presents something of a problem, for despite the uniform characteristics that can be used to characterize the adolescent, adolescents, like humans of any age, are notably variable. It is impossible to talk about any group of persons without flirting with stereotyping. At those points where we have overgeneralized, have implied a uniformity where there is actually diversity, and have inferred defining characteristics from limited data, we confess to the flirtation. We can only warn our readers that all such generalizations, uniformities, and definitions are suspect. Our justification for categorizing is that categories are useful in helping to frame one's responses; that is the sense in which we did it.

While adolescents are not necessarily characterizable as happy persons, they appear, at least in school, to be trying hard to be happy. The great majority of them seem fully immersed in the fun culture of schools. That is not necessarily a negative avocation, unless one supposes that teen-agers generally could find something better to do with their time than seeking out entertainment for themselves. There are adolescents in school who are serious scholars; accomplished musicians, writers, and artists; clever politicians; and highly skilled employees. Sometimes, perhaps most often, these talents are related to or have been developed in schools. That seems to us so perfectly proper that it is amazing that schools do not provide more activities for all adolescents that more directly relate to adult activities in our society. That notion has some serious drawbacks obviously, not the least of which is a possible confining vocational taint to school curriculums. However, our society seems to compound the disturbing breach between youth and adulthood which makes it difficult for many adolescents to see without distortion what being grown up means. Although the fun culture of the schools provides important socializing effects of benefit to participating adolescents, it does not seem to be a prime environment for socializing youth in more serious, if not more important, aspects of life.

Our underlying intention in discussing adolescents was to show several ways in which they differ from each other; as we indicated, we were constrained to display these differences in simplified categories. Our own academic limitations were among the constraints. The categories or factors that we chose are subculture motivation, which we reviewed above, intelligence, family and social class, race, language, sex, and cognitive and moral development. Although these are only a few of the possible differentiating factors, they are exceedingly powerful determinants in the life of a person.

A common characteristic of most of these factors is that they are not easily influenced by school experience. The school's ineffectiveness in most of these matters has not deterred its efforts to wipe out the bad effects of low intelligence, poor family background, lower-class status, and black race membership; to accelerate language, moral, and cognitive development; and to magnify the traditional concepts of maleness and femaleness. Many would judge such an enormous deployment of time and talent an unfortunate waste. We find ourselves in substantial agreement with this position.

We do not see any great advantage in training everyone to speak, act, think, and value alike. Most especially, it does not seem an acceptable social task for schools to perform. Of course, as we have said, schools don't accomplish this now, even though they may try. There are conditions, however, in which some standardization is a rational option. Because of these we place some qualifications on our position.

In the United States many idioms and dialects enrich our language experiences. Even to consider ways to eradicate these expressions of cultural diversity smacks of arrogance. If anything, schools should do what they can to celebrate and encourage these language traditions. However, schools are obligated to say to students that Anglo-English is the standard dialect of the academic, business, and professional worlds. For most persons, the use of the standard dialect is nearly a requisite for participation in these worlds. School should be a place where standard dialect can be learned, but not at the expense of other perfectly useful and communicative dialects. An honest statement would be that Anglo-English is the only dialect that teachers in most schools are capable of teaching systematically. Teachers who have the good fortune of teaching in schools where language traditions other than Anglo-English are represented among their students should take the opportunity to learn as well as teach.

We feel justified in generalizing this qualification to other culture traits that appear to be related to social class. We see no particular reason for denying lower-class students access to middle-class values and behaviors if they want to be so trained. Nor should they be denied the knowledge that these dominate the transactions of the academic, business, and professional worlds. Successful participation in these worlds may well require a certain level of cherishing of the values. Schools could be places where students are trained for this mobility, if they so desire. Teachers ordinarily represent middle-class behaviors and values quite adequately.

More realistically, however, schools should not play this mobility game with students. For one thing, there is very little evidence that they are very good at it. Rather than training students in different cultural modes, they succeed mainly in making school a distressing and uncomfortable experience for lower-class students. A more humane approach would be to make schools places where many social and cultural variations are valued and where persons of different social class backgrounds can learn to live together. Specifically, such terms as "culturally deprived" must be discredited as fitting designations for persons who are not middle-class. These terms not only imply that one kind of class membership is better than another but also that the members of one class are somehow better than the members of another.

We are not sure how our qualified position extends to sex differences. We doubt, on the one hand, that the complete disqualification of sex as a differentiating factor in society and school is either possible or desirable. On the other hand, there is little rationality in the gross social inequities that are attached to maleness and femaleness. No amount of rhetoric will make men and women equal competitors in most school sports; nor can it justify the common disparity of expenditures on male and female sports programs in schools. Argumentation will not equalize the childbearing burdens of husbands and wives; nor can it justify the gross differentiation of the husband's and wife's child-rearing roles. The list of sex inequities is long, as we are reminded by leaders in the feminist movement. We have become so adjusted to most of the inequities that we must be sensitized in order to see them. Most of them also have lost their warrant, if indeed they were ever justifiable.

The schools and other institutions perpetuate many sexist norms and practices. Girls take homemaking courses taught by women; boys are on athletic teams coached by men. Elementary teachers are predominantly women; most administrators are men. Girls are encouraged to gain secretarial skills; mechanical skills are promoted for boys. Males are counseled into courses to prepare them for the professional schools; females are counseled toward the liberal arts colleges. Emotional and impetuous responses are tolerated in females; males are expected to be more deliberate and logical.

Schools can do some things in this situation. For example, every course offering should be open to both males and females, including modern dance, child care, auto mechanics, and all other traditionally male or female courses. Although that would do very little to balance the membership in these classes, that along with some moderate promotional schemes, is about all that schools can do. They must await substantial societal changes for more dramatic adjustments.

Also athletic expenditures should be equalized for males and females. That does not mean that girls and boys should be required to compete in all sports. That resolution would result in more discrimination against females. Few girls would make the teams. Equalized expenditures would mean rather, that schools would field only males in some sports, only females in some sports, and both males and females in some sports, including male and female members on some teams. The practice could result in more diversified athletic programs in schools as an added benefit.

Finally, career counselors in schools should not discriminate between the sexes for any career. They should, however, reveal fairly the existing employment practices and client preferences in the field.

Schools cannot eradicate the differences between males and females; and they shouldn't try. However, they can do some things that will help change the traditional sex role expectations that appear unwarranted and unjust in today's society. An initial move would be to alter the sex role expectations that are perpetuated within the schools themselves.

We have referred to race and purported racial differences in this text many times. We have reported various conditions in which race appears to be a factor both in schools and in the society. Most of what we have said focuses on blacks and whites, the major racial groups in the United States. Thus most of what we say here reflects that limitation.

In all the racial situations we mentioned, whites usually have the better of it. Whites do better and stay longer in school and read better than blacks. Blacks score lower than whites on interest inventories, achievement measures, and intelligence tests. Also a lower percentage of blacks than whites go on to college, have high-paying jobs, and enter the professions. A disproportionate number of blacks are in the lower class. Despite all recent improvements in the society, being born black in the United States still adds up all too frequently to social and economic disaster.

For years the society accepted, almost without question, the oldest and simplest explanation for these conditions—that blacks are racially inferior. Variations of that argument appear periodically. One was generated recently within the scientific community. An alternative explanation suggests that the American society is so thoroughly racist in its attitudes and outlook that blacks can probably never achieve complete parity with whites. There are simply too many private and subtle societal controls that are beyond the scope of legislation and courts and are impervious to education. Our preference is for the latter explanation.

Despite wishes to the contrary, the schools can claim very little credit for the recent improvements in the lot of blacks in the United States. The equity mechanisms have been the courts and legislatures. School systems, rather than contributing to black and white equality in these cases, have been thoroughly chastised by the courts for maintaining the socially offensive practice of segregation. Twenty years after *Brown* v. *Topeka*, most American students continue to attend schools that are segregated or practically so. Without the use of more radical enforcement tactics, the number of students attending segregated schools will likely increase over the next few years.

Educationally the desegregating of schools may be of little consequence. It may make very little difference in achievement whether persons attend segregated or desegregated schools. However, there are social reasons for opting for desegregated schools which are presumably more valid. There is the barest of chances that schools with truly integrated student societies could demonstrate how the adult society could also become integrated. That in turn could possibly contribute to black-white equality.

Our position is more aptly clarified by the statement that we are not convinced that race qualifies as a differentiating factor among persons of any age, including adolescents. Racial differences account for nothing that cannot as well be accounted for by cultural differences that have gotten themselves fairly consistently attached to race in this society. Thus most of what we have tried to say about class differences, language differences, and culture differences is applicable to blacks as a racial group. Our society persists in its intolerance of the differences among us. Blacks are disadvantaged in this society and in the schools because of cultural differences that ought to be celebrated rather than discredited. As long as the ruling, white middle class labors under the melting pot delusion that everyone should think, act, and value in its image, that kind of tolerance of differences cannot happen. We would like to think that the schools could someday promote that kind of tolerance.

We suggested also that adolescent students vary in their cognitive and moral development. It is not at all certain that schools can affect this development very much. At best, they might speed it up; at worst, retard it. We would be happy, however, to see school programs that recognize that students do in fact have mental powers other than memory and that these higher functions operate naturally and usefully in fields other than mathematics. That is no great expectation; but it would require teachers who have thought carefully about the purpose of schooling along the lines of the rational framework we offered in Chapter 2.

We would also like schools to engage in moral education in the sense of advancing students' moral reasoning. This developmental approach would not indoctrinate students by giving them a "bag of virtues" to guide their behavior. Instead, it would encourage them toward a fuller understanding of the central moral concept of justice and the use of moral principles in making judgments about their interactions with other persons.

STUDENT RIGHTS

We spent considerable time in this book in developing another student perspective. We have shared the impression with many other teachers for many years that students in school simply are not accorded the most primitive rights touted as so important in our democratic society. With misgivings, teachers have cooperated in the enforcement of *decent* dress codes (shirt-tails in, no slacks or shorts, knee-length skirts, hair above the collar), *nice* behavior (no smoking on school grounds, no cigarettes in shirt pockets, no hand holding in the halls, no gum chewing in class), and *proper* speech (no profanity in school, no criticism of teachers, no written criticism in school newspapers of anything, and so on). Teachers have participated in and observed individual and mass searches of student lockers for contraband of all kinds, from comic books to weapons, with and without locker assignees present. They have seen protests disassembled unceremoniously with the swift suspension of everyone in sight.

Even when there has been teacher sensitivity to the injustices perpetrated on students in school, it has not been effective in bringing about more just conditions. Teachers, in general, have been nearly powerless in such matters. Administrators and school boards, who might have done something, generally did nothing. Much to their credit, the correcting of these matters is being accomplished by the students themselves and the courts of the land.

The fight for student justice focused early on dress codes. The discrepancies between what was being tolerated in an increasing number of places in the society and what was being allowed in schools simply became too great. Hair, and lots of it, and faded, patched, and ragged jeans became the rallying issues in public schools everywhere. Once the dress codes were broken, there was simply no stopping secondary students in their headlong flight to equality. School boards, school administrators, and school teachers were propelled into the twentieth century by a coalition of students, courts, and parents. The shopworn concept of *in loco parentis* became noticeably faded with the participation of parents in many court suits. Parents had long since decently acquiesced to the insistent pressures of their teen-age children.

Some day a proper sociopolitical history of the sanguine sixties will offer some plausible explanations for the effects of this period on the civic awareness of students in school. Undoubtedly, some part of the explanation will include a reference to Vietnam. Perhaps that overwrought, overextended, and overplayed national fiasco gave an entire generation of young persons just time enough to reflect on how much was required of them to earn the rights of citizens in this country, how little was being returned to them in the present, and how long they had to wait for the rest.

In some manner, surely not because they were being taught so in schools, students learned that *in loco parentis* and other such tactics for protecting the young from the realities of the real world, the juvenile court, for example, were a poor trade-off for *due process* where their civil rights are concerned. No credit is due the schools in this regard. In their normal and standard posture, they have been acted upon rather than acting in the situation. The reluctance of school boards, administrators, and teachers to accept the conditions of keeping school with students oversensitized to their civil rights still has a long history to run.

It is not that their reluctance is totally without justification. The elements in the society that make rights feasible for anyone are duty and responsibility. These were active historically long before the concept of rights; and they are generally recognized by adults as part and parcel of rights. It is partly through experience that school personnel recognize that duty and responsibility are not universally admired by the young in our society. They recognize that while rights are enforceable, responsibility is not; it must be learned and internalized by the individual.

We do not deny the difficulties involved. But overall, it seems to us, the argument favors the students. It does not take a high level of moral development to recognize the justice in the students' claim. If, on the other hand, they are less responsible than they ought to be to support this claim, that only defines the nature of the educational task at hand.

Professional Power

In a corporate society it is extremely difficult for the individual to muster enough strength to make his position count. Power is generated by groups organized to accomplish specified ends. This is the way the contest is designed, and this is the way in which the contestants stand a reasonable chance of success. We believe that it is professionally and morally right for teachers to build their corporate strength to secure professionally and morally justified ends. Power tests in the near future are likely to occur in the United States Congress, the state legislatures, federal and state courts, and in the collective bargaining sessions in hundreds of school districts.

The question remains of the ends toward which professional power may be directed. It is understandable that an occupational group that has always viewed itself as underrewarded would assign priority to questions of its own welfare. But after welfare questions, what comes next? What of questions of curriculum development, instruction, and academic freedom? Will control of these and related matters be future goals of teacher organizations? Unwittingly, educators have grown accustomed to sharing with others the most sensitive decisions about what should be learned, how to teach, which instructional materials should be used, how schools should be organized, and most other matters related to the educational enterprise. Then in a display of corporate masochism, they are allowing themselves to be berated in the name of accountability. But questions of accountability are premature and nonsensical without also considering questions of responsibility and autonomy. If educators are to be held accountable for effectiveness of public education, they must have commensurate authority and autonomy[1] to decide what is done in its name. That kind of authority will not be given; it must be taken. When teachers are ready to direct their growing professional power toward resolving the educational issues that are beyond the problems of self-interest, the profession will have come of age.

Changing Schools

Despite trappings of innovations, we see most schools as remarkably resistant to change. There are of course significant exceptions where teachers and administrators have expended great efforts to implement new approaches in their schools. Nevertheless, schools as a whole are much as they always have been both in the ways they are organized and in what and how children are taught.

We believe teachers have the potential for playing a powerful role in changing schools. Albeit, they do not now exercise in a dramatic way their several opportunities to try new ideas in the classroom nor their considerable freedom to change the nature and content of instruction. One explanation is that we are an extremely cautious profession. Teachers have been disinclined to exercise aggression and militancy even in matters of self-interest. Moreover, in an abdication of their professional responsibility, teachers too frequently use administrators, department chairpersons, parents, school board members, and vested interest groups as convenient scapegoats for their own failures to produce change. The fact is that few supervisors and fewer administrators have more than a vague notion of what is happening in most secondary school classrooms, innovative or otherwise. That, too, may be part of the problem—too few schools have systematic procedures for supervising and evaluating teaching. More to the point, even fewer have constructive programs of in-service education which enable teachers to improve their traditional competencies, let alone develop new skills and talents that could lead to radical change. Given the massive funds which are expended for school facilities and instructional salaries, the minuscule resources allocated for staff development is tragic. School administrators should seriously consider alternative plans for the in-service education of teachers. Among those plans should be some designed to "radicalize" their teachers' professional energies.

We have noted the bureaucratic nature of institutions and the tendency to reward those who demonstrate the will and capability for preserving the norms of the institution. Given the institutional character of public education and the mechanistic organization of school systems, it is unlikely that a radicalized leadership will emerge naturally from within. In a changing society, the institutional advantages gained by promoting to administrative and supervisory posts those individuals who "know the ropes" and who have earned advancement through years of dedicated and efficient service are ill-gotten. If innovative leadership evolves through that arrangement, it is a lucky coincidence.

Our preference for rationality prevents us from embracing change for the sake of change. We have no intention of promoting such nonsense. We do intend to suggest, however, that public education, school systems, boards, administrators, and teachers need to develop more supple response mechanisms in periods of social change in order to serve their student clients legitimately. In this circumstance, we are promoting the development of a spirit of rational radicalism in the schools wherein the skills and processes of thoughtful innovation are nurtured and the generation of ideas is encouraged and rewarded. Our prescription has three facets, the development of organizational climate, skill and process training, and the breeding of ideas. Together they constitute the necessary conditions for change for the sake of improvement. We are prompted to say further that when thoughtful individuals are given the freedom, resources, and skills necessary to try and to evaluate their ideas, the first giant step toward improved quality of education is taking place.

The Preparation of Teachers

Teacher training programs in the post World War II years were forced to produce certified teachers in numbers never before imagined in the history of our country. The colleges did an amazing job in staffing the classrooms of the nation during that crisis period. Now, however, the "numbers game" is over. With the number of students in teacher education programs drastically reduced, an ideal opportunity is presented for a reexamination of the ways in which teachers are prepared. Unfortunately, we anticipate that the reexamination, if it actually takes place, will produce little more than a spate of rhetoric and a modicum of altered programs here and there. On that prediction we hope we are wrong. But if the millions of dollars spent in the 1960s on curriculum projects for elementary and secondary schools could produce mostly cosmetic effects, what can an "opportunity to examine" under the poverty conditions of the 1970s be expected to accomplish? Our cynicism notwithstanding, we will suggest some areas related directly to our interest in secondary schools that ought to be considered when and if that massive reexamination of the nation's largest professional education enterprise takes place.

While the professional schools which prepare teachers and the public schools which employ teachers quite obviously trade in the same commodity, it is quite as obvious that they trade in different worlds. The first serious contact of these worlds usually occurs in the last phase of a teacher candidate's program when he leaves campus for his student teaching assignment in a public school. That contact, involving a teacher candidate, a public school teacher, and probably a college supervisor, is hardly plenipotential; nor does that contact ordinarily develop into a sharing situation capable of affecting future contacts of the two organizations. We view the separation of university teacher preparation and the public schools as unfortunate and inappropriate. This view does not deny that universities and public secondary schools have unique functions and responsibilities with respect to the preparation of teachers; but in teacher education, there need to be recurrent, plenipotential intersections of the two institutions.

In general, our view holds that the theory/practice dichotomy is an artifact. Programs in teacher education which are characterized by a thorough immersion in subject matter content and pedagogical theory on campus, followed by an incidental involvement with in-service teachers and public school classrooms where the "practical" is encountered, can only by accident produce teachers who validly can mend the theory/practice schism. The need for participation of public school teachers in the professional preparation of teachers for purposes of identifying necessary competencies and designing and directing commensurate experiences is so obvious that the limited association of teachers with most teacher education programs, once they have graduated, is embarrassing. For one thing, the practicing profession exercises no power in determining who may enter certification programs or who, in fact, may become certified to teach. Progress toward professionalism of teaching necessitates that teachers play a more significant role in controlling entry into the profession.

At the same time, we believe the wholesale abandonment of the public school classrooms by the professional schools in education to be equally reprehensible. There would seem to us no less reason to suppose that professors of education can contribute to the development of public school classrooms as clinical adjuncts of a professional school than to suppose that school teachers can contribute a sense of reality to a teacher education program.

On occasion one hears that some teachers cannot teach because colleges of education have poor programs. If, indeed, the indictment is justified, a cooperative venture in teacher education as suggested above could be remedial. In a larger sense, we would like to challenge the implication that a teacher's education is ever complete. Indeed, many teachers continue in graduate and post-graduate courses for years following their certification. More pertinent and more useful for teachers, however, and also for schools, would be a continuous program of in-service education focused precisely on the professional problems faced by teachers every day. Such a program can provide, as an additional benefit, a mechanism for a more enduring cooperative arrangement between the schools and the universities.

The lack of variety in teacher education programs leads one to assume either that the novice prepared in a standard model could function in any school setting or that all school settings are alike. Neither is true. We are encouraged by some of the new teacher education programs which offer alternatives to the standard model. Some of these involve public school teachers and administrators, professors from education, arts and sciences, and other colleges, and community representatives in designing and implementing preparation programs for teachers of selected school populations. There are two characteristics in these programs which appear to have considerable merit; the "parity" involvement of concerned, knowledgeable, and responsible parties, and the development of multiple approaches to teacher education based on the special needs of student clients.

There are still many unanswered questions about the proper preparation of teachers. There is difficulty in identifying in any systematic manner the personal, social, and intellectual qualities necessary for effective teaching. There are serious questions about the appropriateness of the present academic experiences required in teacher education. Majoring in a specific academic discipline may be more confining than liberating, thereby serving to reinforce rather than encourage thoughtful evaluation of the existing public school curriculum. The relationship is symbiotic.[2]

As with public education, we are, in effect, opting for a spirit of rational radicalism in the realm of teacher education. The option can provide for the ventilation that the professional education of teachers requires in this era of change. In any event, when we cease searching for new and better ways of accomplishing our educational goals, or accept the goals themselves as unchanging, we are surely near professional demise.

QUESTIONS AND ACTIVITIES

1. Select one of the main headings of this chapter and construct your own analysis of the topic or problem. At what points are your opinions in disagreement with the authors'? Do you disagree mainly over conceptions, descriptions, explanations, predictions, or value judgments?
2. Using the main headings of this chapter write your own essay on schools. Are your views substantially different from those of the authors'?
3. What in your estimation is the most crucial problem facing public education in the United States today? Why is this problem more important than many of the others discussed in this book? What might be an acceptable alternative in resolving this problem?

NOTES

[1] Harry S. Broudy, *The Real World of the Public Schools* (New York: Harcourt Brace Jovanovich, 1972), chapter 6, "Accountability—Why Not?" This chapter provides an extensive, penetrating, and thought-provoking discussion of the question of accountability in education.

[2] We are indebted to Professor Orrin Gould of the University of Illinois for this science analogue.

Index

A

Ability, individual; variability in, 46
Academies, 3–4, 10
Accrediting associations, 141–142
Achievement, class differences in, 44–
  47
  racial differences in, 44–47, 74, 76,
  184
    integration, effect, 74, 146
  school expenditures, effect, 146
Ackerly, Robert, 99
Administrators, school, 8, 188–189
  authority of, 88–89
  as change agents, 165, 169
  statistics, 106, 110
  student rights and, 99–103, 187
Adolescents, 64–81, 181–187
  characterization by types, 65–66,
  182
  development differences, 78–80
  lower class, 70–73
  race factors, 73–74
  reading and language differences,
  74–77
  sex differences, 77–78
  subcultures, 66–67
  understanding of, importance, 23–
  24, 80–81
  values of, 64–65
  variances in, 73–80, 181–182, 185
  See also students
Alabama, student rights ruling, 94
Alexander, Hines, and Associates, 155
Alternative schools, 57, 156–159, 179
American Civil Liberties Union
  (ACLU), 95, 102–103, 143

American Federation of Teachers
  (AFT), 115–118, 121
Authenticity problem, 36–37, 38

B

Berkeley, California school district,
  157
Bestor, Arthur, 8
Bilingual schools, 157
Bill of Rights, 85, 89, 91–93, 97, 98
Blacks, 35, 143, 184–185
  in inner city, 34, 41
  language characteristics, 75–76
  segregation of (See Segregation)
  student dissent by, 87
  whites and, situations compared,
  184
  See also Race
Blackwell v. Issaquena County Board
  of Education, 90–92, 96
Bloom, Benjamin, 132, 133
Boston, 2, 4, 53, 147
Brammer, Lawrence, M., 86
Brown v. Topeka Board of Education,
  41, 52, 184
Bruner, Jerome, 163
Bull Island, mentioned, 37
Bureaucracy, school as, 85–86, 167,
  189
Burnside v. Byars, 90–92, 96
Busing, 41, 53–54, 60–61, 147

C

Carnegie Corporation, 144, 145

Changes, in the family, 10
  in schools, agents of, 163, 165–169,
      171–172, 188
    conducive factors, 166–169
    curricular, 55–57, 163
    dimensions of, 162–165
    guidelines for, 173–174
    implementation of, 162–173
    model for, 170–171
    in organizational patterns, 149–
        160, 163–164
    process of, 165–167
    proposals for, 55–62
    related factors, 167–169
    resistance to, 9, 164–167, 188–
        189
    in student rights, 89–103
    in society, 17–19, 36–37, 149
    in teachers, 108, 113, 119
    in values, 9–10, 13, 18
Charlotte, North Carolina, 53
Chicago, 74, 118, 157
Chicanos, 34, 42, 70, 76, 87, 143
Children of Crisis, 45
Cities, problems of, 35–36, 58
  See also Inner city; Metropolises
Civil rights movement, mentioned, 87,
    89
Coleman Report, 47, 73–74, 146–147
Coles, Robert, 45
Collective bargaining, by teachers,
    119–122
Colleges, impact of, on public educa-
    tion, 137–138
Communal society, described, 18
Community involvement in schools, 8,
    58–60, 61, 179
  curriculum decisions, 142–144
Conant Report, 144–145
Conrack, 108
Constitution, U.S., 14, 51, 54, 140
  student rights under, 89, 91–94, 97,
    98, 100
Contract teaching, 56
Copernican system, 9
Corporal punishment, 94–95
Craig, Patricia A., 115, 118–119

Crane, Ichabod, as a stereotype, 108
Crisis period, in society, 9
Curriculum, 126–135
  categories, 126–128
  changes in, 55–57, 163
  commonality vs. generality, 24
  decisions, 128–132
    forces affecting, 137–147
  defined, 126
  goals, 132–134
  historical development, 2–9
  national project movement, 139,
      163, 164
  Seven Cardinal Principles, 7, 27

                        D

Decentralization, of urban schools, 58–
    60, 61
Declaration of Independence, 14
Delinquent adolescents, 66
Desegregation (*See* Integration)
Des Moines, Iowa, 90
Developmental theories, 78–80
Differentiated staffing, 154
Doxiadas, Constantinos, 31
Dress codes, 94, 186
Dropout Centers, 158
Drug addiction, 45–46
Due process, for students, 95–97, 99,
    187

                        E

Education (*See* Public education;
    Schools; Secondary schools;
    Teaching)
Educational parks, 54–55, 157
Educational Policies Commission
    (EPC), 145
English Classical School, 4
Ethnic schools, 157
Evanston, Illinois, Township High
    School, 101
Expulsion, as punishment, 95–96
Extracurricular activities, 8, 99, 127

F

Family, 10, 45
Family Educational Rights and Privacy
    Act, 98
Flint, Michigan, 117
Ford, President Gerald, 54
Franklin, Benjamin, 3
Free schools, 158

G

Gault, in re, 96
Gerrymandering, 53
Ghetto (*See* Inner City)
Glasser, Ira, 85n[1], 88, 94
Goss v. *Lopez*, 95, 97
Great Neck, New York, 159
Griffin v. *Tatum*, 94
Guidance programs, 8, 127–128
Guru Maharaj Ji, mentioned, 37
Guthrie, James W., 115, 118–119

H

Haircuts, as student rights, 93–94
Havighurst, Robert J., 33
Head Start Project, 72
Hearn, Norman E., 150n[3], 164, 168
Hentoff, Nat, 44, 95
Housing Act of 1949, 34, 40
Howard, Eugene, 150n[1]

I

Identity crisis, 38
Independent study, 155
Indiana, collective bargaining legisla-
    tion, 121–122
Indianapolis, Indiana, 53
Indians, American, 38, 70
Individualism, in American society,
    15–16
Industrial growth, 17

In loco parentis concept, 88–89, 94,
    95, 97, 99, 187
Inner city, 34, 37, 40, 41
    language in, 75–76
    schools in, 55–62
        achievement question, 44–47
        segregation, 42–43
Innovation (*See* Changes)
Institutions, changing values, effect on,
    9–10
    function of, 32
    mechanistic, 166–167
    organic, 166–167
    in a pluralistic society, 16
    urban problems and, 35–36
    See also Schools
Instruction (*See* Teaching)
Integration, 48, 51–55, 57, 61–62,
    180, 185
    methods, 52–55
        busing, 41, 53–54, 60–61, 147
    model schools, 158
    results, 73–74, 146
Intelligence, 67–69
    differences in, 46
    race and, relationship, 46, 76
    socioeconomic class and, relation-
        ship, 69–73
Intelligence Quotient (I.Q.), 67
Irving, Washington, 108

J

Jencks, Christopher, 43, 45, 48, 55, 61,
    74
Jensen, Arthur, 46
Jesus Freaks, mentioned, 37
Junior high school, development of, 7
Juvenile court system, 88

K

Kalamazoo case, 6
Kennedy, President John F., 121
Knowledge, nature of, 23

Kohlberg, Lawrence, 78, 79–80
Kratwhohl, David R., 133, 134

L

Language deprivation, 75–76
Latin grammar schools, 2–3, 10, 26–27
Latinos, 34, 35, 42, 143
Learning centers, 157
Learning packages, 156
Legislation, on collective bargaining, 121–122
on curriculum decisions, 140–141
Legitimacy, of urban schools, 42–44
Leone, Andrew A., 93
Lieberman, Myron, 107–108, 116, 117
Lockers, student; search and seizure question, 92–93
Los Angeles Association of Classroom Teachers, 117
Louisville, Kentucky, 41, 53, 101, 147, 157
Lower class students, 70–72, 183
remediation for, 72–73
sex-role differentiation, 77
speech, 75–76

M

"Magna Charta for students," 97
Magnet schools, 157
Masia, Bertram B., 133
Massachusetts Bay Colony, 2
Massachusetts Institute of Technology, 17
Mass society, described, 18
McCoy, Rhody, 42
Mechanistic organization, 166–167
Metropolises, 33–35
authenticity problem in, 36–37, 38
identity problem in, 38
institutional crisis in, 35–36
population statistics, 179
schools in, 179–181
segregation in, 38–42, 179

Military institution, 85, 88
Minority groups, 34, 35, 41n., 58, 180
relevance problems of, 37
See also specific minority groups
Moral development, 79–80
Multicultural schools, 157

N

National Association for Secondary School Principals (NASSP), 99, 100, 145
National Consortium for Alternatives in Public Education, 157, 159
National Education Association (NEA), 6–7, 9, 109, 113, 115–119, 121
New England, 2–3, 5
New Jersey, corporal punishment prohibition, 94
New York City, 35, 102, 130
teachers' strikes, 118, 119
Northwest Ordinance of 1787, 6

O

Ocean Hill-Brownsville area schools, 42, 47, 59
Office of Education, U.S., 51
Open schools, 157
Organic organizations, 166–167
Organizational patterns, innovative, 149–160, 163–164
criteria for evaluating, 151–152
proposals, 152–159
Orientals, as a minority group, 70
Overton case, 93

P

Pairing schools, to achieve integration, 52–53
Parental participation and control, 8, 58–60, 61
Performance contracting, 56
Philadelphia, 3, 130, 157
Piaget, Jean, 78–79
Plessy v. Ferguson, 52

Political involvement, of public schools, 43, 57–58, 115–116
Population growth, 17
Pregnancy–Maternity Centers, 158
Pressure groups, 143–144
Prince Georges County, Maryland, 102
Principals (*See* Administrators, school)
Private schools, 57, 157
Professional status, of education, 107–108
Progressive education movement, 7–9
Protest, student, 86–87, 89–92
Ptolemy's theory, 9
Public education, alternatives for, 51–62, 156–159, 179
  community involvement in, 8, 58–60, 61, 142–144, 179
  decentralization of, 58–60, 61
  establishment of, 4–6
  financing of, 6, 107, 113–115
  lay control of, 113
  metropolitan context of, 31–48
Puerto Ricans, 34, 70, 76
Punishment, 94–97
Puritan ethic, 19

R

Race, achievement and, relationship, 44–47, 74, 76, 146, 184
  behavior differences, 73
  intelligence and, relationship, 46, 76
  See also Blacks
Rationality, nature of, 23
Redistricting, to achieve integration, 53
Remedial reading programs, 72
Richmond, Virginia, 53
Rickover, Hyman, 8
Riordan, Robert C., 156n[10]

S

San Jose, California, school district in, 157
Scarsdale, New York, 159

Scheduling, flexibility in, 153–154
Schools, bureaucratic nature of, 85–86, 167, 189
  as change resistant, 9, 164–167, 188–189
  conceptual dominance in, 26–27
  historical development of, 177–178
  inner city, 42–47, 55–62
  legitimacy of, 42–44
  metropolitan, 179–181
  purposes of, 13, 16–17, 21, 25, 27, 177–179
    social change, effect on purposes, 19, 26
  society and, 176–177
  See also Public education; Secondary schools
Schools-within-a-school, 158
Schools without walls, 157
Schumacher, Carolyn, 95
Scoville case, 92
Search and seizure, student rights concerning, 93
Secondary schools, accreditation of, 141–142
  adaptiveness of, 10
  comprehensive, defined, 144–145
  historical development of, 2–7
  innovative organizational patterns in, 149–160, 163–164
  problems of, 1–2
  public, 4–6
    See also Public education
  rationale for, 13, 16–17
    development of, 21–25
    employment of, 25–27
  Seven Cardinal Principles, 7, 27
Segregation, 38–43, 47–48, 179–180, 185
  of socioeconomic classes, 38–39, 47
Sesame Street, 75
Seven Cardinal Principles, 7, 27
Sex education, 26
Sex role differentiation, 77–78, 183–184
  in educational positions, 109–111, 183

Smith, Mortimer, 159
Smith, Vernon, 157
Snavely, Robert J., 166
Social norms (*See* Values)
Society, attitudes of, toward teaching,
  111–112
  changes in, 17–19, 36–37, 149
  communal, described, 18
  crisis period of, 9
  mass, described, 18
  pluralistic nature of, 13–17
  schools and, 176–177
Socioeconomic class, achievement and,
  44–47
  intelligence and, 69–73
  segregation of, 38–39, 47
  of teaching candidates, 110–112
Speech variance, in adolescence, 75–
  76
Standardized tests, 76, 138
State departments of education, curriculum influence of, 141
Stein, Jesse, 162n^1
Street academies, 158
Strikes, by teachers, 118–119
Student rights, 85–103, 186–187
  educators' adjustment to change in,
    98–103, 187
  judicial rulings, 87, 89–97, 100
  personal rights, 92–103
  protest rights, 89–92
  punishment and, 94–97
  records, access to, 97–98
Students, curriculum decisions and,
  131–132
  grouping of, in classrooms, 146,
    155–156
  lower class, 70–73, 75–77, 183
  nature of; importance of consider-
    ing, 23–24, 27
  powerlessness of, 85–86
  protest by, 86–87, 89–92
  rights of (*See* Student rights)
  statistics, 106
  values of, 134
  See also Adolescents
Student services, 127–128

Subcultures, in adolescence, 66–67
  race, 73
Suburbs, 33–35, 37
  schools in, 168
  white character of, 41, 42
Supreme Court rulings, on integration,
  41, 47, 51–53, 58
  on student rights, 91, 97
Suspension, as punishment, 95

T

Teachers, 106–123
  attitudes toward, 108–112
  certification of, 113, 190–191
  as change agents, 163, 165–168,
    171–172, 188
  changes in, 108, 113, 119
  characteristics of, 109–110
  curriculum decisions by, 130–132
  feminine image of, 109–111
  in inner city schools, 44
  innovative, characterized, 166
  job satisfaction of, 110–111
  male, 109–111, 120
  militancy of, 111, 119–120
  political activity of, 115–116
  power of, 113, 116, 122–123, 187–
    188
    See also Teachers' unions
  professional status of, 107–108
  salaries of, 109–110
    collective bargaining for, 120–
      121
    strikes, effect, 118–119
  socioeconomic background of, 110–
    112
  statistics, 106, 110
  training of, 8, 137, 138, 178, 189–
    192
  value conflicts and, 20–21
Teachers' unions, 108, 115, 116–123
  collective bargaining by, 119–122
  professionalism and, 117–118
  strikes, 118–119

Teaching, attitudes towards, 111–112
  individualized, 155–156
  objectives, 132–134
  performance contracting, 56
  professional status of, 107–108
  socioeconomic classification of, 110
Teaching materials, 138–140
  learning packages, 156
  project materials, 163
Team teaching, 154
Textbooks, 138–140
Thinking ability, as a learning goal,
  8–9, 23
Tinker v. *Des Moines, Independent
  Community School District,*
  90–91, 94
To Sir, With Love, 108
Transition period, in society, 9
Trump Report, 145–146, 154–155

U

United Federation of Teachers (UFT),
  119
United States, colonial society, 3
  core values in, 14–17, 22
  post-World War II, 8
  urbanization of, 31–33
  See also Society
United Teachers of California, 117
United Teachers of New York, 117
Universities, impact of, on public education, 137–138

Unks, Gerald, 150n^2
Upward Bound, 72
Urbanization, 31–33
  See also Cities; Metropolises
Urban renewal, 34, 40, 57
Utah Education Association (UEA),
  119

V

Values, adolescent, 64–65
  American core, 14–17, 22
  changes in, 9–10, 13, 18
  conflicts in, 15–16, 18–21, 65
  student, 134
Vietnam War, student protest against,
  87, 89, 90
  teaching of, 139

W

Washington, D.C., 41–42, 59, 94
Webster Groves, Missouri, 159
West Virginia v. *Barnett,* 96
Wood v. *Strickland,* 97
Woodstock festival, mentioned, 37

Z

Ziegler, Harmon, 109–111, 120